MAYNOOTH AT A GLANCE

*Dedicated to
Catherine M. (Kit) Rossiter,
and in memory of my parents
Gerald and Margaret Ledwith*

Míceál Ledwith

Maynooth at a Glance
1985-94

A SELECTION OF ONE HUNDRED AND TWENTY
OF THE PUBLIC ADDRESSES OF
MSGR MÍCEÁL LEDWITH, B.A., L.PH., D.D., LL.D.,
DURING THE DECADE OF HIS PRESIDENCY AT
ST PATRICK'S COLLEGE, MAYNOOTH

the columba press

First published in 1995 by
the columba press
93 The Rise, Mount Merrion, Blackrock, Co Dublin

Cover by Bill Bolger
Origination by The Columba Press
Printed in Ireland by Colour Books Ltd, Dublin

ISBN 1 85607 155 3

Acknowledgements
Grateful acknowledgement for permission to quote material in the text is due
to Health Communications Inc, Mike Cranfield, Mark Victor Hansen, J Z K
Inc, New Horizon Publishing Company, Richard Bach and Diane Munoz.

My thanks are due to Ms Mary Moriarty, Ms Marie Murphy, and Ms
Brenda Behan, who first typed these texts; to Mr Seán O Boyle and Ms
Maura Laverty of The Columba Press; to Dr Seamus Smyth and Dr Dermot
Farrell at Maynooth for their help with this project; to my brother Tom for
his unfailing encouragement; to Professor T R Drury, Chairman of the
Maynooth Bicentenary Series Committee, who read the page proofs; to the
Chancellor of the National University of Ireland, Dr T K Whitaker, and the
Registrar, Dr John Nolan, for permission to reproduce my Citations for the
Honorary Doctorates of the University; and most particularly to a Very Old
Friend whose inspiration lies throughout all these pages.

Contents

11. Life Changed, Not Ended

12. Epilogue

Introduction

Last year a few friends kindly asked me to consider putting together a selection of talks I had given as President, with a view to publication. When I set about gathering the material, I discovered a total of about three hundred scripts, as like the President of any College, the President of Maynooth is expected to speak frequently, on many different types of occasion, and even sometimes, by the nature of the case, on topics about which he can know very little personally. Normally, as will be seen, they were written under pressure to meet deadlines, but I have left them as they were given, while cutting down the number for inclusion to about one third of the total.

These one hundred and twenty talks were selected for inclusion in this book, primarily to give a brief outline of some of the main areas of the College's work in the last decade of its second century, a decade which saw some very significant changes and developments at Maynooth. Naturally they will be of most interest to those familiar with the College, but it is hoped that they will also provide for others a glimpse of some significant features of this very interesting decade.

CHAPTER 1

Times of Celebration

1: EASTER

The Refiner's Fire
Easter Day
Maynooth College Chapel, Broadcast on RTE Radio 1, 3 April 1988

Some of the most poignant relics from our history are the Penal Crosses. It's said they were made with narrowed arms so that they could be carried concealed in the sleeve in time of persecution.

On almost all of them is a drawing of a cock in a cooking pot. It is based on a story in an early Christian document, the 'Gospel of Nicodemus.' Judas betrayed Our Lord for thirty pieces of silver. After the betrayal he went home to his wife who was cooking a chicken in a pot. He told her what he had done and that there was a rumour that Jesus would rise again after three days. Judas was convinced that if he did Jesus would take revenge on him for his treachery. But Judas's wife said: 'Don't be silly: he could no more rise from the dead than that chicken could rise from the pot.' According to the legend, at that moment the chicken flew alive out of the pot and ran away crowing in the old Irish words which folklore likes to read into the call of the rooster: 'Mac na hÓighe slán,' ('The Son of the Virgin is safe') whereupon Judas fell into despair and, as we know, ended his life tragically, his despair of the mercy of God a far worse sin than his betrayal.

This story fascinated old Irish poetry and folklore. It was their way of saying: 'Don't be such a fool as to think you know the limits of what God can do' – just as so many re-interpret, and explain, and paraphrase the resurrection today into some poor thing they are able to accept. Even fervent believers can short-change what the resurrection really is. Of course Christ's tomb was empty on the first Easter Day; of course he was alive after he was dead, but that's only the beginning of what the resurrection is. St Paul called the

Risen Lord: 'the first fruits of creation.' The age-old plan of God in creation had at long last reached its goal, in Christ first, now in his glorified self, but it is something we are all called to reach as well.

Christ very often said he had to go to his death so that he could be glorified or completed by God, and precisely so that this glorified Christ could then be brought back into the world in a mystical way through the Holy Spirit, so as to be absorbed by us, and draw us up powerfully towards the goal of our creation as well. What we are aiming at, and what the resurrection has shown, is something 'eye has not seen, nor ear heard,' something beyond our imagination and wildest hopes, that God has prepared for those who love him. Christ's risen life is there waiting for us to be shared in the seven sacraments, which are at the core of what the Church is; for the Church is not at its heart the pope, the bishops, the scriptures, the creeds, the priests, or even the lay people; the Church in its innermost heart is the sevenfold sacramental structure which contains Christ's life for us to absorb; everything else in the Church exists only to forward that growth and development. This is the heart of what Easter means for you and me; we have to grow, be purified, cleansed and perfected, to follow God's design in creation for us.

Thirty pieces of silver were the poor instrument by which Christ was betrayed. The prophet Malachy spoke of God as 'sitting as a refiner of silver.' Silver is refined in a white-hot furnace. A moment too long there can ruin it. As it is tortured by the heat of the flames all the colours of the rainbow churn across the surface of the liquid metal as the impurities are drawn away. Suddenly, in an instant, the transformation is accomplished, and the pure silver in the dish becomes like a mirror, in which the refiner sees his image reflected.

It is a beautiful image of God, so carefully watching over our purification, especially in times of suffering and adversity, when we can often feel that we are farthest from God and abandoned. In fact everything is carefully part of a purpose, even when life seems most chaotic; in the end our purified nature mirrors that of God, which is the way we share in the glory of Christ's resurrection. Put no limits on what God can do for Christ or for you, and above all know that the glory of God consists in the fulfilment of his creatures – you and me – as Aquinas put it so beautifully, nearly eight hundred years ago.

So on this Easter morn I leave you with these three images to carry the message of the resurrection: the thirty pieces of silver, the Penal Cross, and the refiner's fire; for in them is the heart of the Easter message. For so long we Christians seem to have felt it almost like a duty to give away our power to others; the power to make us happy, to make us worthwhile, to make us fulfilled; and in doing this we delight to make ourselves victims and to wallow long in useless guilt. Give your power away to nobody; if you do you can never evolve. Do not be a follower, a victim of circumstances or of others' doings. Christianity is not a religion of gloom, despite our best efforts to make it so. To believe we are worthless, miserable sinners, hopeless cases, and nothing else, is not pleasing to God. See in today's feast the power and the glory, which belong to Christ, and to you and me, if we only are willing to leave our crutches of limitation behind. It is meant to lead us, even if sometimes through suffering, and through the dispelling of despair, to an everlasting glory beyond our wildest dreams.

Greatness: The Potential of the Unknown Lived
Easter 1990
Maynooth College Chapel, Broadcast on RTE Radio 1, 14 April 1990

All of us to some degree live by social consciousness. We know what is expected of us; we work hard to get the approval of neigh-bours, we try to do all the best things, to be seen in the right places, be known by the right people. But keeping up with the Joneses is a form of enslavement.

Nevertheless, there is a comfort zone in social consciousness, which is why it is so easy to live there. Everything in our lives has been packaged so neatly that we find we are living in a box. All we have to do is decide what we are going to do to support the box – which protects us from having to change or to think. And very many people live exactly in that way today, conforming all the time – even when they think they are being most original.

But the resurrection is all about change and development, not about conformity – or to put it another way, it is only about confor-mity to Christ. St Paul told us that undreamt of possibilities in life, both in this world and the next, are opening up for us as a result of the resurrection. But people don't take him seriously; they feel he was a dreamer, prone to exaggeration.

Is it any wonder that Christians so often fall so far short of the joy and peace that Christ came to bring? Is it any wonder that Christianity for so many is simply a do-good organisation, or the priest a glorified social worker, and that people have no depth in their relationship with God?

There is nothing in nature, not even a rock, which does not evolve and change.

A caterpillar on its extraordinary path to become something greater – a butterfly – gives us a great insight. It has no awareness of what it will become. It spends its whole day, every day, eating green leaves – to the despair of many a housewife and gardener. If a butterfly were to land on the same leaf it would not recognise it. And yet that is its ultimate destiny – to have wings and lift off and go to far and wonderful places.

But even the caterpillar knows its time and its season, and it knows that something is going to change. Maybe it has become attached to its green leaf, its social consciousness, its comfort box, but it gives it up because of its natural evolution and the hidden intelligence that tells it it is going to sleep and to change into something that it does not yet know.

When it comes out of its chrysalis, it sits there and pumps blood to its new wings, and dries in the morning sun. It does not even know yet that it is going to fly. It just knows what it has to do step by step. And when everything is ready, it lifts off, and that green leaf will never see it again.

Now human beings are the most extraordinary intelligence in nature, but we are also the most foolish. Unlike the caterpillar we do not automatically allow ourselves to change, or to follow the processes necessary to achieve our growth into God.

What we are most afraid of is change. Is it worth the risk and the gamble? But is it not worth losing our box, when there is a universe to be got in place of it?

Change is evoked by the Spirit of God within us, who presses us on to be something greater than we are now, but which is now largely unknown. We fear nothing so much as the unknown, but greatness is the potential of the unknown lived.

There is a great difference between the human being and the butterfly, both on their way to fulfil God's design. Doing difficult things is involved, often without really seeing the reason for them. But what if a butterfly were to act as we often do? What if it were to say: 'I don't like this. I can't do this,' and try to get back into its chrysalis? Fortunately for the butterfly that is impossible because the chrysalis shrivels away. For the human being it is not impossible, in fact it is quite common, and the human being's chrysalis in Christian terms is the box, the image of social consciousness, which is the main obstacle to our gaining the fruits of Christ's resurrection.

No one ever wonders if the caterpillar suffers in all that change.

They only marvel at the miracle of transmutation. What was a dowdy, worm-like creature is now an elegant and beautiful creation, with ebony eyes, long silken antennae, and wings that look like beautiful oriental fans. Does the caterpillar have regrets for the green leaves it used to eat? It does. Is there not a great pain to be suffered in the process of transformation? Yes; and it took losing, working, changing, and effort to achieve it.

That precisely is what a great many of us are not willing to accept in our spiritual development towards God, of which the caterpillar's transformation is an apt image, the struggle and the trust in faith.

The difference between the caterpillar and the human being is that the human being can block the hidden intelligence that is urging it on to something greater; the caterpillar cannot. Worse still many people have given away their God for somebody else's image of God, so they no longer know what they are aiming at, and their faith is emptied of power.

Genesis tell us that God made us in his image. We were supposed to struggle and change to develop this image in us more and more. Instead what has happened? Man has made God in his image. As a result people look up to images of God that have little to do with the real thing. They see him as the old man with the beard, as someone located in a far corner of the universe; they see him as if he were some harassed telephone operator, trying to channel through some cosmic-sized switchboard all the prayers and communications from every corner of this world. It is an image so often tragically insecure, bored, psychotic, vindictive, and fickle. What travesties of religion often float even in religious people's minds? What travesties of religion are often criticised with such great success by those who know no other version of it?

All they have is an image of God which is just a human being enlarged, which so tragically misses all that has been revealed to us of his glory, his nearness, his power, and above all of his boundless and constant love for you and me, of which the resurrection tells us today.

For ages people on this planet have been intimidated into believing things that have no basis in reality. Christ wants us to know that what he spoke is true. He also want us to realise the glory gained for us in the resurrection; that God is omnipresent here within us, and that what is important is living in his freedom, which we continually give away in order to honour our fears, most of which come from the struggle to stay in the box of social consciousness.

If we were to put the same power into growing into the risen

Christ as we put into searching for fame, fortune, beauty, clothing, approval, and all the other things we can have, then we would long ago have become the beacons on a hilltop for which Christ wished. The knowingness that it would have taken lifetimes to acquire, we have been given in moments in the resurrection of Christ. We can be threatened, coaxed, persuaded, pressured, to try to get us to do something, but we know very well that it is only when we ourselves really want our lives to be different that we will change. Understanding and development lie outside the box; the key is always on our side of the door.

A School of Fish
Easter Vigil
Maynooth College Chapel, 30 March 1991

In the remote past stories were the format for giving the most profound knowledge and the wisdom of the generations. The Easter Vigil ceremony is full of them, both visual and literal. In a story the meaning is gained in proportion to the attitude of the hearer. One of the best ways to get the mind working outside its barriers is to give it a story to contemplate. The highly intellectual person, especially those who believe themselves to be such, will of course intellectualise it and ask what it's for. A member of any particular religion will colour it with the characteristics of his own faith, especially if he has a doctrinaire mind. The rich man will colour it his way, society will colour it another, and will disparage it as only a story, something for children, inappropriate, so simple it doesn't require any great intellect. If you present a story to someone simple and illiterate, you are presenting it to someone who has to rely on common sense, and truly simple people have a remarkable ability to break outside the limitations we all impose on ourselves, and to see to the heart of things. The simplicity of children can often do the same.

There is a very ancient story which I would like to put before you briefly for your reflection tonight. It concerns a group of fish swimming about in a school. One afternoon someone posed the question: 'What do you suppose water really is?'

The intellectual fish said: 'Water is that which comprises the essence of all things.'

The religious or theological fish (who always went to the coral reef for services) said: 'It is what the great whale that lurks beyond us gives us by way of life; but you have to be the son of a whale to get it.'

The scientific fish, who had the ability to blend in with everything, rose up off the sea bed, shook the sand off his back, took a deep breath and said solemnly: 'Ah, yes, water. I have studied this matter for some time and my forefathers were all immersed in it. Various schools of thought about water have arisen throughout history, particularly in these latest times, which have their own theories about the nature of water, and indeed I have my own. Water is the very essence our fins are made of.'

And the whole school stared at the three of them in disbelief, and dissatisfaction.

Now there was a rumour of a very wise fish who lived far away, and the school decided to go to ask him. So they travelled off a great distance, and it became so dark the whole school was getting confused. Some felt they were exhausted, and had to linger near an oasis. Others thought they would see better from the top of a mountain, and others said they were all getting lost, and went home; (the same attitudes and excuses that bedevil all who set out to discover truth).

Others persevered and swam on into the darkness, and eventually they came into a shallow place of beautiful aquamarine. In a very small rock there was a tiny hole, and they all swam to the opening in the rock. One suggested they meditate on the wise fish first.

Eventually the wise fish appeared (very scruffy in appearance, and not at all looking like an expert) and they told him: 'We have come a long distance with a question. We have already asked a scientist, a holy religious/theological fish and an intellectual: "What is water?" and they haven't given us very satisfactory answers.'

The wise fish showed no inclination to get involved in a long and weary seminar on the subject. 'Water,' he said, 'is the very thing that surrounds you always and that you live in.' And with that the scruffy fish went back to his place inside the rock, and they saw no more of him. 'Water is what is all around us,' said one of the fish, 'How could that be? I'm still thirsty.'

Now try for a moment not to dismiss this story as beneath your dignity, like the first three fishes. Each element in it conveys a very profound truth about human attitudes in our relationship to God, which was what Jesus emphasised especially in his appearances after the resurrection. The Kingdom of God is within us; we, and everything that exists, are all incarnations in different ways of God's almighty love. So many people today ponder the question of

God; so many find themselves unable to believe, not realising that they have set down ground rules which make belief impossible.

Like the fish they are asking what water is, when in fact they are completely surrounded by it, and it is it that gives them life. They are told they live surrounded by water, but they still say they are thirsty, so that it cannot be.

After the resurrection Jesus gathered his disciples in Galilee for his last teaching before he ascended. He asked them to live what he had taught them. The Father and I are one. The Kingdom of Heaven is within you. Go and do the works that I have done and greater. I have won victory over death and conquered all human fears for you. Fear nothing and stop regarding yourselves as victims, for no progress is possible for a person in that mind. He told them that he loved them and that he would be with them always until the end of the world. And he rose above them and became illuminated with a brilliance that filled the sky; and was raised out of their sight. It was in that moment that the power of Jesus the Christ was released into the world by the Father, and his grace and life permeated the whole of creation, for all who were willing and open to receive.

It is for that reason that God is closer to us than we are to ourselves, in Augustine's phrase. In reality there is nothing but God for all has ultimately come from him, which means that there is really no separation between all that exists; and which is the deepest reason why we are all members of the one body. The theological fish here will know the difference between pantheism, which has to do with God's nature, and what I am saying here, which has to do with the manner of his relationship and presence to the creation.

The most debilitating attitude we can have is one of separation; we feel powerless because we believe we are separate from God; we feel miserable because we think we are distant from his grace and glory, immersed in sin; we attack and belittle others, forgetting we are children of the same father; we abuse the earth forgetting we are intimately linked to it as part of all that exists. The message of Easter was perhaps most memorably spelled out by St Paul: 'In him we live and move and have our being.' It's a pity we spent so much of Christian history denying that profound truth.

I said at the start that the message of a story is different in that what meaning is disclosed depends on the attitude of the hearer. Try not to be like the first three fish, but instead be open to the obvious unobvious, the mysterious union which binds together all that exists, which is the fundamental reality of a faith based on the resurrection and ascension of Jesus the Christ.

Mirrors to Each Other
Easter Vigil
Maynooth College Chapel, 18 April 1992

The world, as St Augustine once said, could have been redeemed by the shedding of one drop of Christ's blood. What was the reason, then, for that awful passion?

The clue to the riddle is in the first message to the Infant Church given by that mysterious figure in the tomb at dawn: 'Go tell everyone that your Lord has become victorious over death.'

St Paul called death man's last and greatest enemy. Christ chose to redeem us through his passion and resurrection so that death could be overcome. Fears in so many incredible forms are the greatest obstacle we have in our growth towards God, and the fear of death is the father of most of our fears. It is the root of our difficulties in growing towards God.

The Risen Lord first met the apostles in the upper room. They were hiding in fear like hunted animals. He gave them the same message. He told them of his love for them, and that the greatest fear they had always been taught was death, and that even their own teachers did not believe that there was life afterwards. He had now shown that death was not a victor. And he taught them that as a result they should fear nothing, neither Rome, nor Caesar, nor Herod, the fire, sword, nothing; for the Kingdom of Heaven was within them, and he besought them to know this and not merely recite it.

You have just come out of a sheltered and blessed time, much more precious than you realise; a few days of peace to reflect on who you are, what you want to be and how you are related to God; a chance to reflect if you ever really knew him before. Soon you'll be back to the hurly burly; the college will have more than 3,000 students, many of whom will not share or perhaps even understand your commitment. It is an image of the situation in which you will minister after your ordination.

At the end of such a time of reflection it is more easy to look with a clear eye on the crippling attitudes that are so often deeply buried in our hearts, and to have the grace to do something about them.

Our inadequacies, angers, insecurities, apprehensions, our judgements, our guilt – they are all forms of fear, and what an effect all of these have. Isn't it absolutely amazing how much we hold on to the very things that hold us back most? It comes from fear. We think these things give us our identity, and we probably feel that if we let them go we will no longer know who we are. And there is a truth in that. For our minds are shrouded in limitation. But it is only ourselves that can shift. For how do you teach knowledge and enlightenment to someone whose mind is closed – especially by fear?

At this Mass of the Resurrection could you focus for a minute on the tendency we all have so much to regard ourselves as victims? It was on this difficulty Christ concentrated when he first met the apostles, when he first spoke to the Infant Church. We blame everything outside ourselves for our problems – our parents, families, our friends, where we live, the society, our local organisations, the lack of opportunity, the government, the job we had in the Summer, our poor formation in secondary school, the system – the list is endless. They are responsible for our unhappiness, our hang-ups, our failures and disappointments, for our limitations, our predicaments, our illnesses. Of course in the process we totally doubt that we ourselves have the power or ability to achieve anything of significance. And the thing that probably is most destructive of all in our relationship to God, gossip and backbiting – another manifestation of fear, which often has such a fertile breeding ground in the relatively enclosed world of the seminary.

The basis for making any progress in life, whether spiritual or material, is to want it and to take responsibility. When you say you are confused or messed up in your mind, who messed you up? Take hold of your responsibility. How do you unmess yourself? Want it enough. There is no psychology to mental health, only desire. There is not one problem whose situation cannot be changed radically by a shift in desire. What you come to know about yourself will be always in direct proportion to what you come to know about God. If you do not really have the commitment to bother learning more about yourself and about God, your wish will be granted and your vocation will die.

We do ourselves the same damage every time we point to someone else's shortcomings, real or imagined, and hotly elaborate on them, because in the process we are losing ourselves. We are losing ourselves because what we notice most in others is the perception of ourselves. Anything you greatly admire in another, or anything you absolutely cannot stand in another person, rest assured that that quality is most likely to be found in a supreme degree in yourself.

Our reactions to others always mirror ourselves.

We are all searching for happiness, in everything we do, (even in the crazy and self-destructive things), and in every person we meet and in every situation we look for. But God clearly revealed in Christ that happiness cannot, in the last analysis, be found outside ourselves. It cannot be found through the possession of things, or of other people, or through rank or position, or even through that deceptive arrogance of a failure that we, perhaps unconsciously, look for. The greatest mistake in the search for happiness is to look for someone or something outside to fill the vacuum we have inside.

The lack we have inside is not of the sort that can be filled with any material thing from outside. And this is why relationships so often do not work; we cling too much and depend on others, and kill the feeling between us. And that is why commitments, religious or otherwise, weaken and collapse; because we use them as a crutch. True and lasting relationships and commitments can only be made when we are independent, standing on our own two feet, when we become unreliant and mature people. In short when we have grown to where we are without fear – that is what we are here for. Instead we are so often insecure, dependent, afraid. Why? Because secretly we hate ourselves. Real happiness has always to be found first within ourselves, but we are afraid to trust that.

Is it any wonder, given the quality of our fearful understanding and fearful preaching of the great fundamentals of the faith, and the rigid and defensive attitudes that can come from them, that so often these great truths are the butt of mockery and derision, or regarded as on a par with fairy tales? And why so many of our contemporaries find God attractive, but the Church, his instrument, irrelevant? There is no mystery about why that is so; spare yourself the agonies of wondering why and lamenting about it; the answer is as plain as can be; and the solution is largely in our hands and in the type of person we are determined to be.

When a person receives the sacrament of Orders he is said to be configured into Christ; he becomes another Christ. That's something that we all greatly desire; but how do you prepare to become another human version of the Risen Lord; how do you know what it is you must do, or how far you have succeeded?

It was all summed up for us this Holy Week. Can you return the betrayal of a trusted friend with a look of forgiveness? Can you pray for and love those who scream for your death, even though they had glorified you a few days before, and not despise them for their fickleness? If so you have put on Christ. You have put on Christ when without bitterness or recrimination you can endure the most cruel death, while being totally innocent. And many who have followed Christ have done that; including some people who sat in those same seats as you do.

Above all you have really followed Christ when you just do not say, but really know, that the Kingdom of God is within you, and that no one has any power over you that is not given from above. That last is a joyful realisation, but, strangely, it is probably the hardest of all to accept. Why? Because we have so consistently made ourselves victims. We have so consistently given away our power to others; the power to make us happy, disappointed, sad, grateful, exultant or bitter; that we are no longer in control of our destiny. And isn't it sad that often when we begin to find joy in our faith so many people begin to feel uncomfortable, and suspect something must have gone wrong? What does it say we have made of the resurrection?

These crippling attitudes that we cling to banish the Kingdom of Heaven from our hearts more effectively than the fiercest persecution. More than anything else it is this which makes Christianity most unattractive to those outside the fold today: the gloom of a lot of its members, their rigidity of mind (so often confused with loyalty), or even worse, their false joy.

Remember that there is a thirst for true spiritual values in the unbelieving world today; that is, values that respond to the deepest needs of the human heart, and which are central to the Risen Lord's message, and above all remember it is a thirst for those values which you can be seen by people to have made your own.

Why is it so many people feel they are capable of guiding others before they have gained the necessary virtues of wisdom, knowledge of God through the scriptures and tradition and their personal discipline and reflection, the love, strength and unselfishness, the ability to remain unperturbed despite distraction and upheaval, the ability to retain an internal peace when all around is turmoil and disorder? When a person has achieved all these things he is then ready to try to help others by leadership, but not before. It is only then that perfect love shall have cast out fear. It is only then we will understand fully why we were redeemed, not with a drop of Christ's blood, but through his awful passion and resurrection.

And he taught them that they should fear nothing, neither Rome, nor Caesar, nor Herod, the fire, sword, nothing; for the Kingdom of Heaven was within them, and he besought them to know this. This is the legacy the first Easter left us. Let's see, then, if we can be no longer slaves to our so many fears but worthy co-heirs with Christ.

How Like an Angel Came I Down
Easter Vigil
Maynooth College Chapel, 10 April 1993

In the middle of all the glory and celebration of Easter remember that what gives rise to it all is a very practical and concrete thing: that is, what happened to the Lord Jesus on this night, when he rose from the dead in his physical body. The resurrection of Christ is telling us things of immense importance about Christ, but they centre on his physical body, more than on what was not physical at all in him; and even more importantly the resurrection is telling us, as all feasts of Christ do, something very important about our own journey towards God.

Parents do not create their children. They create the house, the physical body, but they do not create the person; they do not create the spirit. That comes from somewhere else that is, in a sense, very, very far away. A child is sent to 'study' with its parents by God, as a student might go to study in a foreign country to gain an enriching experience and to grow. That human spirit of ours is mighty and powerful, but it is encased in its physical body, which limits what it is able to achieve in this world.

The body is a glorious thing; it is the material garment of the spirit; the instrument by which the spirit is able to act in this world in which we live; we should love and care for our bodies. But the body can also become a prison; something in which the spirit is bound up, as a butterfly or caterpillar is rolled up and imprisoned in a cocoon. There is a time when the caterpillar should be in the cocoon, but a time comes when it is ready to leave, and then it must break out and go on to a much more glorious life.

Nowadays it is rare for people to break out of their cocoon on their journey towards God; in fact we cling to it in fear, or are imprisoned in it by our anger, greed, hatred, and all the other negative attitudes that are so destructive to us. The body then really becomes a prison, which limits and confines all the wonderful things we ought to be able to do, as a gift from God.

The feast of the resurrection, and baptism, which is the primary sacrament of the resurrection, are all about breaking out of the limits of the material world, and going beyond it to the realms of glory, even in this life. The life of baptism tells us, as all of the sacraments do, that we must raise up the level of life at which we live, to something beyond and above this mundane and often very boring and cruel world. And in baptism is given the power to ascend beyond the level of material life. The material level is the lowest of all the levels that exist in creation, as science now is discovering. But we tend to regard it as the supreme level of creation! – maybe the only level of creation that exists! So many people fail so miserably to ascend in their lives; they never realise what baptism is; they never realise what the message of the resurrection really was about; they never realise what they could become. Instead they allow themselves to become identified with their physical bodies, and with this daily material life as if there were nothing beyond. It is no wonder why there is so much unhappiness, frustration and suffering in the world.

It is so hard for us to realise that we are here on this earth for a purpose; for a transmutation, which is meant to be the last stage of our growth towards God. What the sages and the prophets down the centuries, and last of all Christ himself, especially in the resurrection, have been telling us, is that this reality is within us; in a sense we have to become what we already are; we have to allow it to come forth. And yet we prevent it so often by our crippling attitudes, which prevent our growth in the Spirit.

We all belong to realms of glory so magnificent that we cannot even vaguely imagine them today, even in our wildest dreams, and no matter how vivid our imagination. We have lost contact with what we truly ought to be. We are all so ignorant; we are so silly, so filled with folly; so stupid, so lazy, so ignorant, especially when we imagine we are being most shrewd and worldly-wise; we have forgotten what we are: namely that we are not our bodies, but children of God.

Why do we sometimes look out into a clear night sky, into midnight blue, the backdrop of forever? What do we think we are looking for? A longing? Some tethered memory that almost comes to mind, but when it's focused on the thought flies away? Have we ever pondered why that feeling is there? It is telling us something.

We are the children of God, heirs to the Kingdom of Heaven. Have we ever really thought what that means? Or do we feel it's just a beautiful metaphor; something that uplifts and consoles us, but is not really real?

Resurrection showed us we were heirs to the Kingdom of Heaven; baptism is about taking up and gaining what was shown. The glory of God is within us; there is where the key to the Kingdom of Heaven lies. We can make a home a reality in that world as well as in this. But our eyes are so blind, we are so ignorant of death, so afraid of our shadows. We see only this life, we see only our relationships, we see only our careers, what we look like in the mirror, we allow our lives to be shaped by what others in their limit-ations expect of us, we see only our ambitions in the material world. And most sadly of all, we try to destroy, perhaps in the most subtle ways, anyone who would try to waken us up from this slumber, because if we destroy them, then of course we no longer feel the pressure on us to change. 'Jerusalem, Jerusalem, how often you stoned the prophets that were sent to you.'

This is not seeing what we are. And how can we hope to pass from this plane one day if we cannot see beyond it?

Men and women die so sadly because they see themselves only as man and woman, because they see themselves as ungodly, as stupid, as ignorant, as petty, as vain, as unworthy and worthless, and above all because they doubt themselves. We must realise what we are to achieve in the fruits of our baptism. When we have devel-oped a will that is stronger than the needs of the body, a will stronger than the expectations which society makes on us, then we are on the road to achieving the gift which baptism brought us. Then we are becoming greater than our bodies.

The Kingdom of God is within you. How do we go about culti-vating it and making it grow within us more and more? We have to do it, it is what our salvation is.

We achieve it first of all in this way: by avoiding all the things that drain our power away: hatred, envy, greed, despising, jealousy, anger, and above all, fear.

If we are always waiting to be loved, we will never be happy, because we are relying on something that will always be uncertain. Never rely on the love of others; be content to love them unceasing-ly; perhaps some day someone will return this kind of love to you. If you do this your happiness will be unfailing.

Do not despise anyone or anything in God's creation. Allow. Do not suppress the feelings that you have against them. That is no use. Allow; one of the most difficult of all things for a human being to do! Judge not and you shall not be judged.

When we detest someone it is exactly as if we loved that person; we forge a bond between us. Hatred is as powerful as love. If you hate someone you are binding yourself to that person with chains.

Love your enemies! How difficult, almost unimaginably diffi-cult! If you hate or despise your enemies you draw all their negative aspects towards you and you have no defences, because you have lowered them by hating.

This is why Jesus said to love your enemies. He knew if you detested someone you made yourself vulnerable. To defend yourself you must retreat into the impregnable fortress of love. To love one's enemies is the most difficult thing of all to do, but it is the only defence against enemies.

All the great saints down the centuries overcame their enemies by living such radiant lives of purity, nobility and integrity, that sooner or later all who attacked them came to grief from the backlash of their own vindictiveness. For what you put out to others will infallibly come back to you.

Never, ever, fear. Fear is the greatest drain of all. It is the diametric opposite of resurrection. And all of us are so fearful. Fearful for so many things; for our job, for our survival, for our reputation, for our happiness, for our enemies, when we rage at what we may perceive to be abuses. The biggest feeling in most human lives is fear, however skilfully it may be disguised. Perfect love casts out fear, the New Testament tells us. Above all do not suppress your fears. That makes matters worse. Seek out your fears and confront them. That will destroy them. If we do not they will control us, and who wants to be a slave?

The New Testament tells us that we have a body of pure light, an incorruptible body. But as we became more and more deeply immersed in the denser layers of matter, we neglected our Body of Glory so much that eventually it became incapable of manifesting itself. And now we have to reverse this movement and recover what we have lost. Many people today might prefer to skim over this implication of the resurrection of Jesus. Baptism gives us the pledge and the power to begin that very long and difficult ascent back to where we ought never have left. It is thanks to our Body of Glory that we shall live eternally and recapture the abilities that were ours in the past. We are speaking of trying to get back to the situation that was ours before the fall of man; this is what Christ came to help us towards, and he left us the sacraments, whose entry and beginning point is baptism, to enable us to achieve it. How few succeed! The reason is because of the crippling and limiting attitudes that we hold on to so fiercely. We prevent ourselves.

People often imagine that you have to endure great ordeals, or travel to remote areas where they will meet great mystics, or have extraordinary revelations, to be able to achieve the nourishment of their Body of Glory and understand truth. It is very difficult, because of the centuries of neglect in which we stand, but it is not something that is remote and far away. The paradox is that the journey is within.

Our Body of Glory is like a seed within us and the task of a baptised Christian is to water, warm and nourish this seed. When we

experience a few moments of intense spiritual life, when we listen
to beautiful music, or are deeply moved by something that is said,
or by the sight of something beautiful – it is at these moments that
you nourish your Body of Glory. These feelings of wonder and
love, these emotions, are the particles with which you nourish this
body within you, just as a woman nourishes the child in her womb
with her blood as well as with her thoughts and feelings.

What we have to above all remember is that we are greater than
our body. We are not our bodies. But everyone today acts as if they
were their bodies and nothing more. It is the message ceaselessly
pumped out as us from the TV, magazines, newspapers, even from
the churches who have sometimes sold their birthright for what is
often curiously called relevance. The body dictates; the spirit is the
slave. And when the body dictates it means we try to gratify every
whim it has; the result is disaster for the body. We must love and
cherish the body; but the Spirit must be in control, and then it will
give to the body what causes it to be healthy and flourish. When the
body is in charge of our lives, it causes its own death; it is only when
the Spirit is in charge that the body can really flourish and be healthy.

The Journey Within
A Story for Easter
10 April 1993

Let me tell you a story which I heard once from a very old friend.

One of the greatest ways to get the mind working outside the
limits of its barriers, is to tell a story that conveys a very profound
truth in deceptively simple terms, and let it be reflected on. Christ
himself was a master of the parable. Every part of this story has a
message for our journey to find truth and meaning in this life, as we
progress towards God. Maybe it will help you to remember and
understand better what I have been trying to say to you in a very
short space of time.

Many, many centuries ago, long before the beginning of recorded
time, there was a very wise and prosperous man who lived in the
centre of a far-away ocean, of which very little remains as it was
known in those times. He and his family lived on a small island in
this ocean, not far from a very primitive coastline, in those times
long past remembrance.

The wise man lived there on this tiny island with his wife, four sons, three man servants, four woman servants, and a whole host of animals. He treated his slaves like his own family and they lived very happily. They had a wonderful source of wealth which they used to trade with the mainland. He and his servants used to dive down into the pure waters, pristine and lavender, and bring up sea creatures in their shells. They used to extract from these creatures an ink, that at first sight was black. But as it was diluted and mixed slightly with sea salt, it produced the most wonderful colour. This colour was rare and was sought after by kings, noblemen, and priests ... and the colour was purple. The wise man and his family made their living by creating the colour purple, and being exclusive and holding their secret as to how they produced it.

The wise old man loved his family and indeed treated his slaves, his man servants and woman servants, with equality and respect. And upon the tiny island they lived many days, balmy and sweet in joy, and had many wondrous evenings with jasmine-filled air.

After many years of prosperity there came an immense storm from the north. In all of the wise man's days, old as he was, he had never seen such an ill wind. The rains came and the hail came, and even unclean things fell from the sky. The water rose higher and higher. His house, his cattle, his sheep, his goats, his wild fowl, indeed all the things beloved of him and necessary to him, were washed away and destroyed in the storm. And in the last half hour, the old man's family was swept away by a great wave. Of course he himself was saved, but what did his life mean when all that he had worked for was gone, all that he had cared for was gone, and all that he has lived for was gone ... all of that which he loved was gone?

After a few days of drifting on the sea the old man himself was washed up on a strange shore, only half alive. There was in him a spirit that was like to a corpse, rather wanting to die than live. He was taken to a house and nourished back to health. Some people from the nobility recognised him as the man who created the colour purple. They gave him nice houses and all he could wish for, in the hope that he would reveal to them the secret of the colour purple, for only he knew the secret of its origin.

The wise old man was immediately sent for by very high noblemen who took care of him and nourished him and gave him private gardens, and braziers and sweet wine and nectar. Caring for him enough ... all along wanting to know the secret of the colour purple. He went from one nobleman to another.

Still grey in spirit, one evening he flung himself upon a knoll and buried his face in the shrub and cried out, 'What is truth?

Where are the gods? What have I done wrong that they would punish me with life and let me spend all of the days of my life in such
dire misery and pain?'

And he wandered off, an old man heavy in years, and the sorrow in his heart was nearly more than he could bear. And he stum-
bled upon a Sage of those times, who mixed wonderful herbs, and
prepared for him elixirs and potions, and nurtured him without
one word, into a remnant of health. And the old Sage, always working over his brew, always disappearing for long moments at a time,
and reappearing with strange things in a sack, would simply smile,
and prepare his herbs and give it to him, and never say a word.

All the time the old man was wondering about the meaning of
what had happened to him, and was seeking for truth and meaning
in his life. One day he said to the Sage, 'I will go out of my mind
completely if someone does not tell me soon why I am alive, why all
I loved is lost, why you should bother to take care of me. No one is
able to give me the truth about life, so I do not wish to live.'

The Sage mixed for him a golden elixir and gave it to him saying,
'Drink', the first word he had spoken in the months the old man
had lived with him. He drank and immediately he felt full of good
cheer and was lost in happiness. The Sage said to him: 'You who
seek to understand must go to the farthest mountain range which
looms such a great distance away to the west, hundreds of miles,
and if you survive this journey through such treacherous and sav-
age country you will come to a great mountain, the greatest mountain on the earth. It is covered with dangerous places of all kinds,
and hostile animals, and is shrouded in mists which will cause you
to lose your way. But at the top of this great mountain lives the
Lord, and if you can survive to climb to the top of the mountain, he
will give you the truth.'

So the old man set out on the long journey with several stacks of
wheaten cakes, and herbs, and peppers, and garlic and old cheese,
and the Sage sent him on his way, and he endured great suffering
and hardships on the journey, but he did not mind. All he wanted
was to know and understand truth, for nothing was left of his life.

Eventually he arrived at the base of the huge mountain. It was
glazed in pure crystal and shone in the dim light. The old man sat at
the bottom of it and pondered how he could climb it. Eventually he
thought he would look on the mountain as he used to look on the
depths of the ocean where he used to dive to catch the shellfish
which gave the colour purple; instead of diving down into the
depths, he would now climb up into the heights.

So he climbed and climbed for many days, and was very weary, and all the time got closer to the mists that haloed the top of the mountain. Eventually he reached the top and great and wonderful beings met him who ushered him into a great hall set for a banquet. The hall had no ceiling but the clouds that passed and billowed overhead. There was a great light that seemed to come from nowhere and music was played that enchanted him for it was so strange and so beautiful.

He sat at the banquet of the finest meats and sweetmeats, and of golden liquid in crystal goblets. And there he was seated while musicians played wonderful and strange music, and always with delightful sounds coming from their mouths and lights dancing in their eyes. And to his amazement upon this magical table, there were very, very tiny people, and they were dancing up and down this great table singing their own jubilant song. They were smaller than his own hand. And suddenly the music stopped and a wonderful old man walked into this hall, and he greeted the old man. He said. 'I believe I am the one you have been searching for.'

And the wise old man said, 'Of course, if you can tell me the truth.'

And the old man said to him, 'What is it that you desire to know, for I shall give you the truth?' And the old man started to open his mouth and say, 'Why ...'

And then all of a sudden all of the musicians disappeared. All of the food disappeared. And the wee people disappeared too. And nothing was left except the golden liquid in the crystal glass, and the light that seemed to come from nowhere in this roofless room. And instead of asking this lord, why, he said to him instead, 'Why is truth so hard to find? Why is the meaning of life so hard to find? Why did I have to come all of this terrible journey, and endure so many dangers and such hardships, lose everything I had, my family, my sons, my property, and climb this dreadful mountain to find truth? Why is truth so hard to find? Why did I have to come all of this way and climb this treacherous mountain just to know?'

And the lord looked at him with fire in his eyes, that danced merrily across his face, and he answered the old man by saying, 'Behold, because you have placed the answer here. Because you have placed me here. Why am I on this mountain? Because you put me here. Truth, my beloved old man, is only as far as we perceive it to be and as close as we allow it to be.'

So the old man enjoyed the feast of his life. It did not bring back his family or his house, but it brought him back.

At last the wise old man came to know that the journey for truth and understanding is only as great as our need for it, and when we find it we then realise we had never really left, for it is only a journey within.

The Wisdom of God, the Foolishness of Men
Easter Vigil
Maynooth College Chapel, 2 April 1994

We tend to regard ourselves as excellent judges of what is most wise, appropriate or prudent. Few if any of us, I imagine, if we had been consulted, would have advised God to make his grand entry into the world in a stable; nor would we have advised him that the first representatives of the human race to do him homage should have been the lowest orders of society at that time, shepherds; much less would we have advised that the first visitors from outside should have been those people most despised by orthodox Judaism: three or four Babylonian astrologers, the Magi.

Jesus continued to disappoint the prudent throughout the entire course of his life. Born in one obscure village at the end of the world, he lived in another one as he grew up, the child of a peasant woman and of a labouring man, however noble their ancestry undoubtedly was. He apparently worked as a carpenter and made no public move at all until he was about thirty. Surely it would have been better if he had been born in comfortable surroundings, to people who had contacts, power, influence; if only he could have gone to the best schools, got to know the right people, lived at the centre of political power and used the rapid means of communication that then existed at the centre of the Roman world.

Then for three years he was an itinerant preacher. He never had a family or owned a home. He handled no money, never set foot in a big city. He never travelled during his ministry more than two hundred miles from the place where he was born. He never wrote a book, held an office. In fact, come to think of it, he did none of the things that we regard as essential to greatness.

During his ministry he often associated with undesirable elements in society, even at times with those who were outcasts, was merciful to prostitutes, gentle and forgiving to all except those whose hearts were hardened in self-righteousness. He even called a despised tax-gatherer as one of his disciples; the remainder apparently were common men of little or no formal education; apparently of relatively little moral strength either, for even after three years of constant association with him and benefiting from his teaching almost all had either abandoned or denied him within a few hours of his arrest.

When he was still a young man the tide of popular opinion turned against him. He was turned over to his enemies by a close disciple, who was trying to force him to oppose the Romans and become a political leader to save his people. He said he could have twelve legions of angels at his side to help him, but yet he underwent a mockery of a trial, was cursed and spat upon, was scourged, and after having had a robber preferred to him, was humiliated with the most cruel death imaginable, crucified naked near the city dump, between two common criminals. What prudent person would have advised God that this was the best way to conduct the redemption of the world?

While he was dying his executioners gambled for the only piece of property he had – his coat. When he was dead, he was taken down and buried in a borrowed grave, donated by a man who was too ashamed to acknowledge him publicly when he was alive.

It has been well said of that 'one solitary life' that now nearly twenty centuries have come and gone and today, for much of the human race, he is the central figure; that all the armies that ever marched, and all the navies that ever sailed, and all the parliaments that ever sat, and all the kings that ever reigned, put together, have not affected the life of the human race as powerfully as this one man. For when he came to the tomb in the cold dim hours of morning, remade his body and transfigured it in glory, and when forty days later he elevated himself above his followers and disappeared from their sight in a blinding flash of light, he showed that all the standards by which the world judges quality and assesses greatness, are bankrupt and deeply flawed.

The closer and more uncritically we take over those standards from the world and live by them, as we do so much all the time, then the closer we are to seeing Christ's life and ascension, as so many of his contemporaries did, 'to the Jews a stumbling block, to the Gentiles foolishness.' I have often wondered how it is that the standards of God in planning the incarnation, the standards of Christ in directing the circumstances of his ministry on earth, almost never coincided with what the world would have advised.

At Easter ponder why what is judged to be prudent and effective in the eyes of the world is almost never prudent and effective in God's.

2: CHRISTMAS

Can Anything Good Come out of Galilee?
College Service of Carols, 21 December 1989

'Can anything good come out of Galilee?'

A thousand years before Jesus was born it had been part of the powerful Jewish Kingdom of David, became part of Israel after the death of Solomon, and then fell to the Assyrians, when most of the Galileans lost their identity and became worshippers of the pagan deities through fertility cults. So Galilee had a very chequered history and the cynical comment I quoted at the start from some of the first hearers of Jesus, shows us that it was the last place from which a great and long-awaited religious leader could be expected to come.

In terms of superficial human judgement, Jesus seemed to fail nearly every test. 'Is not this the carpenter's son?' 'Do we not know his kinsmen?' I quote these things that were said, because, like most of the criticisms people make, they usually tell you more about the person criticising than about the person who is being judged.

There is in fact no character in all our history who stands out as Jesus does. We count our time before and after his birth. The divine cannot be grasped in any adequate way because of the limitation of the human mind, so there is always the temptation to accept one aspect of Christ and soft-pedal the rest. And this is true even when we feel we are venerating him, for even in the veneration we can lose Jesus.

He is idolised by many and that is an error. For instead of an idol he should be the ideal; instead of being made into a graven image he should be real and living, for he actually lives today in the same body in which he was crucified. The greatest error is to see his life ending in sorrow and death upon the cross, forgetting entirely that the greater portion of his life is that portion after the resurrection.

He is not a King who can intrude his person upon you, but the all-powerful babe in the manger, who stands ready to help you and heal the world. When he lived in Galilee he could reach only a few. Today he is able to reach all who do not exclude him by the same process by which so many of his first hearers excluded him, because their qualifications were those of a world to which he did not belong.

Many today do not see him because they put him in the shrine of the unapproachable. They surround him with mysteries, and make his miracles something of another order – merely teaching stories – which they are not. These approaches hide the unspeakable love Jesus the Christ has for us all. He is not withdrawn from us, we have withdrawn ourselves from him by the very same veils, walls and partitions, even of the most modern and enlightened theological kinds, which remove Christ from those he loves and leave them no way by which to approach him.

Surrounding the Incarnation in a false mystery leaves the way open for doubt and disbelief; the more images and idols are built, the more he is surrounded by death and made unapproachable, and the deeper the doubt and shadow that will be the case, and the wider the chasm of superstition, and the more meaningless the way of the cross.

The mystery of the Incarnation was given to us in terms that outraged the respectable criteria of most of those who were supposed to know. The richness of the mystery of Christ is hard for us to hold in our minds in its fullness. Some take the revolutionary Christ, and forget most of the rest; some take the pacifist and soft-pedal the remainder. Some take the angry Christ; some the gentle, and forget the one who called Herod a fox, and levelled the greatest insult a Jew could use when he called the Pharisees a brood of vipers. Each feast of Christ through the year highlights some important part of the richness of the full mystery of Christ, so that the dullness of our minds can take complementary views from different standpoints, of something which is too great ever to be grasped in its entirety. Easter highlights his glory, the Feast of the Kingship of Christ, his Lordship, just as the Incarnation, and Epiphany add their own.

At Christmas we see that Christ confounded the so-called respectable criteria of those who were supposed to be in the know, but tragically seemed to be much farther removed from him than even outcast sinners. This is a risk we all run, and, paradoxically, the more we advance in the study of scripture and theology, the more likely we are to fall into the trap of producing images and expectations as the prerequisite conditions under which we will recognise and accept Christ. It is harder to accept him as he reveals himself, for that involves us in continually breaking down the idols which the limits of our knowing constantly erect.

This is what happens when we lost the freshness of that humble mystery of the stable, surrounded by the animals, and those people reckoned among the lowest orders of society. But these were the ones the King of Kings and Lord of Lords had selected to be the first witnesses of his glory: that glory which surprised all by being something of the within; something which was visible only to those not too proud to stoop beneath what they reckoned as their knowledge. The avenue to glory we were shown at Bethlehem, was neither poverty-stricken circumstances, or riches, nor indeed anything external such as riches and poverty are. Glory was shown to those whose hearts were open. The humble conditions were chosen only to serve as a stumbling block that might awaken many.

The Pearl Oyster
College Service of Carols, 19 December 1990

Christmas is the most beautiful time of the year. The Crib, the holly, the carols, the giving of gifts, surprises, visits home, the feasting – all of these caught our memory and imagination in our youth and never really let them go again.

It throws us back to reflect on the mystery of Christ, to see it with a fresh eye. There is probably no more beautiful way to do this than in a ceremony of carols and readings such as we have here tonight.

Christmas lets us see into the heart of things. It was at Bethlehem that we really saw for the first time how difficult it is to understand the ways of God; how he confounds the mighty and brings the expectations of the powerful and the superficial to nought. What man of good judgement would have counselled God to make his grand entry into this world in a stable?

The standards of the world are not the standards of Heaven. To judge by the standards of Heaven is very difficult, but it is the only way in which we can start to transform our lives. Our lives can be transformed by our faith and we must never let the pervasive cynicism of the western world take that reality away from us.

The beginning and the heart of this process is to cease regarding ourselves as victims: victims of our problems, of the people we associate with, of our jobs, of our workers, of our bosses, of the world situation. If we do not cease to regard ourselves as victims we can never begin to know the joy which we are told ceaselessly is the heart of all true religion, and is certainly the heart of the feast of Christmas.

When we experience difficulties we are in the habit of concentrating on them; we begin to think about them all the time, ruminating about all that goes wrong, and that gives us a new cause for worry, anxiety and distress. To look down at our problems is not a good way of dealing with them; we have to try to look up, towards the regions of light and beauty, towards all that can give our soul the stimulus it needs to overcome our difficulties. Cares and sorrows will always exist; Christ never promised to deliver us from them, only that he would make our yoke easy and our burden light. This is the spirit of optimism that we try to recover at Christmas.

We can take a lesson from the pearl oyster. A grain of sand gets into its shell and starts to irritate it. What can it do to get rid of it? Does it let itself get worn down by its difficulties, falling into despair, endlessly indulging in useless complaining and recrimination? No, instead it realises that it could wrap up the grain of sand in such a way that it would be smooth, shiny and velvety, and in that way it transforms the irritant into a beautiful and precious pearl. So every time we have to put up with a painful situation, or with someone we really can't bear, we have to try to look on them as opportunities that can enrich us, if we respond to them rightly. The cynic or the opportunist will never do that of course, forgetting that in reacting to others in a critical, negative or damaging way, we damage ourselves more.

Above all we should remember that people act as mirrors to us, and if we find something that we really can't stand in another person it is most likely that we ourselves have that fault in quite a significant degree. If we can't agree that that is so or can't imagine how that could be, it is probably a sign that the fault has become so much a part of us that it's almost invisible to casual scrutiny.

Isn't it amazing that when we are complimented about some aspect of our character we regard the person speaking to us as so wise and perceptive? But when they point out something unwelcome, we can't imagine how they could make such an error of judgement!

Christ never complained, never concentrated on his worries, and he had plenty. At Christmas we are given the impetus to make a fresh start for in the stable at Bethlehem we have the supreme example of the most sinless, the most beautiful person the world has ever known; someone whose whole being was consumed with infinite love. Love is the opposite of worry, anxiety and endless complaint. Love cannot live in the egocentric person. Egocentricity is the opposite to what being Christlike means, and egocentricity is at the root of almost all our difficulties today.

Christmas is a time for renewal and refreshment, a time for a fresh start, a time when inspired by the emotional ties recollected from the deepest roots of our youth, we try to shake off the old man and put on the new Christ born for us in grace each year at Bethlehem. Let us, College community and friends, join in our service of reading and song in that spirit tonight. Its purpose is to uplift us – to pluck the chords of the innermost strings in the human heart, and to freshen, sharpen and fill with vigour our minds and hearts and wills.

The Christ-mass Tree
College Service of Carols, 18 December 1991

Not very long ago in the history of the Western World there were no museums, galleries, no concert halls; in short no Art with a capital letter, and no Artists. What our museums now exhibit as the art of other cultures and ancient times are religious, magical and household utensils, exquisitely and lovingly made. These are by no means confined to objects of luxury made for the wealthy; they include the pottery, weaving, weapons, jewelry and ritual tools of peasants. If there was any art in such times and cultures, it was simply the masterly production of things needed for everyday life. No one then ever made anything for the express purpose of adorning a museum, of being shown in a gallery, or for being commended in the newspapers. In short the self-conscious practice of art for art's sake hardly existed before the beginnings of modern technology in the widest sense, over the past few centuries. The ear cleansing and eye washing of modern art now taking place in the concert halls, galleries and museums, is probably in preparation for a return to the inseparability of art and everyday life.

We need a similar return to reuniting art with life in many areas of religion, particular in relation to Christmas; it has become a secular feast. In fact quite often Christmas in our world begins in early October and is actually over before Christmas Day itself begins. Christmas has become buried beneath the emotion and the tinsel; the refreshing message of the feast, above all as captured so beautifully in the custom of carol singing, becomes lost as the value of recollection is dulled through nostalgia.

Christmas in truth has to do with something far more deep than sentiment. It is the most beautiful time of the year. The Crib, the holly, the carols, the giving of gifts, surprises, visits home, the feasting – all of these caught our memory and imagination in our youth and never really let them go again. The very Christmas tree serves as an image of what we are ourselves; uprooted from the anonymity of the forest as Christians we are called to a higher destiny; the trinkets and ornaments on the branches represent the victories we have won in our life, as the branches grow more and more narrow until they reach the apex at the top, crowned with the star; the realisation of the purpose of our lives.

Christmas throws us back to reflect on the mystery of Christ, to see it with a fresh eye. There is probably no more beautiful way to do this than in a ceremony of carols and readings such as we have here tonight.

We are entering a new year when many of our most cherished western economic and political institutions will be sorely strained, with the disruption in so many areas that that brings in its wake. We need renewal and strength. Christmas is precisely a time for renewal and refreshment, a time for a fresh start, a time when inspired by the emotional ties recollected from the deepest roots of our youth, we try to shake off the old man and put on the new Christ born for us in grace each year at Bethlehem. It is when we take the beauties of religious art, in depiction, in the beauty of the practise of the Christian life, or in the partaking of beautifully artistic ceremonies such as this, and bring the heart of these art forms in which Christmas is so rich, back from the museum into life.

Let us, College community and friends, join in our service of reading and song in that spirit tonight. Its purpose is to uplift us – to pluck the chords of the innermost strings in the human heart, and to freshen, sharpen and fill with vigour our minds and hearts and wills.

The Winter Tree
A Meditation
16 December 1992

O my Beloved God,
Mysterious One,
Humble me,
That I may be arisen from my limitations.
Greet me this fine morn,
Walk as I walk.
Live in me.
Let your will be done in me this day.
So be it!

The tree as a symbol has always been at the heart of our journey towards God. It was the tree in Genesis that was taken as the symbol of knowledge of good and evil, and of the gift of life itself. It was the tree in the Gospels which Christ took as the symbol of a person who was bearing fruit or not. It was on a tree that the Son of Man died on Calvary. The Christmas tree to-day is one of the most powerful images associated with the feast of the birth of Christ.

Christ always pointed us to learn from nature; there is so much there that is the obvious unobvious.

You can seek out the greatest philosophers, or climb the highest mountain to find the meaning of life. A tree in full leaf in Summer is a magnificent sight. But if you go to the foot of a great oak tree in late December, you will see it at its most real; its bare trunk and branches scoured by the cold north wind. When you come back in March some magic has occurred. It has budded with sap and is clear green. A Spring breeze comes and makes a most pure sound through the fresh leaves. What seemed to be an old and dead being is now resurrected and full of life. Its backbone that was bare is now holding a rich new garment. Where did the garment comes from? Was the great tree dreaming a dream, when it looked to be dead and gone. What the great tree was was a great being dreaming a dream of Spring.

On Midsummer's Eve you can sit beneath the tree again; the leaves now fully grown, and it is the home of insects and birds. This is the cycle. As you examine it more closely you see it has evolved and learned, and developed into the prime of life, with its new and magnificently clothed branches.

When you come back in late Autumn the cold wind has hardened the branches, the leaves that in Winter were once a dream are now edged in gold. Its seems as if they do not want to leave, wrapping themselves curled around the branches, like fingers. The wind blows harder, and the great being shakes off the last trace of its Spring. One great blast and the last golden leaf falls. The leaf has a dream of falling as if it did not want to fall far from what gave it life.

You sometimes never see the beauty of a tree until the leaves are gone. You look at this beautiful thing that no one could ever see because of its burden of leaves; its new body that it dreamed into life when we thought it was dead. When the leaves are gone you see its strength in its nakedness. You never realised it was so everlasting or had such deep and profound wisdom.

The tree is an image of ourselves. What we really are, what is eternal in us, is the bare trunk and branches of the depth of Winter.

What we often think we are are the leaves, the externals, the passing things. If you think you are your leaves you will mourn the insect holes in them, their fading as the Autumn comes, their inevitable death in Winter. How vain we are when we think we are the leaves! We condemn ourselves because we feel we are ugly, because the leaves we have don't appeal to someone else.

But what the human being really is is symbolised in the deep trunk of the bare tree. When you can deepen your life, surrender and go deep inside the trunk of the tree in your consciousness, then you are doing what Christ was born in Bethlehem to bring us to. When we go deep inside the trunk we are steadfast against the storm, when Winter comes and all creatures scurry for cover. It gives a consciousness for inner change and transformation which is what Christ asks of us; a transformation from apparent death into new life as the budding tree of Spring symbolises. Each crisis in life can be a point of growth if we have the right attitude; or it can totally overwhelm us if we decide to let it. Christ asks us not to be frivolous leaves; instead, when we disregard the externals and go within we become as potentially powerful as the oak tree symbolises. His birth at Bethlehem confounded the expectations of the mighty and those who had the reputation of being wise; born in a stable, his first welcome given by shepherds and outcasts.

Leaves are temporal, not everlasting. When you go within you come to know you created all the people who have comes into your life, and all the circumstances, the problems and also the answers. You realise there is nothing in your life you cannot change. Most people see themselves as leaves; Christ wants us to see beyond the appearances, to our real selves; as real, as naked and as uncomplex as the mighty trunk of the great oak in the depth of Winter. When all is said and done, this is the real significance of the tree for Christmas. Doing this is wisdom.

Wisdom is achieved very slowly. This is because intellectual knowledge, which can be achieved very easily, has to be transformed into what we might somewhat inaccurately call 'emotional' or subconscious, knowledge. Once transformed, the imprint is permanent. Behavioural practice is the necessary catalyst of this reaction. Theoretical knowledge without practical application is not enough.

Balance and harmony are neglected today, yet they are the very foundations of wisdom. Everything is done to excess. People are overweight because they eat excessively. Joggers neglect aspects of themselves and others because they run excessively. We eat too much, drink too much, talk too much without content, smoke too much, carouse too much, carouse too little, worry too much. There is too much black or white in the ways we think today. All or nothing. That is not the way of nature.

In nature there is balance. Beasts destroy in small amounts. Ecological systems are not eliminated *en masse*. Plants are consumed and then grow. The sources of sustenance are dipped into and then give a chance to replenish. The flower is enjoyed, the fruit eaten, the root preserved.

The human race has not learned about balance, let alone how to practise it. We are guided so much by greed and ambition, steered by fear. In this way we will eventually destroy ourselves, but nature will survive.

Happiness is rooted in simplicity. Tendencies to excessiveness in thought and action diminish happiness. Excesses cloud basic Christian values. Christ told us that happiness would come from filling one's heart with love, from faith and hope, from practising charity and dispensing kindness. Given those attitudes, balance and harmony will almost certainly follow. These are collectively a state of being. In these days however, they are an altered state of consciousness. It is as if humankind were not in its natural state while on earth. It must reach an altered state in order to fill itself with love and charity and simplicity, to feel purity, to rid itself of its chronic fearfulness.

How does one reach this altered state; and once reached how can it be sustained? The answer appears to be simple. It is in fact the common denominator of all religions. Humankind is immortal, and what we are here in this earth now to do is learn lessons. We are all in school.

If humanity is eternal, why are we doing such bad things to ourselves? Why do we step on and over others for personal gain? We are actually failing our lesson when we do this. We seem all to be going to the same place ultimately, even if it seems to be at different speeds. No one is greater than the other in the eyes of God; we are all his children and loved with a love beyond the wildest dreams of human imagination.

Intellectually we may know all the main answers that our faith gives to the puzzles of life and its problems and its glories. But this intellectual knowledge has to be made actual by experience, by emotionalising it, for want of a better word. There is a world of difference in knowing that there are many hungry and cold in many parts of the world, and actually going out to met them personally in Somalia or the back streets of Dublin.

Memorising the faith is not enough. Lip service without the behaviour is of no value. But to do this, to feel it, requires today almost an altered state of consciousness. It is not the transient state induced by alcohol or drugs, or unexpected emotion. The permanent state which is at the heart of Christianity, and above all at the heart of the feast of Christmas is only reached by knowledge and understanding. It is sustained by physical behaviour, by act and deed, by practice. Understand that no one is greater than the other in the eyes of God. Feel it. Practise helping one another. We are all rowing the same boat. Christianity is above all a religion of practice. Can you gather grapes from thorns or figs from thistles, as Christ asked? By their fruits you shall know them. 'Not everyone who says to me Lord, Lord, will enter the Kingdom of Heaven.' It is taking something nearly mystical and transforming it to every day familiarity by practice, so that it becomes a habit that is the heart of Christianity. The freshness of Christmas so beautifully enshrined in our Scripture readings and tradition of carols restores that perspective to our minds.

Peace and Solitude
College Service of Carols, 15 December 1993

We are gathered for our annual Carol Service tonight, dear friends, at the time when one of the most promising instruments for peace in our country has just been agreed by the British and Irish governments. We pray it will show the way towards a lasting peace. It's very appropriate that there has been such an urge to achieve some significant instrument of peace by Christmas. Peace in its fullest sense was what lay at the very heart of the message of the one whose birth we commemorate; Yeshua Ben Joseph, the incarnate Son of God, who in his human nature came to be called the Christ.

For hundreds of generations the people of the world have cried out for peace, but there has been no peace. Many of the most intelligent and educated men and women have dedicated their lives to the search for peace, and, although it may seem ridiculous, many millions have fought to the death for it in these periodic wars to end all wars.

We have never seemed to be able to grasp the essential message of Christ, the essential message of the first Christmas that was sung by the first carollers, the angels above the stable of the Nativity.

Peace can never be achieved through any direct approach. It is not like gold, which can be obtained by continual digging, nor is it a treasure, which you could discover if you knew where it was hidden. Peace is simply the automatically resulting by-product of complete understanding, between all human beings, between race and race, between state and state, between Church and Church, and between humankind and that all pervading power and intelligence which is God. When such understanding exists, there is no need to search or to work for peace, for it exists automatically, but until such understanding has been achieved, no amount of effort can ever be successful and all agreements and solutions will be built on foundations of sand.

Understanding is one of the most important words in our language which is consistently being misunderstood, or bypassed through the use of other words which may appear to be similar in meaning, but which may actually mislead, such as knowledge, wisdom, love and charity. These are all desirable characteristics, but they cannot take the place of understanding.

When people are commanded to love one another we must be clear on what it is we are asking them to do. Love is not an emotion that is subject to the will. No one can actually love someone simply because they are advised to do so, or even commanded to do so, or because a reward, however great, may be offered. Understanding has to come first, before there can be any genuine love, charity or even wisdom, and most certainly before there can be any lasting peace.

Civilisations have always been built and maintained by people of vision who think and work for the future. What person will be willing to dedicate his or her life and work for the benefit of generations yet unborn if we live in a society from which peace is absent, and that is constantly under threat from political or economic instability, or that offers no hope to the young of what one might reasonably expect from life? Unless lowering of tensions can be achieved together with hope for the future, the motto of succeeding generations is likely to be: Eat, drink and be merry. Some will blame parents for this, others the schools or universities, others blame the Church, the state, or the system. Actually none of these agencies is especially at fault. Youth is particularly sensitive to conditions of insecurity, and never in the history of our race has the future seemed less secure.

When a few generations are reared under such insecure conditions, the state of apprehension will have evolved into one of deep-seated resentment against those elements of society responsible for the danger. The resentment will manifest itself in many ways, but principally in various forms of passive or violent revolt against existing beliefs, morals, institutions, and almost all forms of constituted authority, corrupting even the very notion of God.

In the struggle to rid our society of all these ills – at the heart of which lies the desire for peace – we have the example and strength of the God-Man of Christmas to help us. Jesus came as a brother to mankind, and was a fervent part of it. He lived here as man and experienced all we experienced. He lived our despair, wept our sorrow. He dreamed our dreams and knew our joy; experienced all the perils, the desperation, the fleeting moments of glory that all of us have known. He came to remind us of the wonderful heritage we have forgotton long ago, and to remind us of the wonderful future we are all soon to see. He came to remind us that we have far greater options for our life's expression, and to help us bring forth the knowledge that allows us to exercise those options, if it is our will to do so. And he asked us to apply in our lives, in our own time, and in our own way, whatever understandings are fruitful for us in our own evolution into a more harmonious and a more unlimited and joyful life.

Other centuries witness people's discovery of God in nature, or in God's revealed word among his people, or in people's discovering of God in the unfolding of human intelligence, as shown for instance during the Renaissance or the Industrial Revolution. Our late 20th century must surely be classed as the time in which people are in search of who they truly are in their religion. For the search now, as seen vividly in so many instances today, is no longer *outside* in nature, or in the world of doing, but *inside* of the human person so to speak; fundamentally taking seriously Christ's statement, 'the Kingdom of God is within you'.

This process requires a passing beyond the superficial levels in religion. Discipline, silence and aloneness are basic ingredients. Many people, by no means all of them very obviously religious, are thirsting for this today, many of them unconsciously. Times such as this carol service are rare and special moments. We are lifted for a short while away from the humdrum; the associations of the well-loved words and tunes, the precious passages from scripture, draw up the most uplifting from our memories, and feed again many areas that have been starved of what deep down they most desire.

The true world is not in the marketplace, dear friends. Though it teems there with life, the much grander life is to be found outside of the marketplace; in the quiet and stillness of a church, maybe even at the base of a magnificent tree, or on top of a snowy mountain, where the wind is cold and clean; or in the openness of the bogland, or upon the endlessness of the sea. There is so much more to this life than most of us have allowed ourselves to see. We have yet to really live and investigate it. We must not limit ourselves to the oppressive consciousness of our society, with its judgments and petty ideals, and its mad race against the illusion of time.

We will not truly know life until we have been able to become solitary in such places, at peace with the midnight sky, and the moon that illuminates it until it fades into the brilliance of dawn. Then we will know what Christ meant when he taught us that we should know how valuable we are, and the extent to which we are so loved and needed. Whenever we think there is none who cares, we must know that he does. For he will be with us always as a companion of our precious souls, while pregnant with love and hope and joy, they bloom into magnificent flowers of wisdom, compassion and the love that embraces all life, seen and unseen. There will be times in the emotional storm of that blooming that you'll wish you had never embarked on that path, but far far greater will be the moment when you will realise the image of God within you and know it to be so. These are the thoughts we place before us in this carol service; the ideals which we ask the baby of Bethlehem to strengthen and bring about in our lives.

CHAPTER 2

Friends of Maynooth

The Glory of Life
Friends of Maynooth, Maynooth College Chapel, 4 October 1992

There was once a troubadour; we are told he was a startlingly handsome man, with beautiful olive skin and raven black hair, and eyes as green as river reeds, with very thick lashes. He was very handsome in every way, full of the tone and sinew of youth. And his family dressed him always in the richest of threads and velvets. And he was a dandy among the ladies. He had everything, didn't have to work for a living, and had a host of comrades who loved and adored him.

He went as a brave soldier to war with the blessings of the whole town. When in battle, he was laughing as he engaged the enemy with his friends, and he was looking on it as a sort of game. In fact he was so self-confident in the middle of danger that he was knocked from his horse, and while unconscious was dragged by his foot caught in the stirrup. When he came to, it was night. He was near a small pool of water in a clearing, the horse was grazing, his foot was still caught. He was on his back and looking up into the sky. It was one of those very black nights, with no moon but a few very bright stars. And everywhere there was silence. He gazed up at one of the stars and his whole life and its meaning passed before him for assessment.

He went unconscious again, and the fever raged in his body for weeks. Eventually he was returned to his family, and they kept vigil by his bedside, as they felt each hour might be his last. And there were many visitors, priests, bishops, even a cardinal.

At last, one morning, these river reed green eyes opened up to the sound of a bird on the window singing. All he wanted to do was hold the bird closer to listen to its song. Weak as he was he got out of bed to try to catch the bird, but it fled from him off the sill on to the roof opposite his room. And at that moment he remembered the midnight sky, and the last thing he remembered, was looking up at that bright star while his life flashed before him.

This man was so loved and revered by his family and all the townspeople that they shortly afterwards gave a great party to celebrate his return to health, and all their friends came from far and wide. But he was changed; all the things he used to do with his friends he found he couldn't enjoy any longer. And all the dazzling clothes his parents put on him he had no interest in. All he could think about was that night sky and the bright star; and when they'd catch him in this reverie and ask him what he was so preoccupied about, and he would tell them, they'd shove another brew in front of him and say, 'You'll get over it.'

Every day this man could not wait to get out of the city into the countryside, into the fields of flowers. One day he lay on the ground and put his fingers and toes into the very moist earth of the meadow, and he stayed there with his face in the ground the whole afternoon. Another day he found a stone that was marbled in glittering dust, and he stared at it all day. This was a very different person from the happy-go-lucky warrior that set out for battle a short while before.

He spent all his days in the countryside, and his parents knew they were losing him; that wonderful son, on whom they depended to carry on the family, to take over the family businesses, and perhaps one day to become governor of the province. He smiles at them and he loves them, but they're losing him little by little.

And one day he realised how much he loved God, the God that did not say anything in that dark midnight sky, but was there; that was in the bird that sang a song to his awakening, and in the moist and good earth that allowed him just to lie there, and in the poppies that dazzled his eye with blazing scarlet colours and the humming of bees and the iridescence of butterfly wings. He realised that this God he loved was the unseen gift all around him. His parents thought he had gone off the deep end and threw endless parties to try to get him to snap out of it. They even sent him to talk to the priests, who only shook their heads. Finally, one day at a great party, when he was dressed in the most dazzling of clothes his parents could procure for him, he stripped down naked in front of all the assembly, minister, priests, family, women, friends, goats, sheep, horses, the sky, the earth, the village. Not that he was an exhibitionist; it was a sign that he didn't belong to this kind of life any more. And he ran from the city with a song in his heart to find some cloth of the field to cover his body. And there was a song in his heart, and a gentle spirit that was born of the fever. Later he would find an old place and begin to build it up with stones, through freezing winter rains, and his worship to the glory of God was the kingdom of the earth.

The greatest contribution that that midnight sky made to him was not the image for which he had lived so long, but the beauty within man and woman. The fever burned away the image so that he could see what he had never seen before. He turned the page and changed. His parents could no longer see in him the reflection of the glory they lacked in themselves. His friends could no longer see in him the camaraderie they lacked in themselves. The women could no longer see in him the need for a lover they lacked in their lives. He changed and they couldn't see in him any more what they were themselves. They would have to grow to find in him what was in themselves all along.

What was looking out now from those green eyes was no longer the image, but the magnificent light he had become. He would walk in the fields and the birds and the animals would go with him, and once a great wolf or mountain lion came and lay at his feet. And why did he call things brothers and sisters? Because they were. A wild animal will not lie down beside a person devoted to the image, because the image is the stagnation of regressive energy, copulation, pain and power. But a lion will lie down at the feet of a great light and find a oneness with it, because the light that it sees is the life force of its very being.

This man lived the rest of his life being a glory to the God that had emerged in him. He sang of the glory of life and tried to educate people, not in doctrine, but in a simplicity of knowledge. He lived no hypocrisies but was devoted only to God. He became hated and despised, because he tried to shine in the darkness, while someone else guarded the switch.

This is a true story. The dashing young man was St Francis of Assisi. His feast is today, 4 October, and even though Sunday is a Feast of the Lord I thought it not too inappropriate to remember him at this Mass, for his virtues were truly dominical and very appropriate to our assembly. Not everyone can do as Francis did; the world still has to go on, but we do occasionally need individuals who in a dramatic and striking way embody in their lives a true vision of the world and its values. He dissolved the image to find the light that he was and changed everything. What courage it took to walk away from cloth-of-gold and velvet? To run away naked was not to shock, but to say 'none of these things define what I am.'

And what courage it took to walk into the wilderness not knowing where you'd sleep that night.

This stand against the world will be needed in every age. Most of the afflictions that obsess us today are simply the result of a bad culture, bad living, bad habits, bad thinking. They are not necessarily signs of changing times. Most of modern technology, for example, is enormously useful to us and elevates the level of life. The problem is its seduction, for it tends to siphon off all of the talent and creativity that needs also to go into the direct transformation of human nature. If not, life becomes unbalanced. Behind the development of every great new technology there stands a withered human faculty.

For two hundred years the main work of this institution has been to try to walk to a different drummer; to assert that there are centrally important technological values, but that there are others that must be kept alive and well with them to assure the quality of life and human hope; where there is hatred, love; injury, pardon; where there is doubt, faith; where there is despair, hope; where there is darkness, light, and where there is sadness joy. More than 10,000 priests have walked out of this chapel in which we are, to dedicate their lives to that ideal, not certainly in the dramatic way Francis did, but the gesture was at heart the same. In the last quarter century an equal number of young lay people have left here, in different roles, but by and large, we hope, with the same spirit.

All of you here this morning have also now for several years made yourselves partners in this enterprise at Maynooth, and have truly believed that it is in giving you receive; in forwarding the work of an institution dedicated to the ancient Greek ideal of educating the whole person, where, to a degree probably unique today, the arts and sciences, philosophy and theology, are studied together in a community still small enough and homogeneous enough for that interaction of disciplines to take place that is at the heart of the *universale*, at the heart of any true university.

For these and so many other reasons it is a great joy for us here at Maynooth to have you back once more with us today. And especially for Mass in this beautiful chapel, for the Mass is at the centre of that process of transformation of the human person in which the heart of salvation is found. If we could today suffuse our attitude to God and the world with the spirit of Francis it would make such a great difference to our awareness; our awareness above all of a God who is both immanent in and transcendent of the world. This is, in fact, the heart of what catholicism means, and it was probably never better summed up in practice than in the prayer attributed to Francis.

As I said at the start, stories were often the format in which profound knowledge was given in ancient times, and it is one of the greatest ways in which to start our minds working outside the perimeters of their barriers: to give a story and let it be reflected on; for first impressions will never be the same as the final understanding for the person looking for something else in life other than the expectations of what society has and has not.

Water, Air, Sea and Wind

Friends of Maynooth, Maynooth College Chapel, 23 June 1991

At what must be the pinnacle of the New Testament, Jesus the Christ said to the disciples: 'I no longer call you servants, but friends.'

This was the high point of how he referred to them during his ministry, the greatest title he had given them. So friendship must rank high in what is prized in the Christian dispensation.

This College is involved in many disparate but complementary enterprises, ranging over a great many of the main branches of human wisdom and knowledge, while attending to the things of the spirit to which we all aspire with different degrees of success. All of you are helping to forward that work which has done such a great deal to uplift our country in the past and will continue to do so in the future. For that reason we are all friends here, Friends of Maynooth, in a very special sense engaged in a common task, our eyes fixed on a common ideal. We appreciate what you have done and value your presence here in the College for these few hours when we hope to share with you something of the life of Maynooth in a pleasant setting. When all the hustle and bustle is over we realise '...There's nothing worth the wear of winning/ But laughter and the love of friends' (Belloc: *Dedicatory Ode*).

The New Testament has many levels, dear friends, that lie hidden because of the blindness of our Western eyes. The miracle of the stilling of the storm on the Lake in today's Gospel is a sublime example.

We often consider the accounts of the miracles of Jesus in the New Testament, to be merely narratives of wonder works which he did. They are so, but perhaps in a sense even more significant is the further message they gave to the Eastern mind. And we can never forget that despite the fact that the history and doctrinal formulations of Christianity were mostly forged in the Greek and Latin Western traditions, Christianity is an Eastern faith in its heart.

In terms of that Eastern faith the miracles accounts have many levels – our own level of development and our openness to understanding determines the level which unfolds to us.

If the New Testament, for example, wants to proclaim Christ's divinity, it does not do so in the direct way we would nowadays find more natural and familiar, and say simply: 'Jesus is God.' Instead it adumbrates it – or more accurately, *seems to us* to adumbrate it – in an immensely richer way by letting a narrative carry the message.

In the Old Testament there were some central works regarded as belonging to God alone. Some of them are conveniently listed for us in both the Old and the New Testaments: God was the one who relieved the starving, he gave the bread of life; the blind see, the lame walk, the lepers are cleansed, the poor have the gospel preached to them. These are the signs of the messianic age, when there will be no illness, evil or infirmity. Jesus is pictured as doing all of these things, reiterating the acts of God as seen in the Old Testament.

But one of the most significant properties of God was the one told in today's Gospel reading: the stilling of the storm on the sea of Galilee, and the walking on the water, told in another Gospel.

The Jews of old were mortally afraid of the Deep; they regarded it as the abode of mysterious forces, of demons, spirits, the home of the unknown. The Messiah when he came would have to go down into the Deep to subdue it. But the walking on the water and the control of the forces of nature were the prerogative of God, or of those who partook of God in a very profound way. So, in today's Gospel, when the disciples say: 'Who is this man that the winds and the sea obey him?' they are stating what the Western mind would more comfortably express in the vocabulary of the Creed: He is 'consubstantial with the Father.'

So strange as it may be to our Western understanding none of the miracles stories about Jesus is merely an account of wonders that he undoubtedly accomplished, but is primarily a proclamation of Christ's divinity given to those who have faith.

It is a call to faith, for in the realm of the divine there will always be things we do not know, or have not yet lived and seen. So too in the realm of science: today's metaphysics so often turns out to be tomorrow's physics.

Faith is about the most subtle of things: those which are farthest from us and which cannot immediately be verified. To have faith is to leave space for something invisible and intangible.

If you do not have that, then no matter what success you

achieve, you will be fearful – as were the disciples in the boat – needlessly, forgetting you have the greatest power so close to hand

Christ represents love, wisdom and truth within us. When great upheavals take place in our soul, the only real way to calm is to call on the help of love and wisdom.

Wisdom can make the clouds vanish and still the winds, and love makes the ocean calm. Wisdom acts on the wind, that is on our thoughts, and love acts on the ocean of our feelings.

We can open our minds to see the whole Gospel incident at another level when another very deep meaning is conveyed through a teaching parable. The boat is the mind, within which repose the negative traps of fear, guilt, anger, and aggression, represented by the frightened disciples. But there is also present in the mind the still centre represented by Jesus, the Spirit within, who represents love, wisdom and truth.

The wind is our thoughts, the ocean our feelings, which can be so churned up by what is negative in our minds, especially when we fail to realise the power that we have so close to hand. The Spirit within (Jesus) can control the thoughts (the wind), and through them the feelings (the ocean) and thus transmute the negative traps in the mind (the disciples).

Water, air, sea and wind – these are precious symbols of the acts of God as they touch what is eternal in human experience. The Apostles, faithful to the Eastern mind, were acutely aware of their value, and recorded in the Gospels only those events that were significant on all planes. It is up to us to open our hearts to receive their richness to the full. The preparatory ground feeling for it all is friendship.

Keepers of the Bell
Los Angeles, 25 February 1989

George Bernard Shaw, at the end of a long letter to a friend once wrote: 'Sorry this has been such a long letter; I didn't have time to write a short one.'

It's always difficult to say briefly what is as profound and sincerely felt as the happiness and gratitude which the Catholic Church in Ireland, symbolised in Maynooth College, feels towards all of you, our friends, here this evening. No institution has ever contributed more to the Irish national sense of identity, its cultural richness, and its religious vitality, than has that very complex reality called 'Maynooth,' with its 200 years of tradition, a Pontifical University, College of the National University of Ireland, and one of the largest seminaries in the Western world, with over four hundred seminarians among its 2,500 students – a number growing every year.

I want to thank you all on behalf of Cardinal Ó Fiaich, the College Trustees, and on behalf of the college staff and myself. You have given us a really incredible amount of support here in Los Angeles in our programme for the college's restoration programme, which is now at its half way mark in this city. What can I say by way of gratitude except to invite you to come and see us when you are next in Ireland? You will receive, at a minimum, the 100,000 welcomes! But I think we never appreciated what that phrase really meant until we experienced your hospitality for us in Los Angeles.

The ancient Romans, although I did not know them personally, had a famous one-liner: *Ex Africa semper aliquid novi* – 'There is always something new coming out of Africa.' The words are Julius Caesar's, across the span of 2,000 years.

I was delighted when I heard I was to be guest of honour here and speaker at the opening of this new restaurant, but when I heard my rostrum was to be called 'Engine Company No 28,' I decided, with no leave from Caesar, to alter the classical one-liner to read: *Ex America occidentale semper aliquid novi* – in free translation: 'Los Angeles is always full of surprises' particularly when the Mullin clan is about.

Here in the United States, John Mullin, born in Ireland in 1830, built the Mullin Wagon Road. I hope this new restaurant will be a very significant stop on this particular wagon road in Los Angeles. There are many people who have great influence in this city here tonight – can we move them to have Figueroa named more appropriately!?

In ancient Ireland, in County Tyrone, the Mullins were for centuries the hereditary keepers of St Patrick's Bell, which the Saint used at Mass all through his missionary labours in Ireland fifteen centuries ago.

Sometimes one gets a neck-prickling sense of the significance and suitability of events that happen in the course of history. This was the way I felt when I saw the Mullins become the new keepers of St Patrick's Bell in this city, in a metaphorical, but very tangible sense. For it is St Patrick's College at Maynooth that, above all others, carries on the mission of our national apostle in modern Ireland, and the Mullins were the people who bore that particular bell here in California. Pam Mullin, in a way that I can only poorly express, made this her personal cause in Los Angeles.

Peace to this house. I am here tonight to pay a heartfelt tribute to all our friends in Los Angeles who have supported this first phase of Maynooth's campaign so magnificently. In so doing they have done something magnificent too for the whole of the Catholic Church in Ireland.

In ancient Ireland, when they spoke of a happy evening they said: 'He stayed until the skylarks sang at dawn'; so, skylarks, welcome, and beware!

And something more: when the ancient Irish offered a new enterprise to the future, as we do tonight with this new restaurant and fabulously restored heritage building, 'Engine Company No 28', they said: (and I begin in the Irish language):

> Ag Críost an síol; ag Críost an Fómhair
> In Iothlann Dé go dtugtar sinn.
>
> To Christ the seed; To Christ the harvest
> In Christ's barn may we all come to rest.
>
> To Christ the sea, to Christ the fish
> May Christ catch all of us in his net.
>
> From boyhood to man; and from age to death
> In Christ's strong arms may we be embraced.
>
> From death to light; and to the Light of Lights
> May we be in step with Christ in paradise.

Dear friends, I implore God's blessing and our blessing and gratitude on all of you here, particularly Peter and Pam. May it rest on your friendships, on your loyalties, and on this food which we now sit down to share with our friends.

The City of God
Brooklyn, 9 September 1992

Brooklyn is the only entirely urban diocese in the world.

At first glance we might feel that this must surely be an auspicious thing, for the whole complexity of what we call civilisation came from the city. The change from a pastoral to an urban setting was what brought about the specialisation of labour that first freed people from the necessity of producing their own food, and left the way open for the development of dedicated arts and crafts. As the resources of the city could be marshalled for a common purpose more easily than could a scattered rural population the city also led to the elaboration of a closer political unity.

St Augustine, in his *magnum opus* 'The City of God', a magnificent, if somewhat disjointed overview of Christian and Roman history, used the city to give a theological interpretation to the struggle of conflicting allegiances in society. This he symbolised in the clash of the two cities that constitute the spiritual-material tension which always runs down the mainstream of history.

We cannot afford to forget that Christians first contrasted themselves with 'pagans,' a term which, among other things, was used to describe people who lived in the country. If this is so, then 'Christian' must originally have had the secondary meaning of 'city dweller.'

The Duke of Wellington once told a new member of Parliament about to give his maiden speech: 'Don't quote Latin; say what you have to say, and sit down!'

At the risk of ignoring this sound advice I suppose I could sum the matter up by saying in the words of the motto of the city of Dublin: '*Obedientia civium, urbis felicitas*' – the happiness of a city contributes to the well-being of the citizens, if we twist the meaning around a little.

If all these wonderful things be true of cities then surely we might be pardoned if we imagined that the Bishop of Brooklyn, in whose home we are honoured to be guests tonight, must preside over the most fortunate diocese in Christendom.

But we all know that that is far from the case and that the myriad of problems that face society everywhere today are greatly magnified in large cities. Problems of racial diversity, inequality of opportunity, homelessness, hunger, streams of lawlessness and anarchy, substance abuse, crime of all categories, decline of religion and a thousand other problems, seem to have found their most fertile breeding ground where large numbers congregate.

If the historic advantages of the city have become so overshadowed by the disadvantages, then we know that the only completely urban diocese in the world, must have more than the average share of the world's problems.

This is why Maynooth College owes such a very deep debt of gratitude to Bishop Daily of Brooklyn for assembling this very significant gathering of the lay leadership in his diocese to meet us here to night. He has not been so overcome by the magnitude of his own problems that he has no concern for the wider Church, and particularly for the Church in Ireland, from which came so many of the priests and lay people of this diocese in the nineteenth and twentieth centuries.

For that reason I have great pleasure in replying to your address of welcome by expressing our warmest appreciation of your magnificent kindness and hospitality here tonight, and also in many other significant ways in your help to me for quite a long time.

We all express the hope and prayer that in your future pastoral care here over the years ahead Augustine's struggle of the entangled fortunes of the two 'cities' formed by conflicting loves, may emerge into the happy situation which first caused Christians to proudly label themselves 'townsmen.'

The Longest Procession in History
Immigration Museum, Ellis Island, New York Harbour, 30 October 1993

The English poet, John Donne, spoke of America as 'my new found land.'

The native Irish language speakers of the West of Ireland called America, and still do: 'An tOileán Úr,' the adjective 'úr' meaning new, fresh, original, verdant, noble. So America is the new and noble land.

These impulses of language came to be fact for a single reason: America had re-invented hope.

Two thirds of all the surnames on earth are to be found in the USA – creating the greatest genealogical forest in history. Most of the trees of that forest began here in this great hall of Ellis Island as saplings: transplants from poverty, famine and persecution.

In Ireland, combining the Gael and the English, there are at least a thousand ballads about the glory and the heartbreak of the journey to exile in the USA.

The simplest version of the dream is in the sentimental ballad, 'I'm sitting on the stile, Mary,' where Mary's lover sings to her about the enchantment of America:

> 'They say there's bread and work for all
> And the sun shines always there.'

To go back to surnames: Lazarus, with its biblical associations with rising from the dead, is the surname of the author of the lyric of mercy on the Statue of Liberty.

The Fitzgerald families world-wide all stem from Maynooth; a Fitzgerald, Scott Fitzgerald, defined America as 'a willingness of the heart.'

And speaking of definitions, Abraham Lincoln, in the Gettysburg address, gave all mankind the briefest and noblest picture of what the human soul should be in society anywhere. He also left us the gravest and gentlest face of any public man in history.

The Lincolns pre-dated Ellis Island, but the Lazaruses, the Fitzgeralds, the Jews, Italians, Germans, Swedes, the Irish – the *et cetera* is endless – made their landfall here on this spot.

The early pictures of the immigrants, so many hanging here on the walls of this museum, the classic pictures of the American Indians in the middle of the last century, together with Brady's pictures of the Civil War, in which so many Irish died on both sides, are for me the most moving in their own time, or any time.

We are on the site where the greatest procession in history began: a journey towards liberty and equality, towards opportunity; and in this technological age, towards a country which is an experimental station for the whole earth in all the sciences, and is still young

If the first arrivals here were allowed to syncopate space and time in an effort to see the shape of things to come, they might well have hit on Walt Whitman:

> 'Lo, body and soul – this land,
> My own Manhattan with spires and the
> Sparkling and hurrying tides and the ships.
> The varied and ample land, the South and
> The North in the light, Ohio's
> Shores and flashing Missouri,
> And ever the far-spreading prairies
> Cover'd with grass and corn.'

From this very beautiful and providential land of America, which carries so much of the new world and the old world of Ireland in what makes it up, I want to thank especially those few people whose dedication to the cause of Ireland, to the cause of the Church in Ireland, and particularly to the cause of Maynooth, puts us all to shame.

Nos alegramos mucho de que pueda estar aqui esta tarde su Alteza Real, el Príncipe de Asturias. Nos es muy grata su presencia entre nosotros, Don Felipe. Recuerdo con gran placer la visita que rindieron sus Señores Padres a Maynooth hace unos siete años. Espero que Usted mismo pueda venir un dia a nuestro Colegio, que aun sigue cumpliendo hoy con la misión que desarrollaron en tiempos pasados los varios Colegios Irlandeses, importantes Instituciones situadas en su misma tierra y apoyadas por la siempre generosa Patria de España.

I cannot let this occasion pass either without recognising among us this evening someone whose presence is especially significant in the light of history, the Prince of Austurias, Don Felipe de Burbon y Burbon. The greatest classic of Irish folksongs, written in mystical language, four hundred years ago, during Ireland's darkest days of misery, looked for deliverance to two sources; 'the wine from the royal Pope,' and to Spain, where so many Irish found refuge in those tortured days. I was privileged in my own time so see both the Pope, and the King and Queen of Spain, present in person in Maynooth. For that reason, Prince Felipe, while we at Maynooth were, of course, deeply honoured by the decision of your parents to visit our College during their State Visit to Ireland, even more so it was for us a sign of the completion of a destiny; a profound symbol of something that lies deeply buried in the age old links between Ireland and your country.

Maynooth College was founded on the site of what would have grown to be Ireland's first university, which sadly perished four hundred years ago in the Irish civil wars in the aftermath of the Reformation.

The present 'Maynooth', as it's usually called, was founded by an entirely Protestant Parliament long before the Penal days had ended; its founders saw Maynooth as being the heir to the great medieval monastic schools of Ireland, Clonard, Clonmacnoise, Glendalough, from which the treasures of Europe were brought back again to the mainland after the dark ages, by the Irish missionary monks, who were the spiritual and intellectual giants of their day.

Some years ago I heard the father of the European Community, Jean Monnet, say that if he were to embark once again on the process of the unification of Europe, he would not have started by establishing economic bonds, he would have started with culture.

Surely at the heart of culture must stand those values, principles and vision that elevate the spirit of the human person after the message of Christ.

This is what the present day Maynooth has stood for, now that it stands at the dawn of its third century. It is one of the few really native institutions to have emerged in the history of modern Ireland.

No single Irish institution has done as much for the Irish people, not only in the religious field, but in the areas of local and social and economic development, as has Maynooth. Its founders must have seen Maynooth as the phoenix of the Church in Ireland rising from the ashes of the Penal Days. Inspired people perceive today that what happens in Maynooth in the present is what will happen in the entire Church in Ireland tomorrow. The future and health of Maynooth is the health and future of the Irish Church.

The Muffled Bells
**Dinner to Honour the Governor of Pennsylvania,
The Hon Robert P. Casey, Patron of the Maynooth Bicentenary**
Philadelphia, 27 April 1994

Philadelphia, the city of brotherly love, was founded, like the United States itself, as a fundamentally religious aspiration towards a happier humanity. People have an official view of what a city is. Philadelphia is the mother city of the United States and was its capital for ten years. And it was the State where the Federalist Papers, Founding Fathers, Constitution and Liberty Bell, all came together, and where the human being began to find his true definition, as free and enterprising. And where wisdom began of course the world had to copy. America's emergence from isolationism forced the USSR to see itself in terms of global reality and shaped the Europe that we know today.

As far as enterprise goes, the Americans were already trying to sail from here to China in 1782. A European is astonished to see the speed with which the United States expanded. In 1800 it was within a line drawn from the Great Lakes to New Orleans, but by 1850 the whole West was American. And when the capital of North Dakota was inaugurated, just beyond living memory, in 1883, at Bismarck,

James Brice was there, former President Ulysses Grant and Sitting Bull.

'Who could mock,' someone once said, 'this certain type of American, the one who has mastered the art of living and asserted the power of humanity over what once seemed totally ineluctable facts?'

It was of course in Ireland's darkest hour that countless thousands left their homeland and found refuge and opportunity here, particularly in this great Commonwealth. And among them were the forebears of its illustrious Governor, Robert P. Casey. No prizes for guessing what the 'P' stands for! We are enormously proud to be able to honour him here tonight.

No State of the Union is more historic than Pennsylvania. Here and in the neighbouring areas were the great battlefields of the maturity of this nation, including Gettysburg, the high-water mark of the Confederacy, and the bloodiest battle in all recorded history up to that time. An equal number of Irish fell on both the Confederate and Union sides.

It was through the kindness of John Elliott, and his brother Tom, that I first came to know this State many years ago now. John of course was the principal mobiliser of this dinner. And in addition to the personal debt of gratitude which I owe him, to do justice I want to thank him and Eileen most warmly for this marvellous event which you have put on tonight, and also the marvellous team of co-chairmen whom he has marshalled together, whose hard work made this celebration possible. There are few people outside of Ireland who have so entered into the soul of the spirit of Ireland as has John Elliott. I want to thank most warmly, as well, Lois Egan, for her tireless efforts to make this dinner the success it was; my brother Tom has told me so frequently of the heroic efforts that she has made.

Heritage is the strong suit in Philadelphia, and one of the first historic names which I associated as a child with this city was Commodore John Barry, Father of the American Navy, born in Ireland, in County Wexford, five or six miles from my own birthplace. His bronze statue stands here outside Independence Hall. Thirty-eight years ago I saw General Eisenhower unveil an exact replica of that Philadelphia statue in my native town of Wexford. In 1963 I saw President Kennedy honour his memory there as well. I was delighted when I came here first, as John Elliott's guest, to see that Commodore Barry's name was honoured in the great bridge that bears his name in this city, and I gather there's another interesting story behind the naming of that bridge which John, I'm sure, will be glad to convey to those interested!

President Nixon, whose burial took place today, was also one very proud of his Irish roots. I distinctly remember many years ago his descent from the sky at Timahoe, County Kildare, in a large helicopter which seemed to block out the daylight, to visit his ancestors' home place, very close to Maynooth. He was one of the greatest of those who charted American foreign policy to which the modern world owes so much today. May the Lord receive him into his peace.

Many bonds of heritage link this part of the United States with Maynooth College. Maynooth College is not just an institution. It is a cause, and a truly great cause. The vast majority of the people of Ireland, for two centuries, have owed their nurturing in the faith to priests ordained at Maynooth. And in addition to its religious role in binding up the broken-hearted and raising the helpless from the earth in both good times and bad, it has more than any other native Irish institution contributed to the building up of modern Ireland. The names of the Irish saints that grace so many of the parishes throughout this country is eloquent testimony of the silent footsteps of those Irish priests from Maynooth or from the smaller seminaries in Ireland largely staffed by Maynooth priests, who came here to minister to their fellow-countrymen and build up the Catholic Church in this land. And as we have often said, those who now want to give back something to Maynooth for that, are in fact touching on something far deeper than they may realise.

I suppose, after the United States, the greatest contact Maynooth had was with Australia. Last Thursday I had the great pleasure of seeing Thomas Kenneally, the distinguished author of *Schindler's List*, being introduced for an Honorary Doctorate of the National University of Ireland. He was a former seminarian himself at Manly College in Australia, a College modelled on Maynooth, and he spoke feelingly about what our College has done in his native land. I know Schindler himself wished to be buried in the old Latin cemetery in Jerusalem and that it was Irish priests who worked to make that wish a reality.

Through the inspiration of Bill and Virginia McCann, more than seventy distinguished Americans will be our guests at Maynooth for more than a week in May. I think that's possibly the best evidence that the relationships between Maynooth and the United States is set to grow and blossom for the next two centuries as it has in the past. And on top of the heritage wall at Maynooth is the name of the official Maynooth patron in this Commonwealth: Governor Robert P. Casey. All our forebears, as well as his, would be as enormously proud of Governor Casey as we are. I remember back in 1986, John Elliott phoned me, literally within minutes of the election results for the Governorship here, and gave me the good news. I said we would have to light all the bonfires on the tops of the hills in Ireland tonight, now that a native son had reached the supreme office in this great State, which, after all, we must remember, is three times the population of Ireland in size. I was privileged on that momentous day, 20 January 1987, to attend his inauguration as Governor, at Harrisburg, surrounded by a snow-covered Pennsylvania countryside.

I mentioned that there is a private view of Philadelphia, in addition to the official view, and that private view is my own. I once heard a story that recalls probably the most beautiful and touching of all the virtues. This city has a Greek name and the ancient Greeks called this virtue, *eusebeia*, filial piety in the home. It is a great jewel of civilisation.

The story is this: a man was driving his horse-drawn tram through the streets of Philadelphia, when someone called out to him that President Lincoln had been shot. He stopped the horses, got down and muffled the little bells on the horses' necks, and then proceeded onwards through the April snow.

Beautiful America! The America of loyalty, of filial piety and reverence: the thing which so often escapes the superficial gaze of people who observe this great land from the outside – those who provide a voice for those who have no voice, who stand up for the weak and the down-trodden, when there is no margin in it for themselves. Surely these great qualities of America are the most precious, and surely it is those who possess those qualities who are most close to God. And it is these who provide an enduring example and lift us up by their inspiration. I firmly believe that there is no greater example of what is mighty and strong and powerful in beautiful America, and above all of filial piety, than the person whom we at Maynooth have been deeply honoured by being allowed to honour tonight.

Governor Casey, thank you for the rare leadership that you have shown. It has cost you greatly but has been an inspiration for many. We feel for you a pride which words, unfortunately, can only very inadequately express, and we pray that God will shower you with his choicest blessings for your indomitable leadership, and above all your personal courage and integrity.

A Destiny Fulfilled

Museum of Science, Boston, 1 November 1994

Your Eminences Cardinals Law and Daly, your Excellencies, Ladies and Gentlemen:

We are gathered tonight to honour one of the few really native institutions to have emerged in the history of modern Ireland.

In the Dark Ages the treasures of European culture were preserved in the monastic schools of Ireland, and re-imported into Europe later in more propitious times.

When dark times descended in turn on Ireland itself, it never lost hope. In the words of our most ancient folk song, *Róisín Dubh*, it looked to two sources to sustain its courage: to the 'royal Pope' and to Spain.

In our own time we were privileged to see both the Pope and the King of Spain walk in the cloisters of Maynooth, surely a potent sign for those who cherish any imagination in their souls.

Two centuries ago the founders of Maynooth College saw it as the heir to Ireland's medieval monastic schools. It rapidly became the largest seminary in the world, and its contribution to the making of modern Ireland went far beyond the religious, for its contribution in cultural and social upbuilding was immense.

Over the last thirty years this less obvious role of Maynooth down the years has been made more visible and concrete in its reaching to impart an education of a higher quality and a different stamp to lay people. These have now graduated in numbers equal to the ten thousand priests who have gone out from Maynooth to all parts of the world.

We ask God's blessing tonight on the work of that great institution in all its aspects and on all of you in turn who have espoused its cause by gathering here tonight, and who will enable it to ensure that its future will be as promising as its past is proud.

> O God, our Beloved Father,
> We give thanks for this hour,
> For that which we are.
> We knew not, understood not,
> That which we could be.
> O come forth this hour and support us greatly.
> Allow our minds to open and bloom,
> and our lives to change gracefully.
> Bring forth the joy and make us free.
> We ask this through Christ our Lord.

CHAPTER 3

Opening of the Academic Year

The Unnameable Hunger:
The Whole Law and the Prophets
Opening of the Academic Year, October 1985

If you ask a person what they want above all from life, the reply is likely to contain the wish: 'I want to be happy.' Most people put this at the top of the list; even those who land themselves into bizarre situations, that are often enough just misguided attempts to look for happiness in ways that are ill-judged and unwise. Most people who are aware work hard at trying to make themselves happy. They buy books, attend classes, maybe even change their lifestyles, in an on-going effort to trap that elusive quality.

It is equally obvious that most people for a lot of the time do not seem to be very happy. Happiness seems to be elusive, escaping just as effectively from those who get what they want in life, as it does from those who do not. In fact there often seems to be two main tragedies in life: getting what you want, and not getting it, and it's sometimes hard to determine which is worse. Why do so many who we think have every reason to be content and fulfilled, still feel that there is something important missing from their lives? Is it that we are asking too much when we say 'All I want is to be happy'?

Or is it that it's an impossible goal – something like perpetual youth, or the secret of perpetual motion, something very desirable, but which we are not meant to reach, no matter what effort we expend on it? Or is it in fact possible to find true happiness, and that it's just we are going about it the wrong way?

No matter how hard we work at success – in getting our examinations – in First Arts or Second Science – success normally doesn't satisfy for very long. By the time we get there, having had to sacrifice so much on the altar of success in the process, we realise that success is not what we wanted. We can see that more clearly with people who have money and power: we pry into their private affairs, we see their fictionalised conflicts on television, and we feel if we had what they have, we'd be certainly happy; but we never seem to get the message. They are looking for something more. They know something you and I do not know, and might not even believe if told: that money and power will not satisfy this unnameable hunger in the soul. No matter how hard we work at being popular or successful, and no matter how good we are at it, people hardly ever seem to have reached the point where they can happily relax and feel they have arrived. For we know that if our sense of who we are depends on popularity and other people's estimate of us, our happiness will always be dependent on the co-operation of these other people.

I am speaking about these things today when we have our Mass to implore God's blessings on the new academic year. We are living in very difficult times educationally in Ireland at present – though I suppose people involved in education are prone always to believe that is the case! There are enormous pressures on all third-level institutions in the country to reduce costs, reduce courses, reduce staff, to become more cost-effective. Jobs at the end of the courses unfortunately seem to have become fewer as well, with no particular effort on the part of anybody. The spectre of emigration has started to loom again. It is a great tragedy that each year we lose so many of the brightest and best of our students, the life-blood of our country.

In such a climate it is all too easy to start to look out ruthlessly for number one, and be determined to get to the top no matter how many you have to trample on in the process – and that can be as true of the policy of an institution as it can be of an individual student or staff member.

Or it's very easy to become despondent, to feel our lives are senseless and empty; nobody cares. If a tree falls in the forest and there is no human ear to hear, does it make a sound? If a person lives and dies and nobody notices, and the world continues as it was, was that person ever really alive in the true sense? I think it's not the fear of death, of our lives ending, that haunts so many today, as the fear that our lives will not have mattered, and that as far as the world is concerned, we might as well have never lived. This is a big chasm facing the unemployed, and those threatened by it: because we live in a society that places all its value on brute success, as that is conventionally measured. What we miss most is a sense of meaning.

There is an old Yiddish saying: 'To a worm in horse-radish, the whole world is horse-radish.' In short, if we have never known an alternative, then we assume the way we are living, with all its frustrations and disappointments, is the only way to live. This is the way we allow our lives to become cheapened – even those of you in your teens and early twenties. We assume life has always involved traffic jams, and air and environmental pollution, and frustrations of every kind. We accept it and become passive and inert. Or we drop out in disgust, leave them to it, and flee to a rural environment with a simple lifestyle, where we can grow our own food organically.

Counselling can help us face up to the fact that the world we live in is horseradish. It can cure us of unrealistic expectation about the world. It can teach us to adjust and be less frustrated by it.

But it cannot whisper to us of a world we have never seen or tasted.

Psychology can teach us to be normal, but we have to look elsewhere for the help we need to become fully human.

And the question about whether life has a meaning, or whether our individual lives make any real difference, is fundamentally a religious question. By this I do not mean only the types of questions the Churches are posing or ought to be posing, if they are not. Religious questions are not just about matters of belief, or attendance at religious services, but are fundamentally about ultimate values and ultimate concerns. It is religious because it is about what is left to deal with when you have learned everything else there is to learn, and solved all the problems that can be solved. For religion focuses on the difference between the human and all other species, and on the search for a goal so significant that we make our lives significant by attaching ourselves to it.

The pursuit of happiness is the wrong goal. Don't set out to look for happiness. You do not become happy by pursuing it. You become happy by living a life that means something. The happiest people you know are probably not the most well-off financially, or the most famous or successful – again as these matters are conventionally measured. Neither are they likely to be the ones who work hardest at being happy; by reading the articles and buying the books and latching on to the latest diets or fads. I suspect the happiest people we know are the ones who work hard at being kind, helpful and reliable, and happiness sneaks into their lives when they are busily distracted doing other things. It seems always to be a by-product, rarely a primary goal. Happiness is a butterfly: the more you chase it the more it flies away and escapes.

And unfortunately, we often forget that the achievements which society tends to reward most are normally won at the cost of precisely this diminution of personality. And many aspects of life that could have been experienced and enjoyed lie instead undisturbed in the attic room of dusty memories.

This is what we neglect when we are chasing happiness. We distort our personalities in the strain to become good at certain aspects of our work. We refuse to spend time with our ageing parents, our children, our parishioners; with those who are old, lonely or suffering, because we have to run off to a seminar on the value of human relationships. Is there any end to the blindness we blunder into? There will be times we will leave a sick child at home, or somebody studying for an examination. They might need our help or maybe just our silent presence, but we have to dash to teach religious values to someone else. There will be times when we cancel plans for a meeting or reunion with some group that matters deeply to us, family or friends, while we go off – perhaps to preach at a funeral, maybe even praising the deceased as a man who never let his business interfere with his obligations to his family. And the worse thing is we probably never advert to how much our theory and practice have drifted apart.

I remember once seeing an interview with a person who was described as one of the most successful car salesmen in the United States. The secret of his success, he said, was that he treated everybody who walked into his showroom as if he were his best friend. He said, 'I find out what he's interested in, what he does for a living, and whatever it is, I *pretend* I'm interested in that, and ask him to tell me about it. By the time I'm done, all he wants to do is buy a car from me.' We must of course be grateful for small mercies, and this type of attitude in a person certainly makes a change from those who feel the only way to integrity and personal wholeness is to be truculent and rude. Nevertheless, if this is only a façade, and if it is the only attitude that salesman has time for, we have to say, how sad it is to have to make your living in that way. Why does it have to be a case of 'I pretend.' Is there no room for a genuine interest in what another person is involved in? If we always have to pretend to like everyone, a time will come when we forget what it is like to enjoy another person's company as a friend, not just as a potential customer who can swell our bankrolls, or help us up one more rung of the ladder. Contrived emotion does not have to replace genuine emotion, but it infallibly diminishes the personality. The ability to know what you are really feeling gradually disappears. Is this why there is so much phoney conviviality, and so little genuine friendships in the business world?

And of course society applauds this imbalance, honouring us for our financial success, praising us for our self-sacrifice. The achievements society rewards can very often be won at the cost of diminishing the personality. If so, happiness is proportionately diminished as well. Forces in society will not let us become whole people, because we are more useful to it when one small part of us is over-trained or over-developed. Like hunting dogs geared to bring back the game bird without taking a bite, we become more useful to society by distorting instincts. In the medium term this is good neither for society nor for the individual.

Or we may go to the opposite extreme, because we are young, and feel we have unlimited time stretching way ahead. But as time passes and becomes more precious, we gradually realise that a life of uninterrupted fun is only another way of escaping from the challenge of doing something significant with our life. Having fun is certainly the spice of life, but it is not the main course; and having fun is not the same thing as being happy. Nobody wants to be a puritan, but we know that if there isn't some deeper inspiration in fun, then a lot of the time, when it is over, little of lasting value remains.

Aldous Huxley, in *A Brave New World*, examined the choice facing humanity in the search for true happiness – a fully human life, or the 'mechanised servitude of the anthill.' Shortly before his death in 1963 he said: 'It is a bit embarrassing to have been concerned with the human problem all one's life, and find at the end that one has no more to offer by way of advice than: "Try to be a little kinder."'

Embarrassed? Even relieved? Perhaps. But only if we forget that in that attitude Christ said we sum up the whole Law and the Prophets.

Fighting the Ego or Fighting the Neighbour
Opening of the Academic Year, 8 October 1986

Despite the economic recession we are in, and the great difficulties facing educational establishments and students alike today, education in Ireland has never been more universally available than it is now. We have to work hard to make sure that such availability will become wider. More urgently we have to exert the maximum effort to deepen and use to the full the opportunities that we are being given and which will have been won at such a great cost.

Only an institution of higher learning such as a University can achieve two difficult and very different things – first, enriching our culture by integrating insights in all areas into it; second, training young people to be the future leaders of society. By leadership here I am not referring to high position, but to the quality of influence we exert in the society in which we live.

Training has to do with intellectual deepening or it would not be worthy of the name. But it also has to do with the development of people as persons, an aspect of education that can suffer as a result of economic stringency, and the pressures towards practical training to the exclusion of almost everything else, which the shortage of work almost inevitably produces.

But as Henry Adams said once: 'Nothing is as worthless in education as the accumulation of knowledge in the form of inert facts and the sterile compilation of things known.'

A worthwhile education cannot leave us inert and indifferent. It cannot leave us atrophied or apathetic. If it did it would be the kind of knowledge which Alfred North Whitehead said 'kept no better than fish.'

There are a number of things which block our full development educationally. In the first place, hurry. The person who is always in a hurry, mentally, is very foolish, though it is hard to avoid at times: 'We have given our hearts away, a sordid boon.' We all know we cannot turn back the hands of the clock. But we don't seem to be quite as convinced about the impossibility of turning them forward. The time available is *now*. The time we have is brief – never again in your lives will you have the opportunity of such a long and concentrated period of full-time study, as you have now. Make the best of it, no matter how big a burden you may feel you have to bear. Dream dreams and concentrate on the present; the future will take care of itself then. The long procession of people one meets every year, lamenting how little they availed themselves of their time to study is a strong lesson to us all. Another related obstacle is worry, or the belief that we should all be exempt from worry; I'm not sure which is worse. Worry can kill the soul; it can paralyse all our efforts. There is a good type of worry and a bad type. Nothing creates more deep-seated anxieties in us than the assumption that life should be free from anxiety. Anxiety, after all, is what marks off human beings from the rest of creation.

Abnormal anxieties are to be shunned. They mostly come to us from worrying about our material goals – whether one is popular or not, or regarded as successful; whether one can increase one's social or economic position, whether somebody else is getting ahead. In *Peer Gynt* we are told very perceptively what it is that was wrong with many of the unfortunate patients in the insane asylum. All, fundamentally, were egotists; their anxieties, very often, were not about their neighbours, but about themselves. As he says, unfortunately it is here in the asylum that people are most themselves.

Anxiety about the success of our work, or studies, or employment prospects, about the saving of our souls, about the tension between the spirit and the flesh – all of these are normal anxieties if kept within bounds. And in fact the resolution of them is one of the conditions for spiritual happiness. Abnormal anxieties are to be avoided; the normal to be encouraged. The basic fact we have to face is that we are either at war with ourselves, or at war with our neighbour. A person who does not fight with his own ego fights his neighbour. The cross at the centre of one's own life is the assurance of peace in the individual and success and peace among those with whom we live.

One of the greatest treasures a person can have is often a casualty in education today. It goes under many names; one of them is politeness – the way of showing externally the inner regard we have for others. Good manners are the shadows cast by virtues. In the rough and tumble of college life they can often fall by the wayside.

In some people their innate goodness and greatness inevitably show themselves in polite and civilised behaviour. An interesting story, despite the dated *mores* of those times, is told of George Washington. Many people used to slap him on the back and call him 'George.' Once, however, when he met an old slave, he took off his hat and bowed to the slave, because the slave had saluted him first. A General, who was with Washington at the time, asked him why he bowed to a slave. 'Because I would not permit him to be a better gentleman than I.'

One of the elements of courtesy is attention to detail in kindness to others. The human heart is more satisfied with a hundred tiny delicacies scattered throughout the days and years, than with one sudden outburst and costly token of esteem, usually followed by a lapse once again into forgetfulness. Christ promised that those who would be put in charge of great things, were those who had proved faithful in charge of the small. But courtesy can also show itself in excesses. Courtesy must surely be what St Paul called 'Love without hypocrisy.' Love is to courtesy what the soul is to the body. Without it one can have formalism, stiffness, correctness, but no real politeness. Courtesy is affection, not affectation. This sort of politeness is not weakness but strength. The unsympathetic person is never courteous, and deep inside is fundamentally weak.

These are some of the things that go to make a truly educated person in the full sense of the word. Do not be over-bothered by an environment hostile to these values. Have a direction, an understanding and a meaning, about who you are and why you are here. Build up an educational heritage, not merely of knowledge and information, but of personal values of which you can be proud.

Ars Longa, Vita Brevis
Opening of Academic Year, 7 October 1987

We ask God's blessing today on our new academic year, in what is, unfortunately, a very gloomy economic period. It is a time in which rigid economies are required in all areas of the public sector to prevent our country lapsing into an irretrievable spiral. There are, of course, only two ways of repaying a debt: an increase in effort to raise income, or an increase in thrift in spending. At present we seem to be in the heart of the second option. Everyone is in favour of such measures of sanity, but somewhat less enthusiastically when the economies start to bear on us in a more personal way. I hope the present negative period will not endure much longer, until benefits of a more positive kind begin to show. In the meantime we have to do our bit to ensure we have the most efficient system possible, the highest quality possible, and the will to benefit to the maximum from the scarce resources we have. Very often, paradoxically, it is precisely periods of difficulty like the present that are productive of the greatest minds, and the greatest achievements, just as the hottest furnace produces the purest yield from ore, and the brightest lightning comes from the darkest storm.

All of us here have embarked on a project that stretches far beyond the short-term view. The real object of education is to give people resources that will endure as long as life itself endures; habits that will enhance, not destroy the quality of life; occupations and skills that will render sickness tolerable, solitude pleasant, jobs more prosperous and fulfilling, life more dignified and useful and death less terrible. A true education has the same result as the skills of a sculptor at work on marble from a quarry, which shows none of its inherent beauty until the work of the artist brings out the colours and makes the surface shine.

I use this type of image deliberately to underline the effort needed in true education. We are all very willing to learn, but not always
quite so ready to be taught. A good education at university
requires, in a way that was never necessary before in your lives, a
full-hearted commitment to bring out those gifts of the spirit mentioned in today's reading from the Letter to the Corinthians. A person can casually pick up some lessons at university no matter how
badly the time has been wasted – that is true – but it is a sad road to
follow. As Shakespeare put it, 'How bitter a thing it is to look at
happiness through another man's eyes.' The trouble with experience of this kind is that the final examination often comes before the
first lesson. The time you have is brief – never again during your
lives will you have as long a period for concentrated study. Make
the best of it. One of the basic aims to be achieved as a result of your
time here is to secure good employment, and it is very obvious that
mediocre academic results at the end of your course is not a light
burden to shoulder in the jobs market.

While no university today can spend enough time in trying to
secure the gainful employment of its graduates, equally no university can rest satisfied with merely attempting that. A technological
college that saw its role in very narrow terms indeed, might be so
satisfied. But at the heart of a university there has to be a style of
education which tries to instil some of the 'ars longa' into the 'vita
brevis'; out of the moments, traditions, private records and evidences, proverbs, experiences, words and traditions, to try and
recover something from the deluge of time, as Francis Bacon put it.
Yes, skill, depth, sanity, balance and insight, are slowly acquired,
and like all precious things in life hard to attain, more difficult still to
retain. We should release them reluctantly.

Life can be a very interesting story. We are here and the consequences of what we become are eternal. We are students only once.
The consequences last a long time too. Do not short-change yourself. The earth is alive. It cannot be a very secure place. And we are
all alive, with freedom, and freedom and absolute security cannot
exist together at the same time. In our dealings with others when
we are encouraging them to be free and creative, we always run a
great risk. It is not enough to offer security to those we love; quite
often it turns out to be only an ornamental form of slavery. This
helps us to see why God's love for us also runs a risk. He does not
impose what we foolishly call 'his will,' on us – it is really the man-
ufacturer's operating instructions. The 'glory of God' always has to
be the same thing as the 'fulfilment of the creature.' But we have to

freely choose our own way to happiness and learn the deep lesson that in any walk of life the source of contentment and happiness has to well up from within ourselves. A person who is so ignorant of human nature as to seek happiness by changing anything but his own disposition, will waste his life in fruitless efforts and only multiply the griefs he purposes to remove. For the root of happiness comes from limiting one's desires rather than from trying to satisfy them, but we are slow to realise that.

Above all, one of the fruits of real education must be helpfulness and care for others. Many people all around us, especially during our student days, are suffering from tragedy and real deprivation. Be helpful to others who may be less fortunate than you. Be polite: it is merely an outward way of showing the inner respect we have for other people. I like to think of a polite person as one who listens with intensity to things he knows all about, even when they are being told to him by a person whom he knows knows next to nothing about them at all.

I once came across a word which I am told the Japanese often use to describe gardens: 'shibusa.' It means many things that lie at the heart of being a truly civilised human being: nobility, truth, restraint, elegance, good taste, simplicity. In a sense, therefore, it is a word that speaks all at the same time on the planes of religion, morality, art and etiquette.

One of the elements of courtesy in this spirit is attention to detail with kindliness to others. For the human heart is more pleased with many and continuous small things, than with the extraordinary and rare exception. In truth, this is how the 'ars longa' deepens and enriches the 'vita brevis'.

Victims or Children of God?
Opening of the Academic Year, 6 October 1989

This weeks marks the tenth anniversary of the Holy Father's visit to Maynooth, and to this church. Yesterday morning I had the privilege of concelebrating Mass with him and he recalled his visit. I told him we were having this Mass here today and he asked me, very deliberately, to convey to you his very special blessings and good wishes for the coming year's work.

You may have read in the newspapers yesterday of the struggle of two blind students from County Kildare to get to university. It takes an enormous effort for a blind person to do some short project which the average student can achieve with very little difficulty. No

matter how tough our situation may be, the really precious possessions and abilities are the things we take for granted – to be able to
see, to be able to speak, to hear, to walk – things which we think
nothing of until they are gone. Because appreciation is normally by
contrast, whether that contrast be of the enforced kind which deprivation brings, or whether we can use our minds to stand outside
our situation sufficiently to realise how rich we really are in essentials.

The opportunity to study is what we would like to see as a right
for every young person in Ireland. It is also a great privilege to enjoy
that right uninterrupted by war, disease, disaster and other unfortunate circumstances that plague so many young people in the
world today, and that plagued so many in Europe in the not too distant past. The signs are that it may well do so again in parts of
Europe. The opportunity for three or four years' study is a great one.
We are here only once, but the consequences are long-lived. Do not
short-change yourself by wasting precious years that will not return.

Higher education, in whatever faculty you are, is a highly com-
petitive business today. It is difficult to get in, and it is difficult to
score highly enough to ensure a reasonable prospect of employment at the end, above all the prospect of a way of life that will be
more than a mere job. The ethos of the rat-race can all too easily be
imported into an academic career, where the attitude of dog-eat-
dog and the survival of the fittest, can so easily prevail. If that is the
spirit in which you go through Maynooth, your education will have
failed, no matter how successful you may have been, and no matter
how materially rewarding your future work may become.

Education is about the development of the whole person. You
cannot defer your growth as a person until you have the serious
business of getting a degree and a job out of the way first. Why?
Because it is precisely in these activities that your growth as a person takes place. There is something laid down for each of us to
achieve as we pass through each experience in life, and in the early
years of life these experiences are all the more crucial. If you neglect
them they can never really be made good again. A well-quoted saying puts it very directly: 'I expect to pass this way but once, and any
good thing therefore that I can do, or any kindness that I can show
to any fellow creature, let me do it now. Let me not defer or neglect
it, for I shall not pass this way again.'

Most certainly none of us will pass through the paths of life of
1989 and 1990 again. Do not miss their opportunities to help your
growth as a person, for if you do, you will descend into the mentality
of the rat-race.

Many wise people teach and advise, and many sit there listening to them patiently, waiting to hear – what? – the things they want to hear and to hold on to. They sit there vaguely nodding their heads, until finally they hear something they want to hear, and only then do they perk up.

We are all made in the image of God: we have the divine life within us. We were meant to make this grow and develop, and to live in the joy of this world that belongs by right to the children of God. But this process has slowed down in us until it has almost stopped, and fundamentally it is because of our belief systems and the way in which we hold on to them. Our illnesses, fears, inadequacies, insecurities, and judgements, all these. Why are we so attached to these very things that hold us back? Because they give us our identity, and we feel that if we were to let them go we would no longer know who we were.

Our minds are shrouded in limitation. And how do you try to teach knowledge and enlightenment to a person whose mind is closed? This one central issue I put before you today at the opening of the academic year, because it is one of the greatest single obstacles to the spiritual, material and educational growth in the human being. If we could open our minds to see the way we limit ourselves if would be the very best gift we could give to our education in this new year.

And it is a betrayal of what is at the heart of Christianity: that the love of God and his life is here within us. It is not something out beyond the planets and the galaxies. God the Father, that all-consoling light, is within you. You are that presence, that power and that beauty that comes from him. This is the only realisation on which true growth, true happiness and development can flourish, and above all, on which true education can flourish: the positive attitude and the optimism towards ourselves which will fill our lives with a cheerful spirit and transform everything with which we are involved in a wonderful way.

By way of conclusion let me tell you a story from a very distant time in the past history of this world. It is a story of a mighty warrior, who was on a long march with his army. They came to a great primeval forest, and he led them in through these magnificent trees, as old as the ages. And from being brash and boisterous men, they became uneasy and afraid. Deep within the forest they came upon a great tree – the father of the forest – whose massive trunk even a hundred men with arms joined could not encircle. He assembled the men before the great tree and asked them: in what way is this tree greater than you? He told them they would have to stay there until they discovered the right answer. For hours they thought and thought and grew more frustrated. No answer they thought of could satisfy him.

One warrior said, 'Lord, how can this tree be greater than us, for we can cut it own, chop it up and burn it?' And the leader said, 'Only the human mind could sink so low as to embrace a thought like that.'

Eventually he said to them, 'This tree does not know how to die, you do; it only knows how to live. For that reason it is greater than you. And it is this lack which inspires all your attitudes of failure and limitation.'

The attitude of the mind is what determines all things in life. With it we can scale the heavens and live accordingly, or we can sink into the depths of fear, limitation and despair. The choice is ours, and depending on our choice and how we trust our own capacities, we determine what it is we will experience in all life's situations, and how we will emerge from them.

Power and Fear
Opening of the Academic Year, 10 October 1990

There is a lot to be learned during your period of university education, but one area where we need God's blessing most of all is in the area of personal growth and development. You might end up never thinking much about it, or getting any formal advice or help on it at all. Many people do not realise that there is a skill involved in growing up spiritually, just as much as there is a skill involved in achieving anything worthwhile, and it's about that I want to talk to you today.

What we might call power, for want of a better word, is essential for our growth into God. One of the really great obstacles to growth is fear, and the many activities in our lives that are generated by fear, unfortunately fear of which we are often not really aware, or that, if we are, we suppress, and so continue the enslavement we live in. Power is essential for our growth into God.

For many people power means being able to impose your will on others, but there is no security in that sort of power; it is really only a disguised form of weakness, and a time will come when the disguise will be painfully removed.

True power comes from feeling at ease in your environment.

Fear, or any of the activities generated by fear, cannot produce power: pride, luxury, false gods, dominance. Power comes from very unexpected sources: allowance, compassion, perfection; the gifts of the spirit of which St Paul spoke, the attitudes of a person who has aligned with his soul.

If we want to make progress in the Christian life we have to eliminate crippling attitudes, and it is fear that lies behind nearly all of those; fear that you are vulnerable, that you cannot cope outside the shelter of your home or loved ones; fear that you will not get your just desserts, that people will exploit you; that you will not be allowed to function by others. We would literally stand amazed at the results if we could get rid of this poisonous fear. And as the scriptures say, it is only *perfect* love that casts out fear. We become strong and powerful when we are able to express our energies only in love and trust, and never in fear, helplessness, and the inner terror they often generate. The less empowered you feel the more you will have a need to control that which is external. We really must try not to seek to control, but to nurture, not to dominate, but the opposite – to empower. This is where religion often fails, not in the sense of seeking to dominate, but in the sense of failing to empower which is quite a different thing.

If your love and care for another person or thing is detoured through the wants and needs of your own personality, you are only seeking external power over them. There is nothing there but loss, for when you try to dominate another you may succeed *sometimes*, but you *always* disempower yourself.

If we are in the state of love, we rest on a very powerful inner strength which cannot be removed from us. From this flows a reverence for life in all its forms, for we feel no threat from any of them. We realise that they are all God's creation, and, even if they are unfortunately misled, are still trying to express in a certain way. There is no attraction towards the symbols of external power, nor to competition in the wrong sense. This is a far cry from always trying to do your best; that is aimed at an ideal. Competition aims only at trying to surpass another.

When we learn through a powerful wisdom in this way our vision is crystal clear. This is the real source of compassion, and the abolition of judgement, spite, anger and greed. This is what allows the heart to give out its life giving flow and weakens our many addictions by disempowering them.

From this vantage point it is easy to forgive and forget. Most people who forgive do not want the one they have forgiven to for-

get that they forgave and forgot. This is just another way of trying
to acquire external power over another. When we do not forgive
then we are choosing to carry with us the garbage of that experience. That is why Christ told us to forgive; it is really enlightened
self-interest in its best form, for if we do not forgive we attract to us
once again precisely those things we hold in resentment. We are
accountable for what we experience. When we complain it is
because we want someone else to be responsible for what is happening to us and we want them to fix it for us. It is a form of manipulation, just as it is often the case that the person who breaks down
and weeps in the face of difficulty, seemingly so weak and helpless,
is often a tiger of manipulation inside.

When we realise we are accountable then we release critical
judgement of others and of ourselves. Now we are at the heart of
the *metanoia* of which Christ spoke. We often make decisions when
we are less wise, but to cling to the negative experiences that resulted is not true conversion. Regret is a double negativity; the negativity of clinging to negativity. It can most effectively impede spiritual
growth. *Metanoia* is not regret, but the state of a heart focused on the
opposite.

When we have reached some success in the arduous task of cast-
ing aside fear, regret and powerlessness, we are open to that true
love which is the energy of the soul. There is nothing in the personality that cannot be healed by true Christian love. There is ultimately
nothing real but love. Love is not a passive state, much less the
mawkish sentiment described in the pop world. It is an active force,
the force of the soul; it is in reality the life of the Father, the
Kingdom of Heaven within us, the life of Christ.

So many, even those who would regard themselves as very
faithful Christians, have never realised how these dynamics of true
Christian freedom work, but instead have followed, no doubt most
sincerely and faithfully, what was in the last analysis only a
learned-off religion. But many others, especially the simple and sincere, perhaps even those poorly educated in the conventional sense,
did realise what was involved in the process very well. Their simplicity meant their vision was unblurred. But some others today,
even some knowledgeable in theology, have just substituted new
forms for old constants. Their absorption of the faith was never
accompanied by any understanding of how necessary a continual
growth towards God is, and the things we have to do to bring this
about – the things of which I have been speaking so briefly here.

What I have been speaking of are the dynamics of true Christian freedom. These lead the way to the destruction of corrosive fear. If you follow that path the Gospel serves a warning that you will be hated. To be hated for the right reasons is often a good indication you are doing something worthwhile. These dynamics are at the heart of the Christian message, indeed at the heart of all education in the sense that matters eternally.

We ask God's blessing today on the many new things you will have the chance to learn at Maynooth, but if you miss the chance to learn something of these things, then you will have missed what was perhaps the greatest chance of all in your lifetime here.

This One Planet is Our Home
Opening of the Academic Year, 9 October 1991

The readings of the Mass today, from a Servant passage of Isaiah, to the gifts of the Spirit enumerated in 1 Corinthians, and the Lord's Prayer in the Gospel, give us a sublime charter for the right relationship of human beings to their fellow human beings, and to the world in which we live. It is customary at the beginning of each academic year in all the great academic institutions of the world to ask God's blessing on our future work and to select some headline at which we might aim in the coming year. Of all the tasks that face us today, hopefully as thinking leaders in today's society, one of the most urgent must surely be our relationship to the world in which we live.

The science of doing what is right – often called ethics – is an essential foundation for the building of civilisation. We cannot live at all in the world without an ethical view, even if we reject such a notion entirely. Unfortunately many of the ethical positions that are current today view the world as a piece of real estate, a piece of property, which is there to be exploited. The so-called 'unexplored' areas are looked upon as mere wildernesses, to be exploited, to be possessed and to become 'productive.' We have reached the sad stage when this mentality has become the defining badge of 'civilisation,' that it is all right for the strong to oppress the weak, to destroy the self-sustaining diversity of the systems of nature, the right to send other products of the evolutionary system to the wall of extinction, all in the name of progress.

If we were to let the age of the universe be represented by a twenty-four hour day, all of our history since the industrial revolution would be represented by less than one thousandth of a second, and yet in that relative flash of time the face of our planet has been changed more than in all its previous history – and usually for the worse.

More and more frequently, concerned people have produced television programmes to bring the major question of starvation to our attention. It is said that at present more than forty-five million people are on the verge of starvation in Africa. Given the pattern of bizarre weather patterns and the rate at which the world population is increasing, it seems as if we are going to be faced with a major food crisis by the end of the decade. Somebody gave an example once of taking a test tube and putting in it some bacteria that double in number every minute. If it took, for example, thirty minutes for the test tube to become half-full of bacteria, it would only take a single minute more, for the tube to become full. Half full in thirty minutes; completely full in thirty one minutes.

It has been worked out that eight thousand years ago it took the world population a hundred thousand years to double. Three hundred years ago the population was doubling every thousand years. By the middle of the last century that was down to two hundred years; by 1930, it was doubling every eighty years, and by twenty years ago the world population was doubling every thirty five years. Just beyond the turn of the century the population will double every seven years if things continue as they are. None of the admirable development programmes and famine relief arrangements that we now have can even remotely hope to deal with such a situation.

But closely related to the issue of starvation is the extent of environmental pollution. This is not something remote like the cutting down of the rain forests and erosion in the Brazilian jungles. In the main street of Leixlip, it has been calculated, the average person living there is forced to absorb the equivalent in toxins from air pollution of two packs of cigarettes per day.

In parts of the European Community and also in North America some rivers are so contaminated with oil that they are fire hazards. Others are so contaminated by pesticides, chemical fertilisers, domestic garbage and industrial effluent, that they are dead or dying and dangerous to any form of life using these waters. The proliferation of new and deadly viruses almost certainly can be traced to the ravages of pollution. Crises such as that posed by the new exotic diseases, for which there is no treatment and no antidote, with a 90% fatality rate, should give us all reason for pause.

Not alone are we failing to feed a significant proportion of the earth's five billion inhabitants, but are also failing in important areas that are down the list only because they are less important. We cannot educate, house, or employ these great numbers in any acceptable way as things now stand. Lack of employment is one of the current issues that bites us very painfully here in Ireland, but in other places the pain takes the form of basic survival.

A major difficulty is greed, closely followed by the desire we all have for convenience. If we could make things convenient for people we would probably have them in the palm of our hand no matter what we wanted them to do. One third of the population of the earth is using up three quarters of the earth's produce. The advance of technology is not bad and it is not wrong; on the contrary it is a great expression of what God has given man the capacity to discover, and it does raise the level of life enormously for those fortunate enough to be able to avail of it. But a powerful technology gives the means to wreak even greater and more rapid havoc on the natural resources of the earth; maybe even going so far as to use them up altogether. Because of the dire consequences of such a policy, alternative or less damaging ways must be found, and until they are found limitations have to be placed on what we consume: 'to live simply, so that others may simply live' is no longer just a pious wish, but an imperative, for if things continue, it is not just others who will need to be allowed to simply live; it is getting near that stage for us all.

It has been calculated that in this decade up to ten plant or animal species become extinct every day. Every single species that disappears sounds a note of warning for the human race itself, but when ten species disappear every single day, we have obviously arrived at a very serious stage. What causes this? Forests in the tropics are chopped down with a zeal that will leave little by the middle of the twenty first century, and have we forgotten that then of course we will undoubtedly suffocate? As the forests fall millions of species are losing their habitats, many to disappear for ever. We plough up virgin areas, even though most of them are marginal. Soil, one of the most precious of all resources, is washed or blown away in billions of tons each year because of inadequate developmental or farming policies. We have a sublime example here in the Dublin area of how vast tracts of the most productive land in the country are paved over or developed each year. Some environmentalists fear that the rate of desert expansion will mean we could lose 75% of all arable land in the next seventy-five years.

I am told that if, from today onwards, no more pollutants were to be dumped into the Atlantic Ocean, it would take two thousand years for it to fully purify itself. Horror stories abound of how we ravage one fishery after another, in some cases making recovery of these grounds impossible. Are dolphins, seals and other marine animals to follow the path of the great whales? We desecrate the landscape with waste, quite a lot of it toxic. The catastrophic pollution of the atmosphere has meant that in certain areas it is almost inflammable. All atmospheric pollution since the beginning of time is still here with us. It is washed back down by the rains, or stays trapped in the upper atmosphere, but none of it drifts off somewhere into outer space.

Of course to call attention to issues like these risks being dismissed as an alarmist, a crank, or ridiculed as a wishy-washy 'Green.' Nobody wants to hear things like this, including myself. Nevertheless matters have got to a stage where we can't afford to ignore them any longer. Down the line our very continued existence is threatened, but there are also consequences much nearer home.

The over-burdening of the earth leads to all sorts of other breakdowns. As people clamber for bigger shares of dwindling resources, conflicts break out. More people have been killed in military conflict since the end of the Second World War than were killed in that bloodiest of all wars. The breakdown of our political systems, economic mechanisms and social systems, is the first warning signal of what we have done through abusing the earth. The effect of the modern urban environment on people is sometimes blatant, sometimes more subtle, sometimes it is more personal than widespread socially, but is nearly always negative. As organisms we have to face the fact that we have not had the chance to adapt to the environment that now surrounds us. Our central nervous systems are attuned to an environment that contains a certain amount of stimulation. When that is exceeded the over stressed person tries to run away. This can be done in various ways – by retreating into the past, for example. Violence is solved by calling for more policing. Rebellion is confronted with authoritarianism; a vicious circle.

Others take refuge in the use of drugs, others take to gurus, astrological prophets of the deceptive 'New Age' movements, or the now rarer Marxist simplifiers: all ways of trying to stay afloat in the torrent of a world of technological change. Or others turn to violence, when all reality is seen in terms of 'them' and 'us.' One section of society becomes militant, the other vigilante.

A deep reason lying behind it all is, I suppose, that we have been technological giants, but remain ethical dwarfs. Consequently we have limited our ability to cope in a sensible and mature way such as would respect the quality of life. In these circumstances, to cherish the gifts of the Spirit, and to realise as in the mentality of the Servant passage of Isaiah, that we do not own this earth, but have borrowed it from succeeding generations, and must take care to hand it on to them in good order.

Environmentally the state of the world today is very serious. We hear a lot of the bad news, but when you realise that a great deal of the pollution is caused by the same people who control the means of mass communication, we obviously must conclude that we are far indeed from knowing the full story.

It is a serious situation which demands a fundamental re-think, and the best hope is to take our stand on firm Christian values. If the earth is a self-regulating system of some kind, it also has to try and purify itself, and if so some of the unwelcome and increasingly frequent natural catastrophes may well be due to our own abuse of nature. In a contest between humanity and nature there are no prizes for guessing who will win.

It is futile to point the finger at the great corporations that cause so much of the pollution, and do little ourselves to curb our own consumerism. Likewise we can can often feel that we are too tiny and insignificant to do anything that would make a difference. But when one person unravels a single string that ties the environment together, he usually finds that everything else is attached. Two hundred years ago the man who probably had more to do with the foundation of this College than anyone else, Edmund Burke, said: 'Nobody made a greater mistake than he who did nothing because he could only do a little.'

Destiny and Forgiveness
Opening of the Academic Year, 14 October 1992

The life of the spirit enables us to add something to our instinctive life and live on a higher plane, a plane which is beyond the reach of destiny. But to reach this our spirit has to be given the freedom to put its seal on everything we do.

One of the great cornerstones of Christ's teaching was forgiveness. He made it a cornerstone for a good reason; because the taking of revenge is the most effective barrier to advancement in the spirit.

We are vindictive by nature; the custom since the beginning of time has been to seek revenge for any real or imagined wrong that has been done to us. If someone harms us we must harm in return; if someone hits us, we must hit back twice as hard, two blows, two kicks for each one.

Never fight cruelty with cruelty, anger with anger, slanderers with slander. In that way you identify with your enemy; you face him on his level, instead of on yours. If you want to be invulnerable you must lift yourself, by prayer and reflection, by willpower, up to more pure and noble realms where light reigns. If you carry in your mind the image of your enemy you strengthen it and feed it. Leave enemies, slanderers and detractors behind. Evil projected by an enemy on to someone who refuses to accept it, by staying above that level, in fact turns back to plague the one who has sent it out.

Enemies vanquished by force are never truly vanquished. No nation can be conquered by force, nor by weapons nor by espionage. Eventually the physical victor becomes in turn the vanquished as history has proved over and over again.

In fact, wisdom actually sees our enemies as a blessing, because we can use them to become strong; they force you to work on yourself, to exert yourself, to evolve. The wise person knows that the enemy is a mirror to oneself. What most upsets or irritates you about another person is quite likely to be your own worst weakness.

Instead most people seek revenge in the name of justice; an eye for an eye, a tooth for a tooth. It is not the commandment of Jesus that the world follows, but the command of Moses.

I am not saying, do not oppose your enemies. What I am saying is that you cannot conquer them in the way that comes most natural to you. Kill and you will be killed, especially, as is more normal today, the killing by the biting word, the negative comment, the mean and vindictive insinuation, the smart remark that always has to try to take the good out of something. Kill and you will be killed, on and on, until eventually someone comes along who has more generosity, and forgives the enemy. It is then the chain is broken.

But do you think the hard-nosed man or woman of the world can see that? Of course not. They are convinced that it is the highest form of idealism to be passionately patriotic; blinded by a multitude of disguised passions every day, they do not reason. Of course it is much harder to work on yourself than it is to give in. It takes time and constant effort, whereas to reach for a gun, or to give a blow, or to crush with a vindictive remark, or harmful gossip, is quick and easy.

We prefer ease and rapidity, but they create a self-made nightmare.

We may be content to live like everybody else, and never do anything on the higher levels of existence. Maybe we feel the destiny some people have on the instinctive level is quite nice; the destiny of the rich may, for instance, seem very good, they seem to live in peace and plenty; no one bothers them, they eat, drink, travel – what more could anyone ask for? you might say. But if we had the eyes of the spirit to see with we might judge that the life of a man struggling, suffering, stumbling against innumerable obstacles, and bereft of every comfort, might be far more worthwhile than the lives of those who live in the lap of luxury; why, because they are trying to elevate the level of life at which they live to something greater.

To opt for one or the other of those ways of life is the challenge. Simply to be rich or poor has nothing to do with it. What is significant is our own choice; no one can do this for us. Will we opt to try to grow up more into the likeness of God; or will we choose a pleasant and enjoyable existence, but at the sub-human level? The choice is yours to make. It has nothing to do with *being* comfortably off, or with *being* poverty stricken; you can make the most marvellous steps towards God while being unimaginably rich; you can be as far as imaginable from Christ while being immersed in poverty. No *state* in life, no *conditions* in which we live, can make the decision for God or Christ for us; they may make it easier or more difficult. Poverty makes if difficult for some, more easy for others; riches have the same ambiguity. No *state* in life can ever make the decision for us. What I am saying in plain words is that just because you are in any particular state of life doesn't automatically mean you have opted for Christ; just because you are a seminarian doesn't mean you have opted for Christ; only the character of the way you are living and thinking can do that for you; only the way you live and think can tell whether you are living at the animal level of instinct, although perhaps in a very civilised way, or whether you are trying to rise to live at the level of the spirit.

Many people never realise there is a difference, because they base everything on contentment; if they are content they feel all is well with God and man. The cattle in the field are normally content. There are many different kinds of contentment. And most of them never come near bringing the joy of the Spirit which Christ promised to those who love him.

A Time of Testing

Opening of the Academic Year, 12 October 1993

For people in institutions like this, God is often predominantly seen as the God of examinations, and the Spirit as the one to whom we turn for help in recalling information to help fill our answer books during those dreadful sunny days at the end of May. But the Spirit is really meant to be the one who penetrates our work and understanding as we do it, all the time, and above all has far less to do with the amassing or retrieval of information than with the enlightenment of our hearts and minds. Since the Middle Ages it has been the custom in all the great universities to ask the blessing of the Spirit on their work at the beginning of the year. This time next year we will have begun our bicentenary year celebrations. We give God thanks for this present year which marks the close of two centuries of service to God and country by Maynooth College, and we pray that the enlightenment which should fill all areas of our lives as Christians will come to us abundantly through what we expend our energies on here in Maynooth during 1993-94.

For several years now, but particularly in the last few years, it has seemed as if the whole world were rushing towards a confrontation with itself. In the last hundred years we seem to have progressed farther and faster than in all time preceding that we know about, most particularly in the area of technology. People now remember having lived in an entirely different world, one they had experienced in childhood, when life moved at the pace it took to walk to your neighbour's for company, while others, most of us here included, were raised in the age of TV and telephone, a computer-wise generation, for whom in some parts of the world, reading has become difficult and writing awkward.

Have we ever stopped to ask where the world of computers, the world of the bio-technological revolution will take us in the next five, let alone the next fifty years? Humanity is living at a faster and faster pace, but is humanity any more happy than it was five hundred years ago?

Humanity is being compelled to face tests which strain its level of spiritual understanding to the very limit. Only people whose consciousness is centred on God, rather than on the body, will be able to handle this challenge in the immediate years ahead.

The Western world is in the forefront of the technological evolution, but there has been very little attempt to match it with a comparable revolution in the state of human consciousness. We have a higher material standard of living, where there is a plentiful supply of food and water, available at little personal sacrifice, a life where most of the physical dangers have been removed, where disease only rarely threatens. But if this is the case why are people so unhappy with their lives? Why is there such a rise in the rate of suicide in all western countries? Why are human relationships disintegrating so much? – the Pope spoke so strongly about in the Encyclical of last week *(Veritatis splendor)*.

Humanity to a large extent has lost touch with its roots. Living in a world dominated by technology it is easy to forget when we came and where we go, to forget what is the motive power of all life, what is the source of the energy which completes, creates and controls all things. Above all we have forgotton our own divine link, that every human being is a child of God

Humanity has to try to achieve a change in its consciousness to find a way our of the present impasse. Such guidance can only come from a point of stillness within us. Life is like a rapidly spinning wheel. If you stand on it near the rim everything looks blurred and confused as it flashes past. If we stand at the centre we are in a state of stillness and recollection. This is the only state in which we can hope for true guidance and inspiration from God, but attaining this state is a skill of our faith which we have allowed to atrophy.

It would be nice if we could tune into this divine guidance whenever we wished, but we know we can't. And we realise how easy it is to confuse our own crowded and confused thoughts with inspiration. So we have to empower ourselves, and this is done by purification in thought word and deed. And by establishing that pattern of stillness and silence when we consciously, in a spirit of the discipline of surrender, turn our thoughts inward to the Creator of all life and humbly offer our service to the Lord with no thought of reward.

It is only an aware person who sees the hand of God manifesting itself in his daily life and who acknowledges and gives thanks for that presence. That is true communion. We can choose to walk our path in life hand in hand with God, or not. Indeed that is the only path that a person who is evolving and growing can walk.

It is probably the only way in which we can hope to meet the events of the next twenty years, physically, mentally and spiritually.

The world is already in a time of great testing; for the foreseeable future there is no hint of improvement, much more likely the opposite. It probably will be a time of sorting the wheat from the chaff, when, unfortunately, many will lose their centre, fall by the wayside and perish. But it is also a time of great opportunity and new beginnings, a time of great happenings. In very many ways it is a privileged time to be alive, and we can face it with confidence if we are secure in the guidance of God our Creator.

This work of this institution for two centuries has been to produce leaders in society; in the older part of the College's work through the future priests of Ireland and many other countries; in the newer parts of the College by producing the leaders in society that university graduates should be. For us, in this great two hundred year old institution, to be part of this process, and to begin to give a lead and inspiration, firstly to ourselves, then to others not so fortunate, is the highest role we can aspire to in all we achieve and say during the academic year ahead.

CHAPTER 4

Graduation

Faculty of Arts Degrees
Aula Maxima, Maynooth, 11 November 1987

To obtain a degree is a very significant milestone in a person's life: the higher the degree you are receiving today the less you will need to be told that receiving a degree does not mean you know everything about a subject. What it does represent is the university putting its seal on your studies and saying that you are now equipped to carry on your studies alone. I mean this not as an empty platitude because the only way your teaching and inspiration will have that extra life and sparkle is if you are a person in whom your subject lives by continued interest and reading all your life long. Of Graduation Day it can be truly said: 'Ní críoch ach athfhás' – not an end but a new beginning; and more a beginning than an achievement if the education process has been a success.

You are graduating today at one of the bleakest periods ever experienced in Irish third-level education. Most of the western countries, but particularly our own, are going through a very difficult period. It is the sort of time when the prophets of gloom have a field-day and despondency can all too easily become the norm. It is so easy to feel that our chances of employment for the young are almost minimal. But difficult as the times are, they are not so desperate for people in your position to warrant the mentality that would head for the nearest means of transportation out of the country, once qualified. Our economy is unfortunately small; its ebbs and tides are often dictated by forces outside our control. Our country is not poor but unfortunately we have grown accustomed to living beyond our means and when expenditure exceeds income the remedies are painfully clear: reduce expenditure or increase income. The first is obviously far more easy to do, however painful, than the second. We hope that the stage of savings in which we now are is only a necessary prelude to the recovery of our economy when the rising tide will lift all ships.

The Democratic State is built up from below, respecting and cherishing the institutions and smaller units that go to make it up. The less that families and individuals do for themselves the more the State must provide. In fact the political health of any nation can be gauged by how much the people expect the State to give them and how little they are able to do for themselves.

As the finest ideals decline in a democracy freedom degenerates into licence; anarchy appears. Anarchy has to be suppressed with power so that out of the false freedom that imagines everything is allowable only totalitarianism can ultimately come as an alternative to chaos. The only way known to history in which people can prevent the State from controlling their lives is for them to control their own. I cannot help but feel that some of the greatest problems that are besetting our country today would be helped immeasurably by the sort of leadership and idealism which you graduates are uniquely placed to give. I hope you will see that obligation to give as one of your primary roles in your life ahead and I hope that whatever you have got from your education here you will at least be proud of what you are and determine to give back to your country in terms of inspiration and leadership what it has given in enabling you to reach this day.

At present the departments of State are grappling with the immense deficits that have plagued our country for so long. Reductions in expenditure can go only a limited way as a remedy: the deeper solution has to be the resultant economic upturn.

There are many things we ought not to expect the State to do for us. But education, especially at third-level, is one area which does need the strong support of the State, not only for its proper survival but even more importantly because it is one of the chief areas in which the skills and leadership necessary for economic recovery must come.

For centuries the universities probably relied too much on a feeling of inherited superiority. That has to be replaced by a reputation that is earned. In these days of economic realism it is entirely proper and natural that graduates should question the practical value of the education they receive. On this test I think the universities in Ireland can hold their heads high. But of course there are other matters to which universities must also attend if they are to remain worthy of the name: academic vitality, general education, and disinterested research. It is from these that the fundamental value of a university to society springs, and without which even their job-creating role is threatened, even in the short term.

Despite the present day economic demands, if the universities were to give in to an excessive utilitarianism they could well destroy themselves more effectively than their worst enemies and give rise to the conception that they have little role to play in the building up of the intellectual and moral leadership of a nation.

Far too often the impression is given that university courses today, especially in the non-technical subjects, border on the luxurious. But even a cursory examination shows in fact that the employment level from university courses of all kinds, is quite high.

The production of Arts graduates represents an extremely good investment for money by the State. Five years ago 72% of those Arts graduates seeking employment were successful in obtaining it, one in six being employed in the commercial sector. Last year 75% of those Arts graduates seeking employment were successful, with an additional 3.8% being placed in training schemes. One in three was employed in the commercial sector. In addition it should be borne in mind that the holder of an Arts degree is very flexible and versatile in adapting to employment opportunities – more so than a graduate in a very specific or vocationally-oriented field.

In the Science area five years ago 75% of those seeking employment were successful – one in every two going into the commercial sector. Last year 86.5% of those with Science degrees seeking employment were successful – 70% of them being placed in the commercial sector. The universities also of course are rich sources of consultancy-style work for the benefit of industry and Government administration – the work quite frequently provided free of charge.

I may add a note to say that the Maynooth graduates from the higher Diploma in Education course stand second highest in employment in the country. These few facts which I have selected from many more do not support the mentality of the prophets of gloom regarding the employment prospects of university graduates, however difficult the circumstances we face at this time. And all of this I think we can say has been achieved without losing sight of what the basic work of a university ought to be.

Civilisation in the broad sense must always lie at the heart of good university training. What memory is to the human person history is to civilisation. No one can think profitably unless he goes back into the storehouse of memory to draw out thought and experiences to form the new basis of ideals and leadership, and there is no one who can rightly interpret new events when he recoils from the long-term view. If there is anything that sets the human being apart it is his consciousness of duration. But today the preponderant catering to the lowest in taste, the decline in respect for the role of experience and wisdom, the identification of progress with contempt for the past or shame for our native heritage have all conspired to provide an amnesia which betokens a betrayal of the heritage of civilisation. The universities have a very significant role here in the immediate future.

I would like to pay tribute to our staff who despite the shortage of resources in these latter days have continued to produce a most creditable record of research and achievement in both the Arts and Sciences. Maynooth has just completed 77 years as a Recognised College of the National University even though the expansion of courses and student numbers dates from only 21 years ago. Precisely because of the fact, every post that has been established or filled here over these 21 years has been based on a very real need in the expansion of student numbers and courses. As a result of our recent history there is very little that can be dreamed for in this College by measures of economy.

I can say without fear of contradiction that in terms of productivity for money invested we have one of the most efficient university systems in Ireland here at Maynooth.

I warmly congratulate you all. It has taken a lot of blood, sweat and tears for you to reach this day but even more than yours, I think this is your parents' day. Probably nobody but a parent can fully appreciate what it costs in human and financial terms to bring a daughter or son to the stage of university graduation. I am delighted to see so many of them have been able to join us for this happy occasion and I appreciate the efforts and sacrifices they have made.

And I warmly congratulate you graduates once again. Our country is scarce in all natural resources except the one that matters most – our young people. I believe this country has a great future but I am equally sure it will achieve very little without that life and support which our young population can give. To stick with this country despite the difficulties and disappointments that face us all today and not take what in many ways is the hardest way out and in some ways the easiest – emigration – will take a great deal of effort and sacrifice and rugged determination to make a go of things. But that is the basic shape that patriotism takes for the youth of Ireland today.

I hope that you will take with you away from this College many happy memories and experiences that will help you and shape your life for the good over the years ahead. Sometimes when you look back through the mists of memory and recall the red creeper-covered walls, the morning fog in the College park, the kingfishers in the river by the Library, the sweet aroma of chemicals in the Lab or the Arctic blasts of wind on the bridge over the Galway road – whatever memories you have – I hope you will look back on those who with you inhabited these ancient and historic walls as people who basically tried to aid you to achieve the rich promise of your youth, and that you will above all always treasure this place that was in the providence of God privileged to become your Alma Mater.

University College, Cork
Aula Maxima, UCC, 22 October 1988

Reasonable and sensible people tend to adapt themselves to the way things are. Unreasonalbe people, or so they are often called, try more to shape things to themselves. If so there must be a sense in which we can hope for more from the unreasonable than the reasonable. In that sort of division I suppose you would all have to be classed in some sense as among the unreasonable, but in the best possible sense.

It has taken a lot of patience and effort for you to reach this day. You are painfully aware of the effort it took yourselves in the years of dedicated study without which it is not possible to achieve the standard you have arrived at today, when the university puts its seal on the education and training you have received. Impatience and hurry are often the mark of the amateur, but of course they have a great attraction. But apart from your own efforts it also took a great deal of dedication on the part of your parents, especially, and of your families and friends. This is their day too and I warmly congratulate both you and them for this rich achievement.

Now most of you are facing into a new world to find positions that will give the best opportunity for you to experience the value of your talents and education here at University College, Cork. Experience tends to make clear only what is already in the mind, however dimly. Too often it can be a history more of illusions lost than of wisdom acquired if an adequate preparation has not been made.

We really know the value of what we have gone through only when it has been put through the sieve of memory. I am confident that the high quality of these Degrees of the National University of Ireland will now provide you with the admirable and sure foundation you will need for working in today's world. I hope you will continue to be 'unreasonable' people all your lives long in the sense I mentioned at the start: the most important role education has is to develop the personality of the individual so as to enhance the significance of the graduate's life both personally and for others. This is the basic architecture of a life; the rest is merely decoration and ornamentation – however much of a priority it may seem to have in the conventional wisdom of to-day.

I am here today as Pro-Vice-Chancellor of the National University because of the illness of your own Pro-Vice-Chancellor, the President of University College, Cork, Dr Tadhg Ó Ciardha, and I am sure you would want to join with me in sending him from these ceremonies our best wishes for a full recovery in the near future. I want to thank very warmly the Registrar, Professor Michael Mortell, and his efficient staff, for their kindness and hospitality to me on my visit here to conduct these two conferring ceremonies today.

Beir bua agus beannacht!

Royal College of Surgeons and Royal College of Physicians
Corrigan Hall
Royal College of Physicians, Dublin, 22 November 1991

Fortune has its way with coincidences. Sometimes it works in such a way that coming, on an auspicious day like this, to an event bonding two such historic institutions as the Royal College of Physicians and the Royal College of Surgeons, one may come armed with some historical souvenirs. In this case they will underline the not too distant cousinship between these Colleges and Maynooth, but that rubric, a word which itself effectively means 'red-letter day', I shall leave till the end.

We are in the presence of the Colleges' essential life today – a new flowering of graduates, and as we congratulate them and their families, we should salute and cherish the rock from which they are hewn.

The man in the street, if he is old enough and well-informed, will think of the College of Surgeons under the emblem of 1916 and William Butler Yeats. Lady Constance Markiewicz commanded the College in the Rising. She was one of the Gore-Booth sisters Yeats likened to gazelles. The chronicles recall the embarrassment of the English Officer, as he accepted the lady's sword when she surrendered. On a more picaresque note they also recall the youngster who so disrespectfully cut the College's portrait of Queen Victoria from its frame, and made himself a pair of leggings with his canvas spoils.

But that is not why graduates remember the College of Surgeons in South Africa, Kenya, Malasia, Norway, and Saudi Arabia; in shorthand, *ubique terrarum*. They know it as a home of medicine, a place of vital skills, an atmosphere of charm, a cordial tradition.

The simplest touchstone is to list some of the famous names, since they and their achievements are the College's essence written large.

But before these are mentioned, we should pause over the *genius loci* of the College's architecture. Dublin's epic microscope, James Joyce, boasted that the city could be reconstructed from his writings. Not Surgeons, since the College clock in 'Two Gallants' seems to be all that he recalls.

The College of Surgeons is the last Georgian building in St Stephen's Green still serving its original purpose. The pediment has a unique small medical galaxy; Wisdom between Health and the God of Medicine and the Prince of Medical Ethics, Hippocrates, holds the centre of the Arch. *Laudemus viros gloriosos.* Let us praise famous men. President Whiteway in his day had performed the autopsy on Dean Swift. Gustave Hume added to the gaiety of nations. He regarded porridge as a potent *nostrum* and it was said of him in verse that he 'scoured death with stir-about'. President Hartigan in 1797 had Franciscan leanings. He walked around with a pair of kittens in his greatcoat pocket.

Colles who was President at 29 has his testament in medical history under *fascia* and *ligament*.

Professor Jacob lives on in 'Jacob's membrane'. He had another side. In class, among other things, he 'used to illustrate the fantastic tricks of the monkey tribe'.

Surgeons had their first year of surgery in Ireland in 1785; a first in midwifery in 1789; a first in these islands in preventive medicine. And closer to our own times, a first Professorship in Anaesthesia in these islands, while brain surgery in Ireland was pioneered by Adams McConnell.

In 1885, Agnes Shannon was the first woman medical student in Irish and British Medical Schools.

This class of graduates today, then, can point to a proud escutcheon, *Ars longa, vita brevis*: Life is short, knowledge is slowly acquired, Hippocrates said. The graduates may add: *Nobilis nobis hereditas*: a fine lineage is ours.

I mentioned that I was coming with historic souvenirs and I come to that rubric now, very conscious that I am speaking in the Corrigan Hall.

The Royal College of Physicians had its roots in 1654. The Royal College of Surgeons began in 1789; the Royal College of Maynooth in 1795. George III founded both Maynooth and the RCSI, although in the case of Maynooth he said signing the Act gave him more pain than the loss of the American Colonies. It was the age of Science, Cavendish and Dalton, and the age of Burke, a beginning of tolerance.

Just over a month ago, on Sunday, 20 October 1991, the Fitz-Gerald Castle of Maynooth was handed over to the nation. A FitzGerald of the line was present.

It was John Adrien, an original member of the RCSI, who attended the mortally wounded, Lord Edward FitzGerald, and the College of Surgeons was, in fact strongly represented in the United Irishman.

To the layman, medicine began in the 19th century. It is the age of the apocalyptic names, Typhus, Typhoid, Cholera, and the figure that comes to mind in this connection is your Sir Dominic Corrigan, after whom this Hall in the College of Physicians is named. He had his preliminary education in the lay College attached to St Patrick's College, Maynooth, in the building where my office now stands.

He was a kind of medical Daniel O'Connell, a member of Parliament and maybe the first medical doctor to enjoy mass fame. The *Dictionary of National Biography*, in an otherwise grudging entry, says of him: 'He was the first prominent physician of the race and religion of the majority in Ireland and the populace were pleased with his success and spread his fame throughout the country'. Maynooth's blessing on his head.

I remember once reading with morbid fascination of his days as a body-snatching medical student at Kilmainham, in a paper published anonymously in the *British Medical Journal* just a year before his own death. It gives an idea of the circumstances endured in the struggle to make medicine a science: personified in people such as Sterne, Molyneaux, Willoughby, Petty, Churchill, Haughton, Kirkpatrick and Moorhead.

I may perhaps mischievously claim another link with the

denizens of this more than three-centuries-old institution. It's told of the Battle of Moytura, near Cong, in the year 487 BC, that the leader, Nuadhat, lost his hand there, and had a silver replacement made: the first reference to an artificial limb in Western literature, and now the well-known emblem of the Irish Army Medical Corps and of course featuring in the crest of the Royal College of Surgeons. The College I come from, in Irish is 'Magh Nuadhat,' the plain or clearing of Nuadhat, and may give an odd sense of histori-cal fitness to Corrigan's adolescent journey there and to my being in this position today.

What we have here are the alumni of two of Ireland's most ancient and revered institutions, emerging also as graduates of the National University of Ireland; an institution in turn which perhaps more than any other was dedicated to preserving and enriching the spirit and heritage of this land.

One does not preach to the educated. One suggests.

Let these young doctors, 'by whatever each one holds most sacred', to quote Hippocrates, try to live in the shadow of some abiding canon of care and civilized values. The roles of surgeon and physician are the most humanitarian of all. It is a service to human-ity; never forget the humanity of your patients; it is in that spirit you will become most enriched as a human yourself.

In one tradition it is expressed like this: 'the Lord careth for the strangers: he defendeth the fatherless and the widow' (Psalm 9); 'He healeth those who are broken in heart; and giveth medicine to heal their sickness' (Psalm 149).

On behalf of Dr Nolan, the Registrar, and myself, may I warmly congratulate you all and your families on this auspicious day on behalf of the National University of Ireland, and I thank you warmly for the privilege of inviting us here to confer these degrees.

Faculty of Science Degrees
Aula Maxima, Maynooth, 14 November 1992

Almost six hundred graduates and diplomates receive their *testi-monia* here today. It is the largest number of graduates that we have had in the College's history. It's very happy that this should be so, for this year will see the 80th annual graduation ceremony here at Maynooth since its participation in the National University began. The National University is a distinguished Irish institution which

was established in the early years of this century to preserve, protect and promote the richness of the culture and identity of this
country. No one can deny that in those four score years it has done
so, and done so very well.

However, new times and circumstances have prompted the
Colleges to seek for new circumstances and forms in the submission
made to the Department of Education and enshrined in the Green
Paper, which hopefully, despite the present difficult economic and
political climate, will result in new university legislation in the not
too distant future. Among other things, this will, in effect, result in
the disappearance of the National University of Ireland as we know
it, and will create what will be essentially four independent universities joined in a loose confederation. Of the four Colleges involved
in this process Maynooth has most to gain. As you are well aware,
we have been what is called a Recognised College since the beginning of the NUI. Chief Secretary Birrell, in communication with this
College during the preparations for the 1908 Act, while recognising
that Maynooth would be the largest of the NUI Colleges at that
time, and also the College with the most gifted range of undergrad-
uates, nevertheless recommended accepting Recognised College
rather than Constituent College status as the price of having a private Board of Trustees, as had Trinity College. Over the years this
arrangement served the College well, and through the courtesy of
the NUI we have in practice enjoyed many of the benefits of a
Constituent College, but the arrangement has become anomalous
with the passage of years and radical changes in circumstances. It is
now more than eight years since the College applied to the Senate
for a change to a status more appropriate to its circumstances, and
we look forward to the speedy formation and implementation of
the new university legislation.

*Cuireann sé athas ar leith orm an oiread sin de mhuintir na gcéimithe
agus dá gcáirde a fheiceáil anseo le haghaidh na hócáide, agus is é mo
dhóchas go mbeidh cion ar leith acu agus ag na céimithe iad féin ar
Choláiste seo Mhá Nuad ar feadh a saoil. Ba mhaith liom buíochas a ghabh-
áil leis na céimithe as ucht an saibhreas atá tugtha acu do shaol agus do
stair Mhá Nuad le linn na mblianta atá caite acu inár measc, agus guím
ráth agus beannacht orthu agus iad ag tabhairt agaidh ar dhúshlan an
domhain mhóir.*

In the first place I want to express my congratulations and good
wishes to those who received these Science degrees this morning.
This is your day; today is what the College is all about, and we can
so easily forget that in the myriad of negotiations that have to take

place each year, within our own faculties and committees and with the government and university agencies. We are very proud of you and have every confidence that your future will be more promising still.

This will be a milestone year for Science at Maynooth. The stage has been set over the past few years by the many spectacular achievements of our Science Departments in winning so many prestigious research grants, probably the most true indicator of the quality of the research and teaching in any third level institution for the applied sciences. In fact with approximately £2,000,000 in research grants at present Maynooth has, in proportion to its size, probably a greater such endownment than any of the other universities.

Our new Science building is well advanced in construction under the direction of Vice-President Seamus Smyth, and it will be ready for occupation in the early part of next Summer, ready to receive its first students from the Departments of Biology and Computer Science next September. I want to acknowledge with gratitude the contribution which the staffs of those two departments have made to the elaboration of the brief for the building by Professor Smyth. The campaign to win this building was a long and hard-fought battle against the conflicting claims of many other causes and institutions. But it was a worthwhile struggle, and while some of the Science Chairs here at Maynooth were established just two hundred years ago this represents the first significant building purpose-built for the Science Departments in the long history of Science here in the College.

It has been a year in which many other projects into which an enormous amount of effort had been put over the past few years at last came to fruition, to the tune of more than £13,000,000 of new construction, and close to £2,000,000 of renovation to the heritage buildings of the College. Restoration and refurbishment of old and gracious buildings is normally both costly, and if well done, unobtrusive, so that after much effort and expense you seem to end up with much the same as you began.

But after this ceremony I hope you will be able to join us for some refreshment in one of the more obvious and attractive results of that restoration over the past year, the magnificent Refectory designed by Pugin in the early 1840s, and reckoned to be the finest Hall he designed anywhere. Our new students' restaurant and sports centre have added very badly needed facilities to our campus. Frank Lloyd Wright used to say that while doctors might be able to bury their mistakes all architects could do was advise their clients to plant vines! With the addition to the North Campus last year of the four new apartment buildings, the sports facility, restaurant and science building, it has at long last begun to be possible to create there what will I think, over the next few years, be a richer and very attractive architectural ambience, which in modern form will match the beautiful Georgian and early Victorian buildings here on the south campus for which Maynooth is so deservedly famous world-wide.

The College has responded generously to the Government's request to provide additional student places, particularly in those areas that help forward the economic development of the country. I want to register my appreciation of the very great efforts of both academic and administrative staff which were necessary to achieve this on the meagre resources which the College has for that purpose.

Undergraduate student numbers have increased three times during my own period as President. That was necessary to ensure the College's future and its effectiveness, but it was not an easy task and I wish to acknowledge publicly the very great efforts of a dedicated staff that were necessary to see us through that period. There is little doubt that we are facing a future that is most uncertain and difficult for all the universities, but I know that vibrancy and vitality we have developed over the past decade will be more than adequate to see us through.

I warmly congratulate all the graduates once again, and I hope you will regard Maynooth in the future as always having a special place in your lives. We certainly want to thank you for the richness that you have contributed to the already long and distinguished history of this College. I hope you feel that you belong here, and that you will always feel welcome to come back and visit, and take your relatives, friends, and future families with you. I have been gratified on so very many occasions to hear graduates of Maynooth say how much at home they felt here; to know that they mattered as individuals to the staff members who taught them, and that their all-over welfare was of concern to both administrative and academic staff. That is a precious thing in any setting; it is rare in a modern university. I think it is the single greatest contribution that Maynooth can make to the future of university education in Ireland.

One of the really significant movements of recent years has been the awareness of the importance of the environment, and of the extraordinary damage we have done to it by pollution. Science, I suppose, has a major role here, both in its cause, its remedy, and in alerting us to the seriousness of the situation. The scientists tell us that everything is polluted, the earth, water, the air; and that plants, fish, birds, and human beings are dying because of it. They don't know what to do to stop it, nor how irreparable the damage already done may be. One worrying fact, for instance, is that all of the atmospheric pollution since the beginning of time, especially that of the industrial revolution and of the drastically new kinds we have inflicted in this century, has all just gone up into the atmosphere, where it must stay, apart from what is washed back to earth, because it can't drift off into space. The concerns people have got, thankfully, about the importance of this, will force very dramatic changes in our way of life within the space of this decade, and hopefully will help us realise that the end of each species is a step closer to the end of the human race itself. It is something I would ask you to keep in mind constantly during your careers.

I hope all of you and your guests enjoy your visit here today as much as we do having you and that you will enjoy the hospitality the College has to offer.

Faculty of Arts Degrees
Aula Maxima, Maynooth, 13 November 1993

In the first place I want to express my congratulations and good wishes to those who received these Arts degrees today. This is your day; today is what the College is all about, and we can so easily forget that in the myriad of negotiations that have to take place each year, within our own faculties and committees and with the government and university agencies. We are very proud of you and have every confidence that your future will be more promising still.

With the addition to the north campus of the four new apartment buildings, the sports facility, restaurant and now the new Callan Science building, it has at long last been possible to create there a richer and very attractive architectural ambience.

The new Science building, as the Taoiseach pointed out when he opened it on 26 September last, was the first notable purpose-built facility for science in the close to 200-year history of the science departments here. The campaign to win this building was a long and hard-fought battle against the conflicting claims of many other causes and institutions. Our thanks are due to the Department of

Education and the Higher Education Authority for awarding it to us under the Structural Funds Programme.

While the building has obviously been an enormous addition to the facilities of the Science Faculty here, of course it has also greatly enhanced the entire north campus of the College, crowning the five other fine new buildings erected there in the last three years, more than £13,000,000 of new construction in all.

I want to pay a particularly warm tribute to one person without whose dedicated work our magnificent new science facility, in particular, would be nowhere nearly as impressive as it is: Professor Seamus Smyth, who chaired the design team, and whose imagination, vision, patience, and incomparable skills in dealing with people, were the essential foundation on which this whole project rested. There is no doubt all of us, and the Science Faculty in particular, owe him an enormous debt.

Today is a challenging time for universities. The university was not only born in Europe nine hundred years ago, but it was essentially European. For it was in the last part of the middle ages that the institution of the university gave Europe its first unification. The European university has grown and developed upon an age-old tradition: the autonomy of the institution; the freedom of teaching and research; the training of the political and intellectual élite. Strong in its prestige and in the influence it has exercised on the cultural history of Europe, the university was thought of in the words of A.N. Whitehead, as the 'meeting place of imagination and experience.'

But the university in Europe today is passing through a crisis of identity, which is really a reflection of the crisis of identity of Europe itself, with the rise of so many nationalisms questioning now the very concept of a European identity, the identity in which the last generation put such trust, and which we have refused to forsake. But in the last two years we have all been tempted to abandon these dreams, as we have had to suffer the collective shame of Europe as we passively watched the systematic violation of the right of peoples and individuals to live in peace. Fifty years after the defeat of Nazi-Fascism it has been demonstrated that in the very Europe of Monnet, of Spaak, of De Gasperi, of Schumann, of Konrad Adenauer or Willy Brandt – it is still possible for force to impose itself clearly over the law and human rights.

We often wonder if such passivity in the face of such atrocity means we have lost the right, the legitimacy necessary to conduct a process of European integration which would mean so much more than an unstable coalition of economic interests.

Whatever may be the answer the university and the values which it has nurtured will have to play a central role in the formation of the new Europe, principally by influencing the lives of its staffs and graduates. The creation of the Conference of the Heads of the Universities in Europe was an important step for the universities in the new unification of Europe; towards a recovery of the role the universities had in the old unification of Europe. We had the privilege of having a meeting of that Conference here at Maynooth last May, when 145 of the Presidents of the universities in Europe came to Maynooth, the first time this meeting had taken place in Ireland. In this enhanced role of the university in the new Europe the EC has given a decisive push. The action of the European Commission has taken the form also of a vast programme of co-operation, in the programmes of ERASMUS and COMET. These have had a very significant impact in the lives of the European universities. There are now 2,500 inter-university programmes in ERASMUS and the other programmes, involving 70,000 students in 1993. Two hundred university/industry associations are now created within the framework of the COMET programme, involving 10,000 students. In this way we can hope to develop European co-operation, combining the advantages of identity and of difference. One of the major steps towards this for the universities must be the ECTS system installed in the framework of the ERASMUS programme, enabling the transfer of credits between universities throughout Europe.

The university has just as crucial a role in the new unification of Europe as it had in its first unification. In such a situation there is a need to underline what distinguished European culture, what is it that is universal, that unites? What unites European culture and is universal is the foundation of values and ideals shared by all. What distinguishes it is what Julien Benda was doing in his 'Discourse to the European Nation' and 'The Treason of the Intellectuals,' in a time still marked with the bloody traces of nationalism, a time in which expressions such as 'French science' and 'German culture' or 'Latin civilisation' were still re-echoing cries of war. 'Who will deny that the conduct of a scientific work, the exposition of a doctrine, the development of an idea, should be as different as the work of a Frenchman, a German or an Englishman ...? The difference, well understood, existed in the breast of the spiritual unity of Europe at that time.

It has been well said that even in a university in the thirteenth century, in which lived side by side students and professors of all nations, the commentary on a text of the 'Sentences' or on a verse of the 'Decretals' was not the same it if was the work of a man from Saxony, Ireland, or the Auvergne .... But the thinkers of that time did not concentrate their attention on that difference, at least they concentrated much less on that than now, beyond that it was a bond between them. The impression of these differences faded away for them in a feeling, much stronger, of the identity of their intellectual speculations, their methods, and their ideals.

The unity of Europe will always have to be an extraordinary contrast between cultures, experiences and situations. The evocation of the problem of the tension between identity and difference which characterises and runs through European history leads to the role and place of the university within the European identity, as we plod so messily towards a new world order: a new world order not of the fashion planned for us by the puppet masters who wish to manipulate us into a situation of control from behind closed doors, but a new world order in which the best of human ideals can be realised in freedom for each man and woman.

I warmly congratulate all the graduates once again, and I hope you will regard Maynooth in the future as always having a special place in your lives. We certainly want to thank you for the richness that you have contributed to the already long and distinguished history of this College. I hope you feel that you belong here, and that you will always feel welcome to come back and visit, and take your relatives, friends, and future families with you, particularly next year as the College celebrates the Bicentenary of its foundation by Grattan's Parliament.

I warmly thank your families for the effort they put into keeping you here and am delighted to see so many of them here today as guests. I have been gratified on so very many occasions to hear graduates of Maynooth say how much at home they felt here; to know that they mattered as individuals to the staff members who taught them, and that their all-over welfare was of concern to both administrative and academic staff.

Next Summer it will be ten years since this College submitted an application for Constituent College status in the National University system. As you know Maynooth has been a Recognised College of NUI since the NUI began. Over the years this arrangement served the College well, and through the courtesy of the three constituent Colleges of NUI and the NUI Senate, Maynooth has in fact enjoyed most of the benefits of a Constituent College in practice, and indeed some benefits that the Constituent Colleges themselves did not enjoy. However, over the years the position has become anomalous, and with more than four thousand students Maynooth is now greater in size than any of the three Constituent Colleges were for most of their history. Ten years ago the new Maynooth could have taken a different path from the one it chose. The fact that it did not, and the fact that it has waited for these ten years, illustrates well the regard in which Maynooth holds the National University established through our link of more than eighty years. With the establishment of the National Education Convention recently, in which Professor John Coolahan played such a significant and central role, and the promise of a White Paper on Education in the near future, we are hopeful that the tenth anniversary of our application, now in the form of independent university status within NUI, will not pass without significant progress having been made on this centrally important issue.

In conclusion I want to thank all the members of the Academic and Administrative staff of the College, many of them here behind me on the stage. Without them obviously this day would have been impossible and I want them to know their hard work and dedication are things of which Maynooth is very rightly proud. Things have not been the easiest over the past few years in all the universities, and we owe them a debt of gratitude for what they have achieved. In particular I want to thank the Registrar of the College, Dr Peter Carr, and his helpers who organised all the details of this day. We owe a great debt of gratitude to our friends from the Army who have provided such a delightful musical accompaniment to the ceremony, and to the security staff, our catering staff, and the student members of the Aula Maxima Committee who organised the guests and graduates so well, and have the hall looking at its best for all of the graduation ceremonies we have over these weeks.

Mater Dei Institute
Dublin, 19 November 1993

The greatest challenge which all those who teach religion or theology today have to face, is to be able to convey that their faith is actually an instrument of enlightenment and growth, rather than a burden and an obstacle, which is unfortunately the perception of so many in this country today. The true purpose of religion is to elevate our minds and hearts, to enlighten our understanding; for so many today it seems to do the opposite; it seems only to immerse them in fear and guilt for they have not understood the role of moral teaching and insights into the profound truths of the faith. The point of belief is to make some progress in our growth towards God, which is the whole point of the process of salvation; to communicate this is the great challenge facing all religious educators today in Ireland, no matter at what level.

The greatest way to acquire what we might call growth is not to measure ourselves by comparison with anyone else. There is no one that you can say you are less than, or that you are better than, or that you are equal to, as Christ so clearly told us. The basic reason is that we do not know what other people really are in their heart of hearts, which is where God assesses, but neither, and probably even more importantly, do we yet understand what we are ourselves. So to look at someone else and try to measure how far you have come is being most unfair to yourself.

We really need to discover about ourselves what it is that we love, like or dislike. And what makes us unhappy can be changed by our attitude in the work of a moment.

But it takes great strength and substance for a person to do away with the things of unhappiness by changing this fundamental attitude, because we feel that in so doing we are throwing away our identity. We have kept these things, our moods and temperaments and situations, because that is how we understand what we are; that is what gives reality to ourselves. If we were to think that all in a moment, the objects, memories, personages, houses, clothing, jewels, that make us unhappy, were to be thrown away, how would we identify ourselves? Isn't it extraordinary how much we have let our identities be formed by precisely those things in our lives that create unhappiness?

When you are left bare in this way, you are also left peaceful, for there is no more unhappiness or the reminder of it. What occurs in such a void is adventure.

Everything that creates unhappiness in our lives started out as an adventure. If you have learned to decipher the difference between joy and unhappiness, then you will be very careful into what adventures you enter to participate.

When we have the attitude of surrounding ourselves with joy and things that bring true joy, it is then we will have peace, and it is only at that level we can hope to manifest the whole of the Kingdom of Heaven, because we will have room to do so.

What do we call that state? In the very best sense it is called loving ourselves. I am not speaking of the self-love that is often recognised at the heart of selfishness, but the love of self which recognises that we are all children of God and that there is in us something beyond price, no matter how much our material appearance may appear wretched. True love of self, based on this understanding, is the essential basis for fulfilment and happiness, and when we have attained it, we will also have a compassionate understanding of other people. We may do our best to help others, but then a stage comes when, in compassion, we have to allow them, maybe painfully, to learn the lessons they have to learn, and to learn our own lessons in so allowing.

So if we wish to become greater, and to understand more, using the great instrument of the Catholic faith to do so, the blocks and limitations that hold us within our little shell of limitation will be broken away; but remember they will also tear away our false security. For security is a sort of reflector. When it reflects back an image with which we have become familiar, even if it is one of unhappiness and distress, at least it is known and familiar, and it gives us a certain sense of security. But when change is coming, the reflector of the old and familiar has to be cast aside so that something much grander can take its place.

This very often creates confusion in the faith, when many feel they have made a mistake in embarking on the journey of discovery at all; it often affects people who begin the study of theology, and who mistakenly feel that just because the certitude of the faith was not of the precise kind that they understood in childhood, but of a different kind, there is no certitude at all. That is a great mistake, and it is one example of the confusion so characteristic of the state where many linger who have glimpsed the new, but are afraid of letting go of the old, which is so familiar and secure. They are fearful of further opening the door to the new, of which they have caught a glimpse, because it is the unknown, and they cannot control or dominate it, and determine what is to come. Because of that the emotion of confusion dominates.

We need to realise that in the unknown of opening out to God there is nothing that can do anything to us except make us greater. The unknown is the great adventure; the acceptance, the conquest, the being part of the majestic life to which God calls us. But because it is not old and certain and familiar, it is liable to be fearful to us, precisely to the extent and the degree that our religion is governed by fear and not understanding and true Christian love.

When we realise that there is nothing created that can ever put out our light, when we realise that what is unknown equates with unlimitedness, which equates with manifesting the fact that we are made in the image of God, then we will never really be confused again, but will only want more. Most of you have taken the step towards a challenging and difficult career to day, but one that can be enormously rewarding and fulfilling if followed in the spirit I have just spoken about.

Not so long ago, we had the beatification of the Irish martyrs, among them some magnificent individuals who came from this city, and who stepped into the unknown away from the comfort of all, absolutely all, that was familiar, even life itself. It was because of the strength of the glory in which they believed that they could do that. It's very unlikely that most of us will become signs of contradiction to the extent that people will wish to actually take our lives. But my wish for you today, on this day of your graduation, rather is that you will be able to enkindle a similar dynamism to that which inspired those outstanding people – in yourselves first, and then, more easily, in those to whom you must be in turn a light.

My renewed congratulations to you all, to yourselves first, but also very strongly to your parents, families and friends, who have contributed so much to the achievement that this day marks. May your futures inspire and reward you a hundredfold in proportion always to the extent you have committed yourself, in that spirit of trust and joy that God has unfailingly promised to the cheerful giver.

CHAPTER 5

Honoris Causa

Thomas J. Barrington
Doctor of Laws, *honoris causa*
The National University of Ireland, Iveagh House, Dublin, 13 March 1986

Do bheadh sé molta da mbeinn-se im' thost. (He would be praised even if I were silent). A modest man like T. J. Barrington would, I know, prefer such a course of action from me today, but public men are often denied private choices.

We are honouring a life of the biblical three score years and ten, which began auspiciously with 1916, the date which will always symbolise Barrington's Ireland, the new Ireland he was destined to serve in a striking way.

Born in Dublin, educated at Belvedere and U.C.D., the father of six children, T. J. Barrington was, first and foremost, to use the old phrase, a public servant, and public servants, by tradition almost anonymous, are at the heart of civilisation, of all civilisations.

T. J. Barrington's life spans exactly the history of modern Ireland, an Ireland largely the creation of the Irish Civil Servants, of the teachers and of the Garda Síochána.

Since openings were few in this country, immense talent was poured into the Civil Service. No doubt it had its own dark history of frustration, little room and failure, but it is above all a history of extraordinary integrity and of intelligent service for little gain to a small country. It must also have a history of flair and inventiveness, hidden until recently from the layman. It is with T. J. Barrington that we begin to notice a more public service with emphasis on what, for want of a better word, we may call 'techniques.'

He was founder director of the Institute of Public Administration up to 1977. This makes us aware of a newer and more self-conscious Ireland. Inevitably, complexity, skills, the power to compete – the modern techniques – are in.

If T. J. Barrington and certain of his contemporaries in public service are examined it cannot be denied that by an inward dynamism they promoted the values of what Jacques Ellul, the French jurist and sociologist called, 'man's essential unity' (Jacques Ellul: *The Technological Society*, NY, 1964, p 235), which is almost everywhere threatened by the forces of the modern world. And this was because they retained an administrative humanism which is very Irish, and which could not exist without a superior culture and education, a compassion born of closeness to all the sad exile of our nineteenth century, and the values of what is now called the Judaeo-Christian heritage. These public servants endured a certain material poverty in inverse proportion to their talents, but they gave breathing space to the spirit.

T. J. Barrington was a founder member of the Agency for Personal Service Overseas, and was a Foundation Consultant in Ghana for three years. His guiding spirit is expressed in the significant words of his bibliography titles: ' local,' 'new,' 'democracy.'

If, as administrators, we have so far retained a humane style, we have also a certain charism for helping the helpless overseas. The reasons for this were also forged in our past, but the T. J. Barringtons further enlarged the national soul by the willingness to export with a good heart skills acquired since we emerged from our own third world in the nineteenth century. Our public servants led what is simply instinctive in us to fully social and progressive dimensions, at home and abroad. Openness to strangers is no automatic acquisition of the human heart. T. J. Barrington knows that He whom our ancestors called 'the King of Friday,' abolished strangers and asked for compassion for all. Aquinas said that compassion was love moved by the sight of misery. And that is the crowning factor in that charism which helps the Barringtons, in Philip Larkin's words, to 'robe with destinies the naked of the earth.'

We must also look at a man beyond his vocation and livelihood, and see the frontiers of imagination he has chosen for personal joy, as Horace chose his Sabine farm.

An old Kerry woman, who saw with astonishment the little Inca terraces of dry stones with which he surrounded his second home in Kerry remarked: 'T. J. Barrington has stones in his blood.' She could not have known that his ancestors were master carvers of stone in the County Clare. Years ago as an U.C.D. student, however, it was Kerry's turn to carve affection on his heart. And if in modern Ireland there is any labour of love it must surely be this Dublin man's fascinating book, *Discovering Kerry*.

Professionals, even geniuses, are often one-track men. So that often our experts deliver themselves only of empty platitudes when they stray from their specialities. As was once said in this regard: 'It makes one think back on the collection of mediocrities accumulated by Einstein when he spoke of God, the state, peace, and the meaning of life. Einstein was no Pascal' (Ellul: op cit., p 435).

But Dr Barrington is among Pascal's people. The shadow of *esprit de finesse* has not missed him. Nor has he feared 'excess of love.' Quite simply, as Yeats said, he will always belong 'wherever green is worn.' *(Easter 1916).*

Praehonorabilis Cancellarie, totaque Universitas:

Presento vobis hunc meum filium, quem scio tam moribus quam doctrina habilem et idoneum esse qui admittatur, honoris causa, ad gradum Doctoratus in utroque Jure, tam Civili quam Canonico, idque tibi fide mea testor ac spondeo, totique Academiae.

Seán Mac Réamoinn
Doctor of Laws, *honoris causa*
The National University of Ireland, Iveagh House, Dublin, 2 April 1987.

The most singular cultural gift a university can give is a Doctorate, *honoris causa*. Today the National University of Ireland gives this gift to Seán Mac Réamoinn. He is already a Bard of Wales.

The printed sheets that carry the highlights of a public man's life are generally known to educated people. We know Seán Mac Réamoinn, the lover of the Irish language, the remarkable RTE personality, the editor, the student of religion. That's the professional prose of it: the mystery and the joy is in the binding, in what holds this very unusual man together, the vibrant human pieces.

It's odd to call a man 'Doctor' who considered the finest address in Dublin to be the inside of Nelson's Pillar. It seems too solemn a title for such a darling man. Still, the adjectives that are the Doctor's children in Latin dictionaries fit him very well. 'docticanus,' – 'singing well'; 'doctificans' – 'making learned'; 'doctiloquens' – 'speaking learnedly.' Only one does not fit him in the least, a mere adverb anyway, 'doctiusciale' – 'pedantically.'

Bard, *vatis, file*, go well with him, with those loving eyes and ears and voice that have roamed this land for so long. An Irish landscape lover, first of first cousins of our mother tongue, friend of all our music, *ceol damhsa, ceol sí, ceol éan, agus ceolta na cruinne.*

And it is easy to see him in the larger air of Europe at any time, but especially with Villon, talking about the Holy Spirit with goliards, a friend of troubadours and minnesingers. Nor is it difficult to send him down to Canterbury with Chaucer. He is many-layered with the rich loams of old Christian Europe. And he is 'many-melodied,' like the *ilcheolach* – the harp Aongus Óg had at Brú na Bóinne.

If he had been born in Corkery's *Hidden Ireland*, we would find a gleam of him in the verse of Dineen's that commemorates the Kerry poets near Ó Raghallaigh's grave at Killarney – *Le linn ár ndaoirse b'aoibhinn cóir gach éigeas díobh ag ríomhhadh ceoil.*

They were the men who gave a broken Ireland a pillar of fire in poetry. In our own time Ó Riada and Mac Réamoinn rent the veil between them and us in *Saoirse* and *Mise Éire*.

But 'Doctor' we shall call him, and here we speak of moral beauty. We will not call him with the medievals, *Doctor Angelicus*, or *Subtilis*. A case can be made for *Seraphicus*, but essentially he is *Doctor Humilis Corde*: gentle, very Christian, *grádhmhar*.

Ideally a man's life and achievement should go into a single sentence. Seán Mac Réamoinn guided our Ireland with love away from dream and dust.

Walter Haefner
Doctor of Laws, *honoris causa*
The National University of Ireland, Iveagh House, Dublin, 24 March 1988

We cannot honour Walter Haefner as the Greek poet, Pindar, honoured Hieron of Syracuse, 'Winner of the Horse Race – 476 B.C.' He wished him, in verse, 'the gift of a golden chariot and of horses unwearied of wing.'

We invite him instead, man of culture that he is, to join us in the brotherhood of our Irish culture as a Doctor of Laws of the National University of Ireland.

Walter Haefner does not come to us as an alien. His *Heimatland* holds in the shallows at the East end of Lake Neuchatel, at La Tene, the very early traces of our Celtic ancestors.

That was in the Iron Age. Twelve hundred years later, in the seventh century, the great Irish missionary movement, led by St Columbanus, enkindled the light of faith in Europe. St Gall, one of the twelve monks who accompanied Columban, settled near the Lake of Constance. On this site in the eighth century was founded the great monastery of St Gall. To this day the Cathedral of St Gallen and its very famous monastic library carries the memory and continued educational work commenced by this Irish missionary.

And thirteen hundred years later again, Walter Haefner decided to make Ireland his second home, and we in Kildare are fortunate that he chose Moyglare, the site of the ancient dower house of the Earls of Kildare. Moyglare Stud Farm has been a model for the bloodstock industry over the years. The excellence of the management has produced some outstanding successes. The key to this success was the purchase of animals with good pedigrees, and joined to his foresight in breeding, led to much of the success of Moyglare. Names of great horses bred by Moyglare include 'Assert,' winner of the French and Irish Derbys, 'Be My Guest,' and 'Stanerra,' to mention only a few.

As a keen amateur jockey, local causes and sports have always appealed to and benefited from the support of Mr Haefner over the years. But it is in the area of education that his support has been greatest. His deep interest in our Library and the preservation of our manuscripts had made a lasting contribution at Maynooth to our culture.

Kildare has absorbed many diverse peoples who have come in peace and war, attracted by the green grass and limestone base which have contributed to the strong bones of the horses for which Kildare is so well known. Kildare also always nurtured educational establishments: its ancient seats of learning at Monasterevin and Moone, its Quaker schools, and what would have been Ireland's first University, the first College of Maynooth established by Garrett Óg FitzGerald in 1518, and the present College of Maynooth on the same site, established close to two hundred years ago on the FitzGerald lands.

Walter Haefner has been a princely figure in our culture and society: our educational endeavours and our bloodstock industry bear the signature of his mind and heart time and time again.

He is a very private man. He has found 'a sunny hill in Time,' to quote old Pindar again, in Moyglare. Ancient beeches and oaks surround him. To these he has added grove and clump, a geometry of great fields, marshalled fences, and walls made to the mason's state of the art. And the sun and rain find the bronze of equestrian statues to play on by the windows of the house, facing to the South of this donor of landscapes.

The deep things of a man's heart elude us, but we may intrude to say Walter Haefner must be a man of *Forschung*, but *Forschung* for some inner haven.

His father was a missionary in Tibet. Did he hear from him of Tibetan Shambala, the land that is Paradise but real? Or did his father read for him the Tibetan Bardo Thodol: 'Be not daunted, nor terrified, nor awed. It is the radiance of your own true nature. Recognise it?' I am privileged to present him to the National University of Ireland for a Doctorate in Laws, *honoris causa*.

Geraldine O'Grady
Doctor of Music, *honoris causa*
The National University of Ireland, Iveagh House, Dublin, 6 April 1989

There is an old Irish saying, *Is bocht an Eaglais nach bhfuil ceol aici*: It is a poor Church that has no music. That is true. But if, for the sake of illustration, the word 'church' be taken here as a metaphor for mankind enfolded in its deepest riches, then we may say that mankind is inconceivable without music. Geraldine O'Grady will know the legendary origin of music in the world's childhood, when Pan, in pursuit of the water sprite Syrinx, was left clutching a handful of reeds, and learned to play a lament on a reed pipe, instinctively tutored by the immemorial wind among the reeds. If man, according to Pascal, is a thinking reed, all history is witness that his thoughts have always sought a sister in melody; in *suantraí*, lullaby, *goltraí*, sad music; and *geantraí*, the *allegro vivace* of our Irish ancestors.

And music too has a moral splendour: David cured Saul of madness with the music of his lyre: and the Patristic tradition found Christ-like elements in it. 'Music', says the Pseudo-Justinus, 'for the holy becomes a cure for the distress of earthly life.' For Geraldine O'Grady may I quote Beethoven: 'Few people realise what a throne of passion every single movement of music is, and few know that passion is itself the throne of music, for just as thousands marry for the sake of love, and love in these thousands does not even reveal itself, so thousands have dealings in music and yet do not have its revelation.'

On this rigorous Beethoven score, Geraldine has 'the revelation of music' and her marriage with music is full. She can say, as Pan in Ovid said to Syrinx, who remained with him only as the sound of the flute, '*hoc mihi conloquium tecum manebit*,' 'this conversation with you will continue forever.'

Geraldine O'Grady very simply belongs to an aristocracy and she belongs to a tradition, the scored conversation with the ages.

Schubert was a torch-bearer at Beethoven's funeral: Mario Curio in London continues Beethoven the piano-teacher in a direct and unbroken line through Schnabel, her own teacher. The gift of music comes to us by descent through jealous and dedicated love. And we honour Geraldine O'Grady as a gifted chord in an unfinished melody.

Hers is a household name. *Do bheadh sí molta dá mbeinnse im' thost.* She needs no words of mine. She was one of the very few to remind the world of 'The Harp that Once', before the great crescendo of music in this country, and world-wide, in the last twenty-five years.

Her musical odyssey is well-known: Dublin to Paris under Jean Fournier, the First Prize at the Conservatoire National, following in the steps of Fritz Kreisler and Jacques Thibaud. She has toured extensively in Europe, the United States and Brazil. New horizons beckon, and opportunities open for the violinist whom an American newspaper described as having done more for Irish music in the United States than any other artist since John McCormack. This must have been the reason why Senator Hubert Humphrey once informed the US Congress that 'Geraldine O'Grady is Ireland's musical ambassador to America.'

The major sequence in the universities of the Middle Ages was the *Quadrivium*: Arithmetic, Geometry, Astronomy and Music. Music embodies the first two in its own way, but we honour Geraldine O'Grady as a Doctor for the second pair, stellar magnitude in music.

By way of a very brief recessional, may I quote St Augustine on true music. It is, he said, *praeludium vitae aeternae,* a prelude to eternal life. Yes, great music will always take us to the silence of the mystery from which it comes.

Charles William (Cathal) Gannon
Master of Arts, *honoris causa*
Renehan Hall, Maynooth, 20 December 1989

A Sheansailéir agus a mhuintir na hOllscoile:
Latin is the first language on a grand scale in the musical universe. In the Vulgate Bible one of the psalms opens: *Beatus vir*, and that slips easily into a colloquial phrase in the great language of music, Italian. The phrase is *Beato lei*, which, since we are in the

stream of tradition, can be translated with an old-fashioned Biblical accent as 'most-favoured person'.

And that in terms of talent, will, taste and inspired patronage, is a happy description of the lovely man Cathal Gannon. His life in its private passion has, for all who have an ear for cultural values, the quality of a *bel canto* aria.

A gift for artistic craftsmanship does not go with an ungenerous nature, and for that reason it is most likely that Cathal Gannon would want to hear today the praise of other wise and generous men.

When Desmond Guinness first suggested to Cathal that he try his hand at restoring an old *forte* piano, Lord Moyne, then chairman of Guinness, relieved him of his duties as a carpenter in the brewery and set him up with his own workshop on the premises, with the remit that he should devote himself solely to the making of instruments and their restoration. Lord Moyne opened a Pandora's box, but the opposite of the original: joy and harmony flowed back into the Moyne-cum-Gannon box.

But as we honour Cathal Gannon before this company of family and distinguished friends and academics of the National University, and of this College, some public recital of his achievement is imperative.

In 1950 when the Bach Bicentenary was being celebrated in Dublin, no harpsichord could be found to give to Bach the harpsichord's cohesive *continuo* sound that should characterise the baroque *Concerto Grosso*. That is when the Cathal Gannon we honour was born. Stimulated by this need, he brought all his gifts to replicate the instruments of the past so that we might enjoy the true performance of earlier music.

This *divinus afflatus* took him to the museums and libraries of Dublin, Paris and London. His first major achievement was the restoration of the 17th century Kirchmann Harpsichord in Trinity College.

His home in Castleknock is, in fact, a museum of keyboard instruments and a place of pilgrimage for scholars and virtuosi from many lands.

Cathal Gannon has given this College an 1827 Clementi Grand Piano and a new Italian-style Harpsichord. May he be thanked and praised with strings: with hammers on clavicord and piano, and with jacks and quills on the harpsichord.

In the Greek anthology there is a verse by Leontius on the *Death of Music*:

When Orpheus died, still the muse was left,
But when you died, Plato, the harp was silent,
For until then some small fragments of old melodies
Were saved by your soul and hands.

Today we honour a reversal of the melancholy of Leontius. Invoking the old Irish toast to '*Ceol ár Sinsir*' and – the word came to Italian from Celtic – let us *con brio*, lift a master's glass to Cathal Gannon for the many fragments of the world of old melodies saved by his soul and hands.

Maeve Binchy
Doctor of Literature, *honoris causa*
The National University of Ireland, Iveagh House, Dublin, 5 April 1990

When the poet Yeats was recreating the ancestral homes of the Anglo-Irish as myth, and transforming them by art into elegy, he found a spot 'among the levelled lawns and gravelled ways' for his daughter. He prayed that she would be 'rooted in one dear perpetual place.' 'Perpetual' here means roots in lineage and sensibility.

Maeve Binchy is here today for accolade, and not for elegy. Her name has substantial lineage, and she has made an art of her sensibility.

Her surname, according to MacLysaght, is from 17th century England. The Binchys have remained in Troy. In the plains around Charleville, where the landscape is closed off by the Galtees to the East, Binchy means broad acres, 'hard-riding country gentlemen,' and it is a synonym for eminence in the legal profession. It was the landscape too of DeValera and Archbishop Mannix.

And to 'a scene well set and excellent company' may be added the illustrious name of Daniel Binchy, *enfant prodige* of the origins of our diplomatic service, and a major signature on the scroll of Celtic scholarship since young Irish scholars took the torch from Zeuss, Thurneysen, Pokorny and Kuno Meyer.

Maeve Binchy is a Dubliner. She is on the staff of *The Irish Times*, and was its Woman Editor in 1969, and from her London home still writes a column. She sees herself as an ecumenist between two peoples, and champions the need for English columnists in Dublin, who would build a bridge of common humanity in writing about Ireland, day by day, for intelligent English readers.

It is, however, as a novelist that she is a household word. Her novels have sold millions and have been translated into at least eight languages. This, she says, 'distinctly surprised' her, as her books, she adds, are about 'a lifestyle we all know here.' But she knows, of course, that 'defamiliarisation' is also a secret of art.

Irish writing in the English language has reached world stature in this century: the poet, Yeats; the epic fabulists, Joyce and Beckett; the somewhat dated brilliance of Shaw. Dublin is probably the only capital with three Nobel Prizes in Literature. These stars dictate styles.

The writings of Maeve Binchy have nothing of the bleak Winter trees of Beckett country. Like early Joyce she evokes the average person, fading households, the metamorphosis of exile. She mirrors today in Ireland, and for that she has won substantial acclaim.

Antonin Artaud, the French critic – the man who said there would be no more masterpieces – wants language excluded from the theatre, leaving only 'light, colour, movement, gesture, space.'

That is not Maeve Binchy's school. Children ask for stories, they love the artful jingle of nursery rhymes. They grow up and ask for larger stories. Maeve Binchy stays with language; and with light, colour, movement, gesture, space. She is a realist in the humanist tradition.

Since the novel is inevitably artistic sociology in part, and largely middle-class, and the only art form left with possibilities of epic range, she will, no doubt, find herself in a dissertation soon, on the history of the Irish soul in the twentieth century.

There is a sentence in her novel, *Silver Wedding*, which may be covertly autobiographical: 'After all, here in Piccadilly Circus the whole world could be passing by, and there could be anyone, just anyone, who might see them. Someone from Pinner, or someone from Dublin.'

If it is autobiographical it is a text for today. The accolade we give her recognises that she is not simply 'someone from Dublin,' but a name well-known in Piccadilly Circus, Pinner, and on to the latest translation in Japanese.

Cardinal Roger M. Mahony
Doctor in Theology, *honoris causa*
College Chapel, Maynooth, 3rd October 1991

It was in 1769 that the Spanish Explorer, Gaspar de Portola, visited a mist-shrouded valley in an idyllic climate, nestling between the

Santa Monica and Verdugo mountain ranges, in the unexplored wilds of Alta California. Twelve years later in the centre of this valley was established El Pueblo de Nuestra Señora de Los Angeles de Porciuncula, the town of Our Lady Queen of Angles of Porciuncula. Only sixty years later the Diocese of Los Angeles was established as the Diocese of Alta and Baja California. Its first Bishop was Francis Garcia Diego y Moreno who was consecrated one hundred and eleven years ago tomorrow. He had only five or six priests to cover this vast area, in circumstances of incredible hardship. The labours of Fray Junipero Serra in the same area are well known world-wide today; many of the friars who followed him were Irish.

The Pueblo of Los Angeles served several times as the capital of the Spanish colonial province of Alta California and as a cattle-ranching centre under both Spanish and Mexican rule. In 1846, Los Angeles was captured from the Mexicans by US forces. The arrival of the railroads in 1876 and in 1885, and the discovery of oil in the early 1890s stimulated expansion, as did the development of the motion picture industry, which provided celluloid dreams to so many people all over the world in the early 20th century. More recently, the establishment of radio and television studios and the development of a great variety of industries have contributed to that city's rapid growth. Today, two centuries after Gaspar de Portola, that sleepy pueblo in the mist shrouded valley has transmuted into the capital of the Pacific rim, and the world's leading producer of aircraft, military ordnance, stone, clay, glass, and furniture, and is one of the world's great centres for shipping, industrial, communication, financial, and distribution industries.

It is a vibrant city and full of the vitality that belongs to the new and the strong, but it is also a city rich in culture. It boasts a Botanical Gardens second to none in the world, and several great collections of art. It has History, Movie, Industrial and Science Museums, and many wonderful parks, including Griffith Park, the largest urban park in the world, with a zoo and planetarium. The La Brea tar pits are one of the world's biggest sources of ice-age fossils. Los Angeles has an ethnic variety which has probably never before been matched in human history. There are large ethnic communities mainly from Mexico but also from all over Latin America, India, Japan and China, as well as a substantial American-Indian population. The Sunday Liturgy is celebrated in 42 languages each weekend and in Hollywood High School there are children from 98 different language backgrounds in their homes.

Los Angeles has a renowned Symphony Orchestra, and profes-

sional Baseball, Football, Basketball and Hockey Teams; among the
city's many educational institutions are six world class Universities;
while places such as Knots Berry Farm and Disneyland, which cap-
ture the imagination of children of all ages, contribute to the incredible richness of this city. It was into this wonderful setting that the
Maynooth Campaign for the restoration of its buildings in preparation for its Bicentenary came in the early 1980s. It represented a
partnership here in Ireland, of the Church and the corporate sector,
and had the hope that those of Irish descent and Irish sympathies in
the US would rally to the cause. For two hundred years Maynooth
has produced the majority of the priests who served in the parishes
of Ireland and nurtured through them the vocations of so many of
the daughters and sons of Ireland who went abroad from the other
seminaries in Ireland, and from Maynooth itself in such numbers,
to support the faith, particularly in California and Florida. This project was adopted enthusiastically by Peter and Pamela Mullin, and
later by stalwart friends of the College such as Richard Riordan and
the Leavey and McCarthy families.

The naming of three of our magnificent new Apartment
Buildings after them today by Cardinal Daly is a means by which
we wish to recognise that contribution and perpetuate their memory.
In February of last year, Cardinal Tomás Ó Fiaich, Chancellor of
this University, went to Los Angeles, at the invitation of Cardinal
Roger Mahony who was about to announce the launch of his 'Fund
for Irish Seminaries'. It was Cardinal Ó Fiaich's second last pilgrimage; on his next pilgrimage he died, at Lourdes on 8 May.

Today we are gathered here to honour Cardinal Roger Mahony,
a native of that magic city of Los Angeles, and head of one of the
most populous Dioceses in the world. He was born in Hollywood
in 1936 and attended St Charles Grammar School in North
Hollywood before entering the Los Angeles College Preparatory
Seminary in 1950. He studied at St John's Seminary in Camarillo
and was ordained in 1962. At the age of 38 he was ordained
Auxiliary Bishop of Fresno, and became the third Bishop of
Stockton Diocese in 1980. In 1985 he was named fourth Archbishop
of Los Angeles, a Diocese that contains almost 4.5 million Catholics.
He is aided by seven Auxiliary Bishops, 1,377 Priests, 2,333
Religious Women and 214 Religious Brothers.

Cardinal Mahony has been active within the National
Conference of Catholic Bishops in the United States and has served
at various times as Chairman of the Committee on Conciliation and
Arbitration, the Committee on Farm Labour, the International

Policy Committee on Social Development and World Peace, the *ad hoc* Committee on the HIV-AIDS Statement and the *ad hoc* Committee on the Middle-East Statement.

He has also served as a member of the Episcopal Conference's Committee on Migration and Refugees. The American Board of Catholic Missions, the Committee for Pro-Life Activities, the Committee on the Moral Evaluation of Deterrence and a Committee on Stewardship. In recent years he has been appointed by Pope John Paul II to serve as a member of the Pontifical Council on Justice and Peace, the Pontifical Council for the Pastoral Care of Migrants and Itinerant People, and the Pontifical Council for Social Communications. In Rome, on 28 June last, Archbishop Mahony was elevated by Our Holy Father Pope John Paul II to serve as the second youngest member of the College of Cardinals.

Representatives of all the seminaries of Ireland are gathered here today and students from most of them are receiving their degrees or diplomas as well. It is very appropriate that in this setting this University should convey the highest honour it can bestow on Cardinal Roger Mahony. It is to recognise his distinguished leadership in so many areas and the courageous way in which he has faced the myriad of opportunities and problems in what is, perhaps, the most unusual and culturally diverse diocese in the world, but in particular because of his warm and whole-hearted support of the Irish seminaries and the hundreds of Irish priests who have gone to minister in the Diocese of Los Angeles since its beginnings with Bishop Diego y Moreno.

For these reasons, I have great pleasure, Your Eminence the Cardinal Chancellor, in presenting to you for the Conferring of a Doctorate in Divinity, *honoris causa*, Cardinal Roger Michael Mahony, Cardinal Priest of the Catholic Church and Archbishop of Los Angeles in California.

Máire Mhac an tSaoi
Doctor of Celtic Studies, *honoris causa*
The National University of Ireland, Iveagh House, Dublin, 11 April 1991

A Sheansailéir agus a mhuintir na hOllscoile:
Since no one is an island, it is not possible to honour an individual in sheer isolation. Inevitably, we find ourselves honouring also a tradition, an environment, a chapter in history, a cultural style.

This is even more the case in a country as small as ours; an island, and a *gens curiosa suorum*.

In Máire Mhac an tSaoi we meet a dynasty, two dynasties even, since her husband, Conor Cruise O'Brien, too belongs close to the quick of Ireland's political and cultural history. We should, however, employ the word dynasty here with certain nuances. The word is normally a denominator of royal power or of certain political successions, and Máire's father was in fact a patriot and statesman but also a man of letters.

The core of the word dynasty is *dunamis* which means as well intellectual power, art or craft, magic, even the value of a note in music. This is the cluster which is really native to Máire, the world of cultural inheritance. She is also a Gaelic scholar and was a diplomat. She watched young African nations grow, observed the crucible of the United Nations, but if the internal evidence of her Gaelic poems is examined she is, as one of her Munster poets might have phrased it, most at ease with the 'Bridle of Pegasus.' And she has been a *miglior fabbro* to many young Gaelic poets.

Her mother was a Gaelic scholar and academic at University College, Dublin. Her charming uncle, Father Maurice Browne, chronicled the family in *The Big Sycamore*. Another uncle was the Pope's theologian and a Cardinal in Rome. Generations of schoolchildren went to *'cathair áluinn aoibhinn Andes'*, to Valparaiso, with her poet uncle, Monsignor Pádraig de Brún. He was a Sorbonne Mathematician, Professor of Mathematics at Maynooth, President of University College, Galway; a polyglot, translator of the Ancient Classics, Dante and Racine, and a legendary memory-man. There are still witnesses who can remember him quote word-perfectly Bardic poems, Timon of Athens, Sophocles in Greek, finishing with Holderlein's stanza on the swans. He is buried in Glasnevin as permanent chaplain to an heroic age.

Níor thréig Máire a dúchas: and she has refused to accept the advice of Mahon O'Heffernan in the 17th century: *'A mhic, ná meabhraigh éigse'*, 'Forget poetry, son.'

And if we are to link Máire to our poetic past, as we must, the surest encomium we can find for her may be in the *Book of the O'Conor Don* in the poem *'On a Gaelic Miscellany'* (c 1607).

Meic ollamhan Innsi Fáil
beid romhaibh lán do lúthgháir
god choimreic ó bheól go bél.

The sons of the poets of Holy Ireland
Will precede you with great joy,
Quoting your verse from mouth to mouth.

Pistol in *Henry V*, thinking he is speaking a foreign language, says 'Calen O Custure me.' Scholars translate it, *'cailín óg, a stór'*. In fact, the earliest modern Gaelic song is believed to be *Callino Casturame* in Queen Elizabeth's *Virginal Book*. Máire Mhac an tSaoi has remained constant to that lyrical blood-group in her *Lament* for Séamus Ennis, the great piper:

De shians croit, an gallán cloiche rinnce;
Ach, a ríphíobaire Éireann, clois duit
Ní dán arís choíche.

Orpheus of the Burren, you made dolmens dance,
King of Ireland's pipers, your chanter's lost in clay.

And she is full in the heart of woman and full in the turbulence of our time in *'The Hero's Sleep'*, *'Codladh an Ghaiscigh'*.

Féach, a Chonchúir, ár mac.

Look, Conor, here's our son.
He did not come the usual road,
He came from unknown light.

Máire Mhac an tSaoi is a romantic, if by this we understand an informed imagination illustrating the roots of human existence.

Should she choose to face towards a mirror this testimonial scroll, that numbers her among the Doctors of the National University of Ireland, it will not be vanity if she reads there, as an accolade addressed to her, the words of Ezra Pound:

To have gathered from the air a live tradition,
Or from a fine old face the unconquered flame.

Jack Devereux
Master of Arts, *honoris causa*
The National University of Ireland, Renehan Hall, Maynooth,
18 December 1991

Mr Jack Devereux, a fisherman and former lifeboat man, was born eighty one years ago, in the village of Kilmore Quay, in the Barony of Bargy, County Wexford.

He is the custodian of the two most important traditions of that historic barony: recognised by scholars as the principal informant regarding the old dialect of English spoken in the place until the mid-nineteenth century, and the leader of the Kilmore Carol Singers.

With regard to Mr Devereux's importance as an informant in dialectological matters, he has been consulted by people such as Dr T.P. Dolan and Dr Diarmaid Ó Muirithe, of University College, Dublin; and Ó Muirithe has recently published a glossary, mainly collected from Mr Devereux, in a special edition of the *Irish University Review*. The Kilmore fisherman's contribution to the branch of English scholarship has aroused the interest of many outstanding scholars the world over; I may mention the late Alan Bliss of UCD, Professor Tanaguchi of Tokyo, and Professor Markka Filppula of Helsinki among them. Mr. Devereux is unique as an informant on dialect matters. He is the last of those whose conversation was laced with words which Chaucer would have considered archaic; the dialect after Mr Devereux's day will be as dead as Chaucer's: schooling, and other influences of modernity have seen to that.

As for the Kilmore Carols, they have been sung in the Wexford fishing village since the first of them was composed and published in Ghent by the exiled Bishop Luke Wadding in 1684, 'for the solace of friends and neighbours in their affliction,' as he himself put it. Bishop Wadding's Carols were added to in the early 18th century by a Salamanca graduate, a Father Devereux, and the resulting corpus of carols, disseminated in manuscript form down to our own times, are known simply as the Kilmore Carols. The entire body of carols has recently been published by Ó Muirithe and Seoirse Bodley; the book contains songs no longer sung in Kilmore, and two carols never before published. These two were contributed by Jack Devereux, whose father and grandfather have sung the carols before him. Indeed, Mr Devereux's own *Manuscript*, dated 1803, was one of those used in the compilation of the book.

Many times in the past the Kilmore Carols have been in danger of extinction. I need not dwell on the difficulty of singing them in public in Wadding's time and later, nor on the changes in fashion which threatened them in Victorian times, when some Pastors in Kilmore made it known that they would prefer a change to modern hymnody. That these beautiful songs, two of which have recently been included by Thomas Kinsella in *The Oxford Book of Irish Verse*, are no longer endangered, is due in great measure to the personality and the perseverance of Jack Devereux.

He and his singers have sung their carols on Norwegian, Finnish, German, American, British and Irish radio and television programmes. They have been honoured by performing them at concerts in London, and, on one memorable occasion, in Trinity College, Dublin.

I am pleased to propose that the man who, more than any other, has ensured that this noble tradition has survived to the end of the twentieth century, be conferred with the degree of Master of Arts, *honoris causa*, as a testimony of the gratitude and appreciation owed to him by the people and the culture of this land.

Gerard Quigley
Doctor of Laws, *honoris causa*
The National University of Ireland, Iveagh House, Dublin, 9 April 1992

Aoibhinn beatha an scoláire. That is true: but the scholar is the teacher's child.

The verse quoted comes from the growing darkness and anonymity of our 17th century, and it survived as a token of a people's hope, as a measure of their love of learning, and as a portrait of a mind where a 'fistful of quills' takes the place of the farmer's horse and harrow. Within that open and secret vocation Gerry Quigley has lived his life.

The teacher, the hedge school, learning under duress, the Latin tag in the mountains, and so on, were welded by history into our national image. By now it has settled into a gracious inheritance.

In honouring Gerry Quigley with a doctorate, the National University of Ireland honours also thousands of the unknown who plied and ply the art of teaching, and at the level of the elementary school in particular.

We are not thinking of the research scholar, nor of the great library, but of first beginnings, the foundation in lucid essentials; how to read a page, acquire a child's calligraphy; touch the hem of the national annals; calculate bushels of corn and milk accounts; direct a child towards the map in sight and sound of what exists, what has light and what should be our duty to life. As sure as the dawn sends on the sun, the teacher sends on the child.

Once again in our day, history has been stirred and the mystery of the teacher's vocation powerfully evoked in Brian Friel's 'Translations.' There the teacher is custodian, a lost and embattled custodian perhaps, but always a fulcrum of the values all other values must presuppose: custodian, and physician as well, to the self-understanding of the human soul.

Gerry Quigley is native to the valley between our two traditions. He understands what his Gaelic cousin, Sorley Mac Lean, the great poet of the Isles, has to say: 'The old wound of Ulster is a disease suppurating in the heart of Europe.'

But he also knows it as a valley of loyalties and affections. Gerry Quigley shares the same geography of blood as Louis Mac Neice: the Belfast between 'the mountains and the gantries': the nostalgia for Carrickfergus:

The pier shining with lumps of crystal salt:
The Scotch Quarter was a line of residential houses,
But the Irish quarter was a slum for the blind and halt.

As a public figure this sensitivity has enabled Gerry Quigley to shine in social ecumenism and to be a *pontifex*, a builder of bridges.

The teacher did become a public figure. His *curriculum vitae* has at least thirty important entries. It is fitting in the 160th anniversary of the National School system that the INTO – the eyes, ears and conscience of the system – should be honoured in the man who became General Secretary in 1978. He retires this year following 39 years of major leadership. and to our pride, he is now President of the European Council of the Teaching Profession (WCOPT), and is a member of the World Executive.

Before the public, he is seen under the rubric of trade unionist, a shorthand term which covers a vast and serious enterprise. Trade unionism is in fact one of democracy's greatest gifts to the modern world. It restored to society the equality that the guilds gave to the Middle Ages, but on a more far-reaching scale. The INTO has a current membership of 25,000. At a period of great change and challenge for education it is important that the profession of teaching be safeguarded and promoted as an attractive career for the brightest, most imaginative and concerned of our young people.

Gerry Quigley's preoccupation was justice and autonomy for his profession, since no element in society can live without justice and appropriate stature. That he is honoured here to-day is a just measure of his success.

He was adopted by social neighbours for his expertise: a random list includes UNESCO, Ulster Television, The Economic Council, Anglo-Irish Encounter. and, back to the centre again, he was National President of ICTU. *Uasal é ag dáil na saoithe*: a nobleman in the court of the wise.

The man is a teacher. Somewhere on earth there was a teacher, and then there was Dante. Somewhwere on earth there was a teacher and then there was Einstein. Somewhere on earth there was a teacher and then there was Aogán Ó Rathaile. But these are *cláracha binne*, signal summits, and they create their own lodestones. Today, however, we are honouring the day-in day-out teacher, the one the millions know: the citizen who humanises through literacy, passes on skills, and leaves the young with the souvenir of a caring personality. The fact is that civilisation begins again to find its vocabulary in us on our first day at school as children.

As Gerry Quigley looks in his mirror tomorrow morning the words of Yeats in 'Among School Children' should come to him:

I walk through the long schoolroom questioning:
   – the children's eyes
In momentary wonder stare upon
A sixty-year old smiling public man.

Peter W. Mullin
Doctor in Philosophy, *honoris causa*
Maynooth College Chapel, 10 October 1992

'America', said F. Scott Fitzgerald, 'is a willingness of the heart'.

Fitzgerald, who satirised a certain side of the American character in his masterpiece, *The Great Gatsby*, has always remained in my mind for that opening sentence, and I chose it, because in my experience it touches America's most vital vein.

The President in the White House is indistinguishable from everyone else as far as appearance goes. He is not a King and he has no uniformed siblings in the shape of Duke or Duchess, Earl or Lady, Baronet, or even a Guardian of Royal Swans. He wears a suit like everyone else.

This is an American way of saying 'all men are equal'. But where all men are equal, does anyone attain a certain eminence? Yes: obviously through skill, imagination, labour and enterprise. Naturally, someone will say, 'this is a profile of the millionaire'. Agreed. Wealth is a necessity for all development. But the millionaire, the man of power, may well choose to refine his achievement on special lines.

This is done and America abounds in what its real title of honour is, apart from decorations for military exploits. I speak of the role of benefactor. Peter Mullin is a benefactor *par excellence*. There are of course benefactors everywhere, but history, nature, youth, political ideals, the frontier spirit and vast resources have given the title benefactor an almost uniquely American flavour.

The opposite of love, Carl Jung maintains, is power. Wealth is power. But when a wealthy man reverses his power back towards his heart, a benefactor is born; a Peter Mullin, who has done and is doing so much to help this University.

But that is only a part of the story. He is a benefactor, Catholic and fully. In 1988, for example, he became the founding father of an Educational Foundation to provide policy, discretion, and financial support, to assure continuing quality Catholic education in the Archdiocese of Los Angeles. And by his side, in this free gift of time, skill and resources to God, with apparently boundless energy, is his wife, Pamela.

He is also Director of a Foundation to help Irish Seminaries, and to help Maynooth in particular. Pamela and Peter lived in a very warm part of the heart of late Cardinal Tomás Ó Fiaich and this association now continues in the person of Cardinal Daly.

For good measure and to give you a portrait of the American benefactor, I add that Peter Mullin is on the Board of Trustees of the world-famous California Institute of Technology, of the Good Samaritan Hospital, the United Way of Los Angeles, and chairman of the Foundation of The Music Centre of Los Angeles. He goes all the way from quarks to Beethoven. 'Quark', incidentally, was a word borrowed from Joyce's *Finnegans Wake* by a Jewish professor at Caltec.

Peter Mullin is also a Knight of Malta, and if he walks around our cloister, he will recognise the famous cross in the portrait of a fellow Knight, and alumnus of Maynooth, Bishop Moriarty of Kerry. And Peter Mullin, in his private soul, cherishes the fact that his Jesuit uncle was a missionary in China.

In centuries gone by, the Mullin clan were the guardians of the Bell of Saint Patrick. At the close of one of the blackest periods in our history, this College was established to be the heir of the ancient Irish schools of learning. It was not by accident that its founding fathers, among whom was the great parliamentarian Edmund Burke, named it for Saint Patrick. In the great renewal which has taken place here in recent years, particularly in the Seminary and Pontifical University because of his work, it was very appropriate that perhaps the most distinguished bearer of the Mullin name today, should symbolically become the custodian of that dull-toned Bell which expresses so poignantly the indomitable spirit of the mind and heart of Ireland; a spirit which probably no other native Irish institution did so much to cherish and foster as did Maynooth.

I leave you to reflect on why we honour Peter Mullin, while evoking for him the sights and sounds of America, as Walt Whitman felt them:

Pictures of growing Spring and farms and homes,
Lo, body and soul – this land,
My own Manhattan with spires and
the sparkling and hurrying tides and the ships;
The varied and ample land ...
And ever the far-spreading prairies covered with grass and corn.
W. Whitman: *When Lilacs Lost in the Dooryard Bloom'd*.

Karl Lehmann
Chairman of the German Bishops Conference.
Doctor in Theology, *honoris causa*
Maynooth College Chapel, 16 October 1993

We have with us today a very distinguished churchman, who is also a distinguished German, and a very distinguished European: Most Rev Karl Lehmann, Chairman of the German Bishops' Conference. Bishop Lehmann was ordained priest for the Archdiocese of Freiburg in 1963, and holds doctorates in both Philosophy and Theology. He was Assistant to Prof Karl Rahner and later Professor of Dogmatic Theology at the University of Mainz, and Professor of Dogmatic and Ecumenical theology at the University of Freiburg im Breisgau. He was appointed Bishop of Mainz ten years ago and has just completed his first six year term as Chairman of the German Bishops' Conference, and is beginning a new term.

I had the honour to serve with him as a member of the International Theological Commission before his appointment as Bishop of Mainz. He is also a member of the Congregation for the Doctrine of the Faith.

All those here in this Chapel today, particularly those graduating, owe him and the Church in Germany which he represents here, a great debt of gratitude, for the way in which the German Church has supported the work of the Pontifical University. For that reason it is marvellous that you all can have a part in honouring him now in this your own ceremony.

When this College was established just two centuries ago at the close of the long period of the Penal Days in Ireland, its founders, among whom was the famous parliamentarian, Edmund Burke, liked to see it as the heir to the Irish medieval monastic schools. From them the heart of European culture was re-imported into Europe by the great Irish missionary saints, such as St Gall, and St Killian, many of whom had such close links with present-day Germany that their names and their memory are deeply inscribed there to this day. We wish to honour Bishop Lehmann today by bestowing on him our highest honour, and through him we honour the Church in Germany, of which he is the head, for its interest and support of the work of the Church in Ireland, particularly that of this College, thus strengthening and affirming those ancient bonds that link our two nations.

Als Maynooth vor knapp zweihundert Jahren gegrunded wurde, zur Zeit als die lang anhaltende Periode der Katholikenverfolgung in Irland zu Ende ging, pflegten die Grunder, darunter der europaweit bekannte Parlamentarier, Edmund Burke, in Maynooth den Erben der mittelalterlichen Klosterschulen Irlands zu sehen. Von diesen Schulen aus war der dort behwarte Kern der kulturellen Tradition Europas von brossen Missionaren wie dem Heiligen Gallus, und dem Heiligen Kilian aus das Festland zuruckgebracht und von neuem verbreitet worden. Bis heute noch werden jene Iren an verschiedenen Ortren Deutschlands verehrt, und wird ihrer Bemuhungen um Wissen und Wissenschaft in Sinne des christlichen Glaubens gedacht. Wir wollen Bischof Lehmann ehren, indem wir ihm die hochsts akademische Wurde verleihen, die dieser Universitat zur Verfugung steht. Damit wollen wir auch die katholische Kirche Deutschlands ehren und ihr danken fur ihr bestandiges Interesse an der Kirche in Irland, und ihre solidarische Unterstutzung unserer Arbeit. Auf diese Weise wollen wir die weit uber ein Jahr-tausend wahrenden Banden zwischen den beiden Volkern bestatigen und bekraftigen.

Herr Bischof, ich freue mich, Sie zu diesem feierlichen Anlass hier in Maynooth sehr herzlich begrussen zu durfen.

CHAPTER 6

Distinguished Visitors

President of Italy
Francesco Cossiga
Maynooth College Chapel, 8 June 1986

Your Excellency, we are deeply honoured by your visit to us today and it recalls for us the many joyful associations which this country has had with Italy, and particularly with Rome, for so many centuries.

Even in the darkest times of our history the youth of Ireland always thrilled to the tales of the great Roman authors, Livy, Horace, Juvenal, Virgil, and their foundational ideas which went to make the bedrock of so much of contemporary European civilisation.

Before you became a member of the Italian Senate your fame was long established as a constitutional lawyer and it was these wise gifts and skills which you brought to Government. Of you it could be well said what Solon pronounced in Athens nearly two and a half millennia ago; that he had given the Athenians not the best laws but the best they were able to receive. This tension between the ideal and the feasible, the art of the possible, is what perplexes any statesman in any country, and the true test must surely be the tenacity which keeps that idealism alive despite so many contrary currents in diplomacy and statesmanship.

Presumably there was a time in human affairs when no preparation was thought necessary for any art or craft. One simply plunged ahead, and while gathering what advice and counsel one could along the way, one learned largely by doing. But it seems to me that while education and training is now accepted as a preparation for nearly all fields of endeavour, politics, in a lot of people's minds, seems to be one of the few remaining areas for which no formal preparation at all is thought necessary.

By contrast the breadth and range of your own experience has brought a very great treasure to the politics of Italy, and your wisdom, prudence and initiative have given you the class of world statesman, not only by virtue of office, but by the character of everything to which you have laid your hand.

Your wise leadership of Italy has always been based on the realisation that wrongdoing could be avoided only if those who were not wronged felt the same indignation as those who were; that it would be preferable for ten guilty persons to escape than that one innocent should suffer, and that justice and freedom for all can never be advanced at the cost of the loss of justice and freedom for even one person, no matter how expedient or fashionable it may appear to be.

We are honoured to have you with us today and ask God's blessing that your leadership will long continue to inspire your own countrymen and also those of us who have grown to know and respect you from afar.

The King and Queen of Spain
Maynooth College Chapel, 2 July 1986
(English translation of the address of welcome given in Spanish)

Your Excellency and Mrs Hillery, Your Majesties, Céad Míle Fáilte!

I do not have to remind you of the antiquities and glories of your country. You know too that Spain was the first son of Rome in military and imperial skills, and in the uses of the Latin language. The Emperor Hadrian, in fact, is a towering exemplar of the whole process.

So I go to Latin to unfold a greeting for you. The Roman historian, P. Velleius Paterculus, wrote of a Spaniard. *'Balbus, non Hispaniensis natus, sed Hispanus'* (Vell 2, 51). If two words were needed to imprint Spain on Balbus, two more become your Majesties, *Hispanorum Hispanissimi*, the King and Queen, the mind and heart of Spain.

A philosopher with a Spanish name, Santayana, said that those who did not learn history were condemned to repeat it. He was speaking in a semi-tragic way, but there is a also a repeating of history that is joyful – a Summer of memory.

Kinsmen of your own, King Edward VII and King George V of England, visited this College also, long before your time. It was founded by the Irish Parliament in the reign of your ancestor King George III.

As a boy you will have read of Rodrigo Diaz de Vivar, El Cid, the prototype of Castilian chivalry. Even if the canvas was much smaller, Irish boys too had their Cid, Red Hugh O'Donnell. The earth of Spain holds him in your kingdom, in Simancas. So also the great O'Sullivan Beare, whose portrait, painted at Salamanca in 1614 during his exile there, stands before you in the sanctuary.

Salvador de Madariaga once said that when an Irishman enters a room, the room changes. Be that as it may, your visit to Ireland and to this College is an historic and precious binding for many pages of our island history.

Spain was our protector. I need not rehearse the causes or recall old agonies and the promise of Spanish havens, three or four hundred years ago.

A Gaelic poem, *Róisín Dubh*, the 'Dark Rose', a pseudonym for Ireland, recalls the graciousness of Spain, in the way that is most fundamental to history, a snatch of memory in verse among the humble of the land:

A Róisín, ná bíodh brón ort fár éirigh duit –
Tiochfaidh do phardún ón bPápa, is ón Róimh anoir,
'S ní sparáilfear fíon Spáinneach ar mo Róisín Dubh.

Be at peace, my dark Rosaleen,
To the East, the Pope in Rome is on your side,
As the choicest of wines from Spain you now abide.

A part, too, of the territory of Spain is here. Our Atlantic waters hold the dead of the great Armada, sailors of Spain, of the same seed as those who first circumnavigated the globe, nineteen men on the *Victoria* on 6 September 1522.

To speak of the dead is to speak of the spirit, and it was Spaniards too who voyaged to the rarest frontiers of the spirit: Madre Teresa of Avila, and San Juan de la Cruz. And in our time it was Spanish artists who broke down the limit of form, looking for a new way to mirror the soul of modern man.

Today, in your presence there is a group of priests, the last of those who studied at the Irish College in Salamanca. As a body they are the most tangible living expression of the historical marriage of faith and loyalty that makes the sound of the world 'Spain' so pleasing to the Irish ear.

When Miguel de Unamuno was Rector of the University of Salamanca he said that he loved to see the young Irishmen walking the streets of the city. May something of the enchanted eye of Unamuno always remain in Spain.

Your Majesties, may I bid you very warmly welcome to Maynooth.

The President of Ireland
Dr Patrick J. Hillery
Maynooth's First Honorary Doctorate
College Chapel, 27 January 1988

Your Excellency, towards the very end of the Bardic period, in the early 17th century, an unknown poet wrote unfinished verses called *The Empty School*. With the subtle imagery of his craft, he wrote of the cultural and educational desolation of the peoplre of Ireland, as even their Bardic schools perished. He laments the passing of homes of learning, remembering the 'red and shining embers' of:

'Those sanctuaries where we took rank, these forges that sustained the loving companies of artists, houses that bound comrades together.'

About one hundred and fifty years later, here in the sanctuary of Maynooth, the forges began to glow again, the empty school to fill, in spite of the inevitale compromises that always accompany the disinherited in transition. It happened here, on the site of the early 16th century College of Maynooth, which in happier days would have grown to be Ireland's first university. In 1795 the scattered Irish fires in Rome, Louvain, Paris and Salamanca found here again a native focus.

President Hillery, I warmly welcome you here for this very significant day in the history of Maynooth, when we proceed to the award of the highest honour we can bestow on you, the University's first Honorary Doctorate.

The Archbishop of Boston
Bernard Cardinal Law
30 June 1989

Your Eminence, and fellow pilgrims from Boston, welcome to St Patrick's College, Maynooth. This College incorporates in its structure the National Seminary for Ireland, a Pontifical University, and a College of the National University of Ireland, taking them in the chronological order of their appearance. Cardinal Ó Fiaich whom you have already met is Chancellor, and a former President of the College.

In this College over 10,000 priests have been ordained to serve the Church in Ireland and abroad. Great missionary movements have had their genesis here – to India in 1838, to China in 1917 and to Africa in 1932. An even greater number than that went directly from here to the United States, but it would not be accurate to speak of a mission there, for they went to the US to accompany and follow their own people who left their homeland in such numbers in the years following the Great Famine.

However, the arrival of the Maynooth priests in the US was not just something caused by the Famine emigrations, for they had been arriving there for many years before that. The great John England was Bishop of Charleston from 1820 to 1842, and his Co-adjutor was a Maynooth man, Bishop William Clancy.

In Boston one of the early Maynooth connections was Rev Dr Thomas J. O'Flaherty, who was both medical doctor and priest. He was ordained in 1829 in Boston following his earlier studies at Maynooth. He was Pastor of Old St Mary's in the North End from 1841 to 1846. Bishop Fenwick of Boston in 1825 had only three priests to serve the Catholics of all six New England states, but by 1846 he had increased that to thirty nine, of whom twenty five were Irish – many, such as Fathers O'Reilly, Brady, Daly, Flood, O'Sullivan, Drummond, Walsh and Smyth, had studied here at Maynooth.

Father William Moran from my own Diocese of Ferns, ordained at Maynooth in 1835, arrived in Boston in 1843. In 1850 he became the first resident Pastor of St Peter's in Sandwich on Cape Cod. His parish took in the whole of Cape Cod from Plymouth to Kingston to Provincetown and Nantucket. He built St. Peter's Church in 1854. All through the 1840s and 50s Bishop Fitzpatrick brought out many more Maynooth priests to serve the growing Irish population of the Boston area.

In our own time two Boston priests, Fathers James Haddad and John Mulvihill came here to do post-graduate studies in Theology.

In 1981 when Maynooth turned first to the United States for support, your predecessor, Cardinal Medeiros, welcomed us, and we have acknowledged his great contribution to our cause by dedicating a room in our new Pope John Paul II Library in his memory. Later I will be asking Your Eminence to bless a plaque to mark this dedication. I take this opportunity to thank you publicly for your own magnificent and continuing support.

The name Law has a long and honourable connection with Ireland, and people of this name have been prominent in the Church, the Army and business all through the eighteenth and nineteenth centuries down to our own time. You yourself, Your

Eminence, have enhanced this family reputation by your great work for the Church in the fields of communication, ecumenism and reconciliation. In 1985 at the World Synod of Bishops in Rome I was delighted to hear your proposal for a new Universal Catechism of the Catholic Church. (I had a tiny little part to add to that, as I had the privilege that evening, as Under-Secretary of the Synod, to be the one who recorded your proposal for the official record in the Protocol!). I think the new Catechism will have an enormous and positive influence all through the Church of the next century.

This pilgrimage by such an influential group of Boston people, which is working to further the cause of peace and reconciliation, will do much to bind the wounds in our sadly divided land. We need this support so badly in Ireland today, where, as in very many places in the world, traditional values are on the wane and the problems associated with large-scale emigration seem to be returning.

Today you go to visit Clonmacnois, one of the great seats of early Christian education. Monks from this and other great Irish schools of the 6th century went out to rekindle the light of faith in Europe which had been devastated after the decay of the Roman Empire.

We like to see Maynooth's role as carrying on that great tradition. The College aims to educate future leaders of society, both clerical and lay, who will work in the Church, the schools and the missions at home and abroad, who will also work in the fields of science, administration and management both in Government and the private sector. We see them as a force for stability, reconciliation and prosperity both at home and abroad.

I have made the Bicentenary of the College a focal point by which we hope to fit the College in every way to meet the challenges of the 21st century. This is an enormous task, involving the renovation of most of the extensive heritage buildings of the Seminary, to name just one task. The National University section of the College has great need also of extended facilities, particularly in the Science Departments, while residential and support facilities such as restaurant and sports facilities are also very badly needed. These are the more public immediate tasks we face in the years ahead, but there is also the even more important task of ensuring an expansion of the academic subject areas we offer to students, and an enhancement of the ones we already have.

Due to the support of our good friends here and in the US we have confidence that these goals will be reached. I thank you most warmly for what you have already done, and may I say again how delighted we are that you were able to come to see us despite the hectic schedule your group is following.

Delegation from Churches of the USSR
Led by Metropolitan Sergey of Odessa and Kherson, The Ukraine
Maynooth College Chapel, 5 November 1989

True freedom comes from within. Down the centuries people who have lived under the most repressive regimes known to history have managed to remain fundamentally free, because it is impossible to imprison minds and thoughts. Your visit reminds us of this basic fact. Real freedom comes only from within, and it has to be acknowledged from within, by knowing that you are always free to have principles, that you are always free to be honourable and noble in your character, and that you are always free to love and respect yourself and others. This is what being unlimited is; this is real joy, and it is the only thing that will allow you to be in the Kingdom of Heaven, which is, indeed, within you. You can be free in the most restrictive regimes, you can be enslaved in the most liberal.

True freedom opens us up to wonderful knowledge, so much so that we no longer desire to subdue. When we realise the real power we have we no longer need to convince ourselves of it by conquering others. Laws govern only the outward actions of men, not their thought and feelings. To enter the Kingdom of Heaven the laws, the only laws, you need to obey, are to love with all your heart the Father, who indwells in you through His Spirit, and to love your neighbour as yourself.

To truly obey the laws of the Father is to obey them not only in the physical, but, above all, within the soul. If you ever think a thought against another, it is the same as having done it. By virtue of that thought you have separated yourself from the Father's Kingdom within you.

The Kingdom of Heaven is truly within; it is there that joy is born and it is from there answers come. The Kingdom of Heaven is not some far-off place to which we will arrive as strangers once our life departs this plane. You are already in it, as Christ emphasised. For it is basically the capacity to have peace, love and joy in your life, and if you do not enjoy that it is time for re-adjustment. That is why real freedom has so little to do with physical liberty or oppression: it is an internal thing, and to the extent that we have joy, hope and peace in our lives, to that extent we know that we are realising God's Kingdom within us. To the extent that a Church has that love, hope and joy, and allows it to others, to that extent it is fulfilling Christ's desire, for these things come from real freedom which at its heart is not an external thing at all.

This poses a real challenge to every Church that has ever lived in any circumstance down through history, because the superficially favourable or unfavourable circumstances in which it tries to express its mission are liable to be a very poor indicator of whether it is fulfilling the charge Christ gave it. This is a thing for which we must be always on the watch, especially when we realise how true the paradox is that the most difficult circumstances for being faithful to Christ's mandate are often the circumstances in which we are enjoying the most of superficial liberty and freedom.

Dear Visitors, your presence today among us at this historic moment registers the glad fact of the renewed place of religious belief in the Soviet Union, and the difficulties you endured for so long with fortitude, to bring about this day. We hope that that liberty will spread ever more widely and more deeply, so that all those who hold sincere convictions of good will can freely express them. We pray that you, in your new freedom, will stand bravely for this so as to help the Kingdom of God come to bloom in the hearts of your brothers who do not yet enjoy this freedom to the full.

We are deeply honoured to have you with us for these two days in the College and particularly to have had His Eminence the Metropolitan preside at Vespers last evening; to have him light the great candle, the symbol of Christ in the Byzantine Evening Prayer, while that most ancient of the Church's liturgical hymns, the Phos Hilaron, was being sung.

The Metropolitan's words of blessing and encouragement for our students and staff which he asked me to convey to you here this morning at Mass, were most moving, as was the news of the three hundred seminarians in the Orthodox Seminary at Odessa. We give thanks to God for the very positive outcome of this shared visit to Ireland, and pray that it has provided a solid basis for mutual love and understanding between both our Churches and our countries. This College, by its prayers and its work, always stands ready to play whatever part in that process it may be allotted in the Providence of God.

Archbishop Edward Idris Cassidy
Deputy Secretary of State, The Vatican
Diamond Jubilee of Establishment of Diplomatic Relations with the Holy See, 20 November 1989

Your Excellency, your office in Rome is high, and your presence does us a great honour.

For, without bothering with the subtle punctilios of rank in the Vatican, I can safely say that in common estimation you are regarded as third in line from the Holy Father in the daily all-encompassing '*solicitudo omnium ecclesiarum*,' of which St Paul speaks. We are honoured to have you here on your visit to mark the Diamond Jubilee of the establishment of diplomatic relations between Ireland and the Holy See.

You know at your desk every morning what we know only in a glass darkly – the sometimes joyful, sometimes sad, dynamism of the Church '*ubique terrarum*'.

It may be a question of a Cardinal from Mozambique, a Community of Nuns from Ireland, a Bishopric in a troubled border ethnic region. You deal with Kings, Presidents, Governments. Presumably before you reached here you and the Cardinal Secretary were making 'glasnost' and 'perestroika' captives for Christ in Roman Latin as new perspectives open up outside the Brandenburg Gate.

And, since I have quoted St Paul, may your labours find their solutions under Paul's warm rubric: 'All that is true, all that is noble, all that is just and pure...whatever is excellent and admirable' (Philippians 4:8). You serve the protocol of Christ.

This evening, however, we have less universal thoughts as well. You are here '*i gceart-lár do dhaoine*' in the Irish language – 'among your origins'; an anthropology not found in the 'styles' and 'titles' of the Vatican.

You are an O'Cassidy – descended from the *Ollamhs* and physicians of the Maguires of Fermanagh.

The Gaelic poetry of Giolla Moduda O'Cassidy, who died well over eight centuries ago, is still preserved. And Rory Archdeacon Cassidy of Clogher is said to have assisted Cathal Maguire in compiling the fifteenth century *Annals of Ulster*. Had you been born in those times you would have lived for a time in a 'sept' or enclosure, 'out of the reach of noise,' where you would have learned 'Rhymes, Syllables, Quartans, Concord, Correspondence, Termination and Union, each restrained by peculiar rules,' for this was the process by which the ancient Celtic noblemen became acquainted with culture and civility.

And every Saturday and on the eves of Festivals, you and your fellows would have dispersed 'among the rich farms of the country and been made much of.' So, we here have declared a festival this evening, but have left the Quartan, Termination and Union to the absent rich farmers!

Tonight, in Maynooth, which is one of the sanctuaries of our manuscript inheritance, I will remind you of the cultural fragrance of your ancestry in a poem by O hEoghusa in the Bibliotheque Royale in Brussels.

It is 'On the Recapture of Enniskillen,' and was written to Hugh Maguire; but tonight *O'Cassidy pro Maguire valet.*

Happy the face that looks on you
O fortress of the warm streams,
Protecting gate of the province,
How pleasant it is after your hardship,
O snow-white fort of Enniskillen,
Home of the Princes of the Race of Donn.
You who were unknown for a short time,
Forget now thy sore heart.

From your birth in Sydney, and ordination for Wagga-Wagga (literally 'the voice of the crows'), your experience of the Church has been gained in India, Ireland, Argentina, China, Bangladesh, Burma, South Africa, Lesotho and The Hague. On this wide canvas of distinguished service you have worked with significant Irishmen, and with one person who has a very significant Irish connection. You had in India Monsignor John Gordon from Co Clare, and when Pro-Nuncio in China, you had as Counsellor Monsignor Tom White from Co Laois. You had Monsignor Gerada as a colleague in India.

Of the ten thousand priests and bishops who have gone out from Maynooth over the last two centuries for service all over the English-speaking world, a considerable number made a major contribution to the establishment of the Catholic Church in Australia. Only this morning in the post I had a request from the Assistant Secretary of the Australian Bishops' Conference, seeking some details on thirteen Australian Bishops who had been educated at Maynooth, and who were the last few members of that distinguished group on which they did not yet have full information.

This is just one fact that illustrates the deep bonds between the Church in Australia and the Church in Ireland. And so you are bound to us by two deep bonds; Australian and Roman, which accounts for the great sense of pride we all felt here last year on your appointment as Deputy Secretary of State, the highest position a person of Irish descent has ever held in the Roman Curia.

I would like to propose a toast to you in terms of a blessing and encouragement for your future work. I would like to do it in the words of Cormac, the greatest of the Celtic Kings, who reigned in

Ireland before the birth of Christ. When asked what disciplines and qualities he had imposed on himself as a preparation for assuming the responsibilities of kingship, he answered:

> I was a listener in the woods,
> I was a gazer at the stars.
> I was blind where secrets were concerned.
> I was silent in the wilderness.
> I was talkative among many.
> I was stern in the battle, gentle towards allies.
> I was a physician of the sick.
> I was weak towards the feeble; strong towards the powerful.
> I was not arrogant though I was wise.
> I was not given to promising though I was powerful
> I did not deride the old though I was young.
> I was not boastful though I was a good fighter.
> I would not speak of anyone in his absence.
> I would not reproach though I would praise.
> I would not ask but I would give.
> For it is through these habits that the young
> become old and kingly warriors.

These were the qualities the Celts prized before the coming of Christ, and the attributes the Celtic Church cherished in turn. May these gifts in the future continue to bring you joy in the service of the Lord.

Bishops in Liverpool
Archbishop Derek Worlock
Bishop David Sheppard
24 April 1991

I am introducing a very distinguished partnership to this meeting of the Theological Society tonight: Bishop David Sheppard and Archbishop Derek Warlock. I know their list of invitations to speak together is long, and that they have jumped an indecent percentage of the queue to come here so promptly in response to your invitation.

Lord Longford said of Archbishop Warlock that he has changed more in his life than any other Catholic he knew. He has had a most unusual training; his parents were both converts to Catholicism, he was the only Catholic in his preparatory school. Immediately after ordination he began his career that was to see him secretary to three

Cardinals. He was an expert at the Vatican Council where he became a friend of the bishop who is now Pope. His great concerns have been the laity and ecumenism. He became bishop first in Portsmouth, then in Liverpool, where all his talents were stretched to the full.

His concern for social issues has obviously led to his being attacked frequently. One famous attack listed him among the 'meddling bishops' saying that one of the curious things about many verbal political bishops is that they appeared to have no sense of Christian priorities. They pronounce constantly on matters which are not really of immediate concern to the episcopate, such as details of economic policy, while seeming to remain totally silent on issues which are, or ought to be, their particular province (Journalist Paul Johnson). This did not deter Archbishop Worlock, nor indeed did it accurately reflect the quality of his ministry. His outstanding care for the spiritual and material well-being of all his flock is something that has won their undying loyalty and admiration.

Many people may be surprised to know that Archbishop Worlock played rugby for Rosslyn Park. However, his partner tonight, Bishop David Sheppard, needs no introduction to those in some degree familiar with the world of sport, as he was Captain of England Cricket in 1954. At Cambridge in conjunction with Archbishop Warlock he said of his conversion: 'I had few connections with the Church. I believed in God in that unsatisfactory sense of agreeing to the Christian faith – faith in a God who seemed distant from my everyday life. I didn't agree with several things the preacher said from his pulpit, yet somehow a whole tangle of loose threads seemed to come together … alone in my room that night I prayed as I had never prayed before. I realised that faith is not just assenting to some historic beliefs or moral code, but about opening the whole of my life to the Living God.'

His passionate belief that the main task of Christians is the personal redemption of their fellow man and woman. His labours in London's East End are legendary among so many who in the worldly sense never had a chance.

I am delighted to introduced Archbishop Warlock and Bishop Sheppard to speak to you on 'Christian Partnership in a Hurt Society.'

Conference of the Heads of the Universities in Europe (CRE)

Pugin Hall, Maynooth, 6 May 1993

President Seidel, Your Excellencies, Ladies and Gentlemen:

Somerset Maugham said that there were three rules for writing a novel, but that unfortunately nobody knew what they were. This is the third time I have addressed our distinguished group of visiting University Presidents, Vice-Chancellors and Rectors, so there must be at least one rule obvious to all to cover this situation: to be brief!

However, for tonight's formal Conference Banquet we have been honoured by the presence of some very distinguished company: I want to recognise in particular Dr Patrick J. Hillery, President Emeritus of Ireland and Mrs Hillery; seventeen of the European Ambassadors accredited to Ireland, including the Dean of the Diplomatic corps, Archbishop Emmanuel Gerada; the Chancellor of our own National University of Ireland, Dr T.K. Whitaker; three representatives of our Board of Trustees, Bishop Michael Harty, Bishop Michael Smith and Bishop Donal Murray; Mr and Mrs Paddy Dowling, and almost all the members of our own Academic Staff here at Maynooth.

The CRE is the largest and most powerful university organisation in the world; that it has grown to its present stature is largely due to the the wise guidance and energy of Professor Heinrich Seidel, President of CRE and President of the University of Hannover. With the opening of Eastern Europe I believe the CRE has an additional enormous potential in the years ahead. It is the first time this Conference has been held in Ireland. With more than five hundred universities now in its membership it is unlikely we will see it here again for a very long time if we have to wait our turn!

When I was a member of the Permanent Committee of CRE I issued the formal invitation to come to Maynooth, to President Seidel at our meeting in Lisbon three years ago. I did not expect the Conference to come here so soon, and I want to express my gratitude in particular to President Seidel and Dr Andris Barblan, for accepting the invitation so promptly, and through their staff at Geneva facilitating the many necessary preparations for this meeting.

These are interesting times for third-level education in Europe; in fact there is a surprising coincidence of concerns between Europe and the USA. This was readily apparent at a Conference I attended on behalf of CRE at Williamsburg, Virginia, last February, where 20 European University Presidents met 20 US University Presidents to discuss issues of mutual concern and interest. We are delighted to have with us as an observer, President Robert A. Scott, representing the transatlantic counterpart of CRE, the American Council for Education.

There is enormous pressure, all over the Western world, but particularly here in Ireland, to move on a large scale towards professional and applied subjects. There are no funds available at all from government for research in the humanities; even in the scientific areas there is no endowment for pure or basic research. All of us are painfully aware of how necessary it is to foster economic growth and to create more employment. That is true in varying degrees all over the Western world, but there is a great danger in preoccupation with technical training to the extent we have seen so widely in recent years. Professional knowledge and practical skills cannot be responsibly communicated without a background and formation that will spark creativity in the new situations that always continue to open up beyond the immediate crisis. Students who are trained within a very narrow range have little adaptability for the new circumstances that develop with the passage of time, and miss almost entirely the grasp of the interrelatedness of all knowledge, and the maturity that comes of the clash of mind with mind from the different disciplines, which Cardinal John Henry Newman regarded as at the heart of true university education.

The universities in Europe for nearly a thousand years have been the guardians of many things, principally of those things most precious to the human spirit. It was not by knee-jerk reactions to every passing crisis that that proud record of continuity and guardianship was achieved, but because people at the helm, despite the storms and crises through which they were passing, kept their eye firmly on their ultimate goal. If the universities should lose sight of their true purpose they will damage themselves more significantly than their most powerful opponents could ever do. Only dead fish swim with the stream.

But, on an even more serious note, I believe there is also a fundamental need for us in the universities to re-examine and re-assess what the education we give is all about. Many of our Western institutions have grown so tired and so stale. This examination is not a luxury, an optional extra for us; it is what students are already sensing and questioning concerning the value of the all-over formation we are giving them, and while the content and quality of what courses cover may be excellent, there is a sense of loss of something extra, that is to an extent intangible, while being very really felt. But I know it is hard to turn to such issues when all of us Presidents and administrators are constantly dismayed that there is so much month left at the end of the money. It is hard, but I believe it is not something we can defer if we want responsibly to carry on the torch of a thousand years that has been passed to us.

What do I have in mind? Ever since it was realised that the powers of the mind were so effective in acting on the material world, human beings have cultivated the intellect as if it were the be-all and end-all.

But then we have to ask, why it is, despite all the knowledge and intellectual development, that human beings are not in an awful lot better state than in fact they are? In fact the number of delinquents, criminals, and all the others that society regards as failures, are constantly on the increase. Cruelty, hatred, jealousy, greed, aggressiveness and violence seem to flourish everywhere. Civil disorders, rebellions, wars, famines, are becoming more and more common; in regions like Somalia so many starve, in Ireland the EC pays us not to sow crops. All of the Western economic systems seem to be in simultaneous decline, and to be in such a precarious state that even a major natural disaster would cause untold economic havoc. We will go down in history as the generation that has almost succeeded in destroying the earth through pollution, because we have for too long regarded it as something alien to be subjugated and exploited. One cannot help wondering how it is that the intellect not only seems to be powerless in the face of those manifestations, but maybe even seems to contribute to them.

It's not difficult to meet large numbers of people, who can claim to be well educated in the sense in which we normally use that word today, but whose lives seem to be just as meaningless, just as discontented, and maybe even somewhat more dishonest, corrupt and undisciplined, than even the worst of those who have never had any reasonable chance of education. In fact they probably may be a little worse in this regard, because their better level of knowledge makes them all the more crafty and successful in their enterprises.

There seems to have been one essential point that has escaped us: the intellect and the capacity for information has been developed to an extraordinary degree in our modern educational systems but the need has not been felt at all to cultivate at the same time, a faculty that could illuminate and give life to all that knowledge. And now everybody is caught up in the system, even those of us who claim to have a higher inspiration; they have become so intellectual that they no longer have a place for any higher aim.

Learning is a marvellous thing; but it cannot rescue the world. On the contrary if people have only learning on its own they normally use it to subjugate others, even if this is done in subtle ways. Education as it is too often seen in our society has become a strange thing under various pressures of late; and it's becoming even more strange with every passing day. The creation of jobs is an absolute priority for Ireland now, as it is for all of the European nations, and so is the economic development of our nations. But has that to be done at the expense of the irreplaceable, those things that are most precious in the human heart?

Development of the intellect on its own in this way is bringing ruin on the world. Several civilisations through history have taken the same route we are taking now, and they paid the price for it. Learning has to be animated by the spirit. Our misfortune too often has been that in developing the intellect we have severed our bond with the earth.

Down through history all who have learned to work for the elevating and improvement of the level of life in our society, and the growth of the spirit in the human person, have become capable of marvellous accomplishments: among them in a striking way are the great philosophers, scientists, artists, and the humanitarians. All the others, the warlords, the conquerors, the deceivers, have only laid waste the earth for selfish ends. History has little to lose from forgetting them: those who work for a higher inspiration are the ones who help humanity to advance. That ideal, I think, must be close to the heart of that wonderful product of our civilisation, the Western University. I know its an ideal close to the heart of CRE.

Many people have thanked me very generously in the past few days for the hospitality and organisation of this Conference. In many ways I am the one who least deserves to be thanked. You all know nothing is impossible for the man who doesn't have to do it all himself! I am far from claiming that we exist in this College in a state of paradisal bliss, but I am realistic enough to know that we have here a very committed, positive and dedicated staff. The normal reaction to any suggestion or initiative is nearly always positive and helpful. That is a rare thing; and it is certainly the greatest treasure a College can have. I am glad of the chance to say that here tonight when most of our academic staff are present with us.

President Seidel, may I once again thank you most warmly for the great honour you have done us in taking the Confernce here to Maynooth, the first time the Conference of CRE has met in Ireland. We greatly value your presence and know your visit will be a happy event on which we will look back with the greatest of pleasure for many years to come.

CHAPTER 7

Diaconate

The Rich Young Man
St Mary's Oratory, 29 March 1990

Anyone who would come to a ceremony like this, without fear and great soul searching, has not realised what it is about, and certainly has not prepared for what he is going to do. Fear and apprehension are normal and essential for the undertaking of any commitment of this kind such as Diaconate and the Priesthood, because there is no such thing as absolute certainty in this world, so that no possible doubt about anything could ever exist in our minds about it again. The more simple a thing is, like a problem in mathematics, the easier it is to be certain, the more complex it is the more difficult certainty becomes, and there is no more complex thing than taking on a life's commitment such as the sacrament of Orders involves. Having decided, in our imperfections and weakness, leave it aside. A person who continues to worry and vacillate after the amount that is necessary and unavoidable, is really not a worried, concerned and weak person, but actually somebody very arrogant, who believes that he has to carry the whole world on his shoulders, and ultimately has little or no trust in God.

During the last journey Our Lord made through Judea in the final period of his life, he came to a small village between Samaria and Galilee. Here it was he healed the ten lepers and was questioned closely by the Pharisees on the question of divorce. And here took place the touching scene of the mothers bringing the children to Jesus for his blessing. 'Let the little children come to me, for of such is the kingdom of God.' There is a lesson there for you; what you have committed yourself to give all other things for, is the Kingdom of God.

The Gospel goes on to tell us that as Jesus started to leave, a young man came up, and falling on his knees, asked, 'Master, what shall I do to gain eternal life?' 'If you will enter into life keep the commandments.' 'Master, I have kept them all ever since I was a child.' The Gospel tells us that Jesus, looking on him with great love said: 'One thing is lacking if you want to be perfect. Go, sell what you have and come follow me.' And the young man went away sad, for he had great possessions. And Jesus looking around at his disciples said: 'With what great difficulty will those who love the things of the world enter the Kingdom of Heaven.'

Jesus was not talking about having things, or not having things.

Not having things can be just as great an obstacle as having things, as far as gaining the Kingdom of Heaven goes. It depends on the attitude. What a contrast between the children and the rich young man. The difference is that they were simple and pure in their attitude. The young man failed, not because he was rich, as some broken down spiritual theories so often try to make out, but because his commitment was divided. What ever you do, do not go into the sacrament of Orders with a commitment divided. The reason is that the Kingdom is within you, and it has to grow and develop, and the only way it can develop is by the force of the will to pursue it. You cannot stand still in reaching for the Kingdom of Heaven.

This pure commitment has many ways in which it expresses itself.

It is first of all a life of protest; not in the sense we find so often today, the cliche ridden, ready to jump on every bandwagon, but in the strict sense which means 'to declare publicly.' Your person will be a public declaration to society of the proper attitude to things, to people and to sexuality. As long as society needs such a public presentation, then the life of the priest or deacon will be necessary, and the wearing of your clerical dress with pride will be a sign of your commitment to that ideal.

What way do people look on things? Are things a means or an end? Does what you possess become the measure of who you are? Are people loved and cherished? Or are they rather used and exploited. Is sex equated with love? Can a person love fully while abstaining from sexual activity? We say that people are to be loved and served by our obedience, that they are more important than things as we show by our detachment, that they can be loved in an unlimited and not sexual way by celibacy, for Christian love as expressed in the term *agape* means having the same attitude to people and to the environment as the Creator does: it has nothing at all necessarily to do with emotion.

Let me quote an example I once saw a writer give which I think makes the point well. There are two famous and adjacent seas in Palestine. One is fresh and fish live in it. Splashes of green adorn its banks. Trees spread their banks over it. Along the shores of this lake children play today, as they did when Jesus walked there. Jesus loved this lake. He could look across its silvery surface when he preached his parables. On a rolling plain not far away he performed the stupenduous miracle of feeding the 5000 people. The River Jordan fashions this sea with sparkling water from the hills. People build their houses near it, and birds their nests. Every kind of life is happier because this sea is there. It is the Sea of Galilee.

South a short distance away is the second sea. It too is fashioned by the flow of the Jordan. Here there is no splash of the jumping fish, no fluttering leaf, no song of birds, no children's laughter. The traveller seldom passes and the air hangs heavy. Neither man or beast, nor fowl stops to drink, for this sea is full of salt, decay and stagnation. It is the Dead Sea.

The Sea of Galilee, the Dead Sea. What causes such an immense difference between them? Not the river. It is the same. Not the soil. It is the same. Not the country of the climate. It is the same.

The only difference is this. The Sea of Galilee gives, but does not keep the Jordan. For every drop that flows in, another flows out – out to the second connecting sea. But the second sea is shrewder, hoarding its income jealously. It will not be tempted into any generous impulse. Every drop it gets, it keeps. Galilee gives and lives. The Dead Sea gives nothing, but tries to have everything, and as a result it kills itself.

It is a parable of the children and the rich young man. A lesson for those who would look for the kingdom of heaven; and who cannot see in simplicity that it is under their noses

One of the greatest examples of Christian living in the pastoral scene was St Augustine. His memory and example is as alive to-day as it was fifteen centuries ago. Why? He was close to God and also close to people.

His closeness to God made him a man of intense prayer. What is prayer? Not the mouthing of many words, such so-called prayer can be the most effective barrier to God imaginable. Prayer has to have sincerity, the sincerity of the children. It has to have a passion in it. Augustine was a man of extraordinary apostolic activity. As Bishop of Hippo he often preached twice a day. He often preached seven days in succession. He constantly complains of lack of time. He wrote 93 works, 250 epistles and hundreds of sermons. His literary output is six times that of Cicero. He had a delicate constitution, not robust, often worn out by work. He suffered all the infirmities familiar today – varicose veins, pleurisy, hoarseness.

On this very significant night, I leave you these three images for reflection to inspire your ministry: the children and the rich young man, the two Seas on the River Jordan, and Augustine, who in his life so eloquently expressed what the two previous images symbolised.

Golgotha
St Mary's Oratory, Holy Saturday, 30 March 1991

It would be hard to think of a more appropriate time of year in which to receive Diaconate than just after the ceremonies of Holy Week. When we think back on the poignant events that we recall in Holy Week we see in these last days of the life of Jesus on this earth all of the things that threaten us and take away our peace, and all of the ways and the strengths that are available to us to overcome these troubles.

On Wednesday of this week Jesus came to the Garden of Gethsameni, so full of fear that he sweated blood, a medical condition so rare that it's almost unknown, and occurring only in circumstances of the most acute apprehension. He asked of the Father that this trial be taken away from him and that this fearful death be avoided. But within a short while he had reconciled himself to his fate and what it was meant to achieve, and walked towards the gate of the Garden, where the noise of the approaching soldiers could already be heard, and said, 'So be it.'

Judas came with the soldiers and said, 'Master, I love you,' and greeted him with a kiss. Jesus was taken to prison where he was kept overnight, and in the morning was taken to the Council to hear the charges read against him, to which he replied not a word. They didn't know what to do with him, so they took him away and scourged him with the cat-of-nine-tails, the severest of all beatings. But he never uttered a sound, as the scriptures had foretold and as we heard sung in the beautiful motet yesterday; *'Coram tondente se obmutuit'*... '(like the lamb) before the shearer he was dumb.' So much so that the scourgers felt he must have a devil.

He was taken before Pilate, whose wife the previous night had a dream that Jesus had cast a mighty shadow over the whole of Rome, which trembled underneath him. His wife asked Pilate not to hurt this person whoever he was because a power walked with him that was greater than was ever seen in the world before. Pilate was very much afraid, for he knew his wife was a wise woman and a seer from dreams many times in the past.

Pilate saw that this man looked like a king; in fact no king he had ever seen had such stature and such a radiance without ever uttering a word. Pilate was familiar with the many gods of Rome and the lore and mythologies of Greece, so he understood these gods and their heavens. He wanted to know if Jesus was the king of those heavens, but he replied that his was a kingdom that lay beyond all of these. 'Of which God are you the son?' 'I am the Son of the only God there is.' When Pilate threatened him for not answering all his questions he said, 'Do you not know I have the power to release you or to crucify you?' To this came one of the most terrifying answers ever made, and at the same time one of the greatest consolations ever given to you or me: 'You could have no power at all over me were it not given from above.' 'I find no fault in this man.'

He was sent to the governors of the Temple who were corrupt.

They found great fault in him, for he went against all their teachings and openly said he was the Son of God. He said he came to fulfil the Law, and yet the Law was changed according to his wisdom.

When they offered him to the same crowds who had cheered his entry to the city four days before, they screamed, 'Crucify him.'

And they took in his place Barabbas, a criminal, a Zealot who had openly plotted the downfall of Rome.

Jesus never looked at the crowd. The old women in black screaming 'Crucify him.' And children screaming, laughing and yelling 'Crucify him,' not knowing what they were saying.

Jesus was returned to the prison and contemplated all those people, many of whom had been followers of his very teachings, but were now so caught up in fury. He asked for the forgiveness of all of them, and for his forgiveness of them. And he worried about them. They had seen all these miracles, and still wanted him put to death. He knew most people want to see miracles only for entertainment's sake. What would it take to convince them? And he prayed for the whole of humanity.

It was now daybreak and the flat roofs of Jerusalem were filled. Jesus was taken from the darkness of prison to the lighted courtyard where a crown woven from the briar bushes of Gehenna was mashed into his head.

The procession to Golgotha began, led by the soldiers on horseback to separate the crowds, with the footsoldiers behind. The heavy cross was a terrible burden. His eyes were filled with blood, he had difficulty seeing where he was going, and he was being whipped to keep up the pace. As they opened the gates of the city the mob screamed with gleeful joy, and children jumped up and down and laughed at the procession, not knowing what they were seeing.

Old women screamed at him with venom: 'Messiah, Messiah; look to your God, you who call yourself a King. Burn us all. Why are you doing this?' And then they would laugh. And all the time he managed to keep in his mind his love of these people.

At a steep place he fell and as they beat him to make him rise a wonderful woman came up with a cloth and wiped away the sweat and blood from his face, and he looked at her with great gratitude and blessed her for her loyalty and kindness in a time of such disgrace and danger. As he fell again and was beaten to get up, a Nubian from Salem was taken from the crowd and given the cross to carry, for they saw he was too weak to reach Golgotha on his own. The tattered Rabbi was whipped into position at the front of the cross.

This was a humiliating death, for all were there to see, and there is no privacy in this dying, for the crowds have to be pacified. Ahead the two crosses bearing the thieves are already in position.

As Jesus came to Golgotha his mother, Magdalen, Martha and the disciples are already there. Judas looked on from afar; all his plans in ruins because Jesus never lifted a finger to defend himself, nor uttered a word of explanation or excuse. This was he who in a moment could have had twelve legions of angels to defend him.

He lay down willingly on the cross and the spikes were hammered into his arms and feet. Continually he looked up to heaven and was in communion with the Father, to draw strength for the ordeal and never losing sight of what he would achieve, for the glory of God was in him.

Then the ropes were pulled and the cross raised. While the body is flat the suffering is more bearable; when the cross is raised to the vertical the body falls forwards under its own weight, and there is tremendous stress placed on the arms and the spine. All the muscles are in agony with this torture and the bodily functions fail.

From the cross Jesus looks at his mother, the one who was miraculously impregnated in the Temple by the seed of the Spirit, and who had given birth to the Holy of Holies. Now she watches this very special child crucified before her eyes; the conception, the miraculous birth, the exile in Egypt; the struggles to understand as his glory was more and more revealed when he grew; the strains of his public ministry; all these thirty three years had come to this.

There was one soldier standing by watching who began to be

very troubled in his heart and to be frightened. He knew a great error had been perpetrated. Ominous clouds were beginning to form in the East. And Jesus strained to look over his shoulder at all the people in Jerusalem who had lined the way out from the gate, and he prayed for them and he loved them. The morning has waned, the darkness is coming, and the light is getting more dim. Mary is watching; Magdalene cannot believe that all this has occurred within the space of a few days. Judas by now has hanged himself. The body is in severe agony; he is given vinegar but no water to drink.

Birds are fleeing from the place as the skies darken. People sensing a storm are running back to the city. Jesus is feeling his agony and is saying in the words of the Psalm: 'O Father, you have never forsaken me … for I have gone through all things. Give me the strength to endure what I am suffering, for I greatly need that strength.' And great strength was given to him, and an early death, for he had suffered enough. And Jesus said: 'It is finished; unto Thee I give back my soul and my spirit. To God I go back, for I have fulfilled my promise.'

The cross was taken down, he was wrapped in the burial cloth and laid in the tomb of Joseph of Aramathea, which we are told Lazarus had paid for; a poignant reversal of events the previous week when Jesus had taken him out of his own tomb; for it was the raising of Lazarus that precipitated his death.

A large stone was rolled against the door of the tomb on the orders of Herod to prevent any fraud or trickery which might be tried to prove he had risen from the dead as the prophecies rumoured.

The terrified and superstitious guards on this night were surrounded by a great light and thunder and Jesus came and made his body anew, and fixed himself in transfiguration, for he was not of this world, and yet not wholly in the other.

In the morning a woman came to see the tomb and found only the linen cloths; she met whom she thought was the gardener, but when she saw his face his beauty was terrible and she knew the Lord. He told her he had risen from the dead, but to tell no one, even though he knew she would do exactly that.

When the incredulous apostles had been summoned and came to the tomb they were told that the Lord had risen and had become victorious over death. Later he met them in the room where they were hiding in fear like hunted animals; the scepticism of Thomas was confounded. He told them of his love for them, and that the greatest fear they have been taught is death, and that even their own teachers did not believe that there was life afterwards, which he had now shown. And he taught them that they should fear nothing, neither Rome, nor Caesar, nor Herod, fire, sword, nothing, for the Kingdom of Heaven was within them, and he besought them to know this.

When a person receives the sacrament of Orders he is said to be configured into Christ. What that means is encapsulated in the events of this Holy Week. What happens when you put on Christ? You can see it in these events you know so well, and which I have summarised for you. You have really put on Christ when you can return the betrayal of a trusted friend with a look of forgiveness; when you can pray for and love those who scream for your death, even though they had glorified you a few days before, and you do not despise them for the fickleness. You have put on Christ when without bitterness or recrimination you can endure the most cruel death, while being totally innocent. And many who have followed Christ have done that; including some people who sat in those same seats as you do. Above all you have really followed Christ when you just do not say, but really know that the Kingdom of God is within you, and that no one has any power over you that is not given from above. That last is the hardest of all for we have so consistently made ourselves victims, so consistently given away our power to others, the power to make us happy, sad, grateful or bitter; that we are no longer in control of our destiny.

That is the great path you are setting out on this Easter Monday. From what I have said and from what I have recalled of these most significant features of Christ's passion and death, you can see that the putting on of Christ is not something that happens once for all when the bishop lays hands on you in silence next Monday; it can only happen when you have imitated those things Christ came to teach; when you have not simply learned them – that you have already done – but have lived them. Then and only then will you know what *diaconia* really means, and then and only then will you know what it means that the Kingdom of Heaven is within you, when you can be a light to all the world. You have chosen the most sublime life that there is on this earth; you can know the greatest joys or the greatest sorrows in this life you have chosen tonight: the key is in your own hands. If you are generous in your commitment and do your best, the satisfaction and happiness you will receive cannot be matched in any other life in this world. If you are mean, half-committed, grudging, calculating; so will be the joy which comes back to you from God; for as we give so do we receive.

The purpose of swearing these oaths of freedom and knowledge this evening, is so that the Church can be sure you are entering the Diaconate with full freedom and generous in the knowledge of what you are undertaking. It is natural that you feel perhaps nervous, even still a little uncertain, but the time for that is now over. You have made your decision; it is done with human frailty, but with the help of God. Go on now with confidence and with a cheerful spirit and rest assured that the degree of joy and confidence with which you proceed will be the measure of the happiness you will know as one who has taken on Christ.

Joy in the Service of the Lord
St Mary's Oratory, 27 March 1992

I want to congratulate all our candidates for Diaconate assembled here tonight. It is a great milestone in your life; the greatest in your life so far. It's normal to approach Diaconate and this ceremony with a great deal of soul-searching, and probably a great deal of apprehension; it is a serious step, but like everything else done in the service of the Lord, it should be done with a light heart. The God whom we serve is the Christian God, the God who showed himself in Christ, and who said, 'My yoke is easy, my burden light'. We are those for whom to serve is to reign.

So approach this ceremony, and Diaconate itself, not with worry and apprehension, but with joy in your hearts that you have reached this very significant stage, firstly, in your service of the People of God in the Church, but, and more basically, a very significant stage in your own evolution towards God.

Because the things which you are declaring yourself free of and clear about tonight under oath have far more to do with your own personal growth towards God than with the service of the people. And you can never serve the people properly until that personal growth has first taken place. Too many hungry sheep today are looking up and are not fed, or are fed with a rigid dogmatisim which has little in common with true Christian teaching. There is a great polarising tendency beginning to develop in the Church today which has to be resisted: people veering to the extreme right and the extreme left, and too few remain in the middle.

The Church asks the dedication of celibacy from its candidates for Holy Orders. As you know it is not absolutely necessary that this be so. The Church could change that requirement. But the

Church for a very important reason asks for the dedication of celibacy, not as a sacrifice or as a penance (those who feel that way are on the wrong track and would be advised to change), but as a sign of contradiction to the world, as a sign of values that are higher than the material, and as a means of openness towards union with God far more deep than is possible otherwise.

Most of the values of the world today are based on what the physical body can experience; it is a focus that is addictive, based on the senses. Power, sexuality and passion are the reasons for living: material wealth, security, freedom from pain, procreation. It is not a bit strange that our generation, which has almost succeeded in destroying the earth through the abuse of the environment, has become totally addicted also to the abuse of the sensual body, as if the human being were nothing more than that.

We have the gall, then, to wonder why our lives are not fulfiling, why we are not happy, why the young are so discouraged; why so few seem to have any worthwhile goals at which to aim. Even the most thoughtful of the materially minded among us have no higher ideals in life than a little love, a little companionship, and, at the end to die in reasonable comfort with no regrets.

Why is suicide so prevalent, despair so rampant? Why are our prayers not being answered? In that last question there is a clue to why the world is in such confusion at the present time.

In prayer, as in nearly everything else, actions speak louder than words. Prayer is about focusing our consciousness on what we desire, and that is what the character of our lives does, and much more powerfully than the formal prayers that most people mouth. It is confused lives, not words, that send up the most powerful prayer of all, and bring about and deepen the confusion with which we are so familiar. The problem is that our prayers are being answered, and all too effectively. We cannot hope, when we turn to God with a few mumbled aspirations that are probably totally at variance with the character of our lives, that those few words will speak more loudly and eloquently than the message of the way we are living more than 99% of the time. The problem is that our prayers are being answered. But our focus is on materialism and on ways of life that lead to confusion, so that is what our prayers bring about. We are not aware of the very powerful prayers we are making by the way we live.

How do we awaken from this mess? Only through 'love' – after 'God' surely the most abused and misunderstood word in the language. In the way it is humanely interpreted we only think we can love as long as it tastes good, looks good, or feels good: it is all understood sensually.

To awaken some from this fixation it may take the stimulus of a terrible disease or enormous suffering, that prevents the fulfilment of the sensual desires and changes their focus. It can often take something superhuman like that to turn us away from our addictions; to see a loftier horizon, beyond our anger, rebellion, selfishness and sensuality; to see where the highest form of love lies.

Or it can come through a powerful message like the one that a life of really dedicated celibacy can give to the world. This is what your celibacy should loudly proclaim: that God was more important to you than the taking of a wife, your journey more important than the womb, the ascent towards God personally more important than the fulfilment of children. The energy that could have been expressed in sexuality you have instead opted to elevate so that it can open more centres of spiritual awareness and capability in your being.

Many do not see the purpose of celibacy in this prophetic way; and then, inevitably, it becomes a burden, an outdated thing, something meaningless. It is something that came from 'giving up.'

The message of your life is far more powerful than anything you can ever say. A dedicated and living celibacy says that you have put your focus on the spirit instead of on the body. It says you have seen the illusions underlying so much of the modern way of life, and when you see illusions you are no longer captivated by them, and can lead yourself and others by a different path.

When your peace and commitment come from within in this way, they cannot be taken away from you, as every joy and happiness based on material things can. Your apparent solitude in the celibate life isn't the lack of happiness, but the result of happiness.

So, to summarise: Your celibacy is meant to be a sign to the world that you believe you are not your body. So many of us live as if we were our bodies and nothing more; the slightest pain, or discomfort has to be satisfied, the slightest pang of hunger relieved; the slightest insult, real or imagined, avenged; the slightest inconvenience reacted to with impatience, the slightest tiredness alleviated. If this is the way you are, you are a materialist and your spirit is a slave to your body instead of its benevolent master. The only way the body can be really happy is when the spirit is in control. The modern way of life sets about looking for happiness in the opposite direction: it's not possible to find it there.

There are higher ideals and higher realities open to us when we are able to overcome our slavery to the body. This is too large a subject to go into here now, but a dedicated celibacy in this perspective is one of the most powerful ways of liberation.

But many who are in the state of celibacy are not visibly dedicated: they do not seem to be reaching for something higher – namely that much more intimate union with God that celibacy makes possible. Instead it looks like something that for them has become a sacrifice, a form of privation. That is not the true purpose of celibacy.

If your celibacy is fully lived it is a loud sign of the love of God in you which can awaken in a marvellous way the same thing in others, and take them out of their fixation with the material world.

If you can reach that, not alone will you be a sign and a consolation and a hope for the world, but you will also find great hope and fulfillment yourself. Your peace, joy and fulfilment can never be taken away from you as joy based on material things can, because it comes from within. You really have to try to reach that level if you have not already done so. If you do not your celibacy becomes a burden, and burdens are never easy to bear.

It is a hard journey, because we have become so identified and buried in the material, but it is always a joyful and fulfiling one. It's a journey that's going to take everything you've got to make it; all the passions you have ever had for others or for other things or causes, all the energy wrapped up in unfulfiled dreams and fantasies, must now be transmuted and elevated to serve this purpose. It will take sacrifices on the personal level; the idea behind it all is to move your focus to a loftier place.

That brings a joy and fulfilment beyond compare, and much more besides. It is the joy that comes from always moving on to the new horizons, always deepening your understanding of what your life of celibacy means. It is the very opposite of stagnation and the boredom and disillusionment that so often tragically people allow to come with the celibate life. It is the spirit that I know you all have at this time and I pray tonight that it will never wane, but always remain with you and strengthen the illumination that your years of joy in the service of the Lord can bring to others; but only if you have first brought it to yourself.

A Different Life
10 April 1993

Often we have this ceremony of the swearing of oaths of freedom and knowledge outside of a time of retreat, and then I usually give a short address. During Holy Week there is a danger of being over-preached at, especially from myself in this present week, which must surely strain the tolerance of any congregation; but then, I know you are people of immense fortitude. However, may I just make a few short points to you which I feel are really crucial to you at this juncture tonight.

First of all, it is really important, despite the soul-searching and apprehension that must be there before a serious step like this, that this is done in a spirit of generosity and with a light heart. Everything that is really great in this life, has to be achieved with a light heart. God has not great love for the solemn and gloomy heart; too often it's the sign of a person completely self-absorbed.

Secondly, remember your celibacy is a generous gift; the ultimate sign of the wonderful dedication you have made of your life. Make it and be glad; you will receive in return a hundredfold, if it is made and kept in a generous spirit. Do not see your celibacy as a sacrifice; if you do you do not have the generosity which should characterise this free gift of love. If you see your celibacy as a sacrifice you will always resent it in some shape or form. If you give a gift to someone out of love, especially if it has cost you personally rather more than financially, you don't keep reflecting on the gift you have made, assessing the cost, gauging the sacrifice, pondering the alternatives, the reason why you did it – perhaps even if you were wise to have done it. How you would feel if you were given a gift in that spirit? It hardly deserves to be called a gift at all. But that precisely is often what priests do when they engage endlessly in reading and discussing and pondering the meaning of celibacy. Psychologically and spiritually there are great dangers in that. Decide to give your gift, give it and be glad. It is a noble and wonderful thing; you should see that from the mere fact that the mentality of the world today cannot understand it.

In addition to its being an immensely powerful sign of your dedication, a sign of contradiction to a world that badly needs such a sign, celibacy also has a prophetic and much deeper purpose. In addition to your dedication I hope you may come to see that prophetic meaning too, but it takes a great effort to escape the prison of our limitations in order to catch sight of it. What I mean is that the energy that could have been expressed sexually you have instead opted to elevate so that it can open more centres of spiritual awareness and capability in your being. That is the primary purpose of celibacy, but the one most often forgotton or overlooked. In ancient times it was the reason why celibacy was first practised for religious purposes. It was often later copied in an external way by groups who had lost the understanding of its original and deeper purpose, as indeed we have lost it to a large extent today.

Your celibacy says in a very powerful way to the world that you have seen through the illusions underlying so much of the modern western way of life, and when you see these illusions you are no longer captivated and hypnotised by them, and can lead yourself and others by a different path.

May I put in one word for you in your future ministry with regard to youth and by that I mean even people well into their twenties. This is a very difficult age in which to learn the lessons of youth. It must be one of the most difficult times in history. As you look around you you can see so many signs of what looks like the demise of Western civilisation. The reason is that society has for too long pursued the path of the intellect alone, without the balance of spirituality. A wholly materialistic society has been created, in which the chief aims are the self and self-aggrandisement.

Young people are growing up today with a great deal of freedom which was not available in ages past, and with the opportunity to pursue a great deal of whatever they want. But they have not been given the essential motivation to guide themselves. You have only to look around you to see the many paths young people have followed in their desperate search to discover a meaning in their lives. They have adopted many beliefs, created many secular and religious dogmas, followed many cults, and lived their lives in ways which seemed extraordinary to the older generations who did not have the same amount of freedom when they were young. The older generation cannot understand why young people need to pursue such aims, but they are not aware of the lack of motivation within the young people of today.

The basic motivation of a lot of young people is self-gratification. Many of them also lack awareness, for basically, unawareness is selfishness. It is ignorance of the needs of other people, it is thinking only of the self, to the exclusion of all those around. Young people today are to a great extent selfish. They are increasingly not being taught the values of living a a true family union. They are not being taught the values of living in a true group or society. They have only been taught to imitate their parents and the society around, which teaches that they should look first to the self, next to the family, next to the country, and only then to the world.

Hand in hand with the breakdown of modern civilisation has come the decline of organised religion. Only if you do not understand the causes of this will you become unduly upset and disturbed and discouraged by this decline. Unfortunately, whatever you may think of the decline of organised religion we have to realise that the chances of anything coming to replace it are small. Because of this the spiritual guidance which is the essential birthright of every young person has been missing. This is becoming more and more the case here in Ireland, one of the last countries to experience it. So you have the young people of today, living in an age which to a large extent supports their whims, searching around for a form of guidance and a purpose to their lives which appeals to the ego, to the self; all exacerbated by the chilling prospect of an unavoidable unemployment. I am far from saying that this is true of even most young people in Ireland, it is not. But it is what is coming more and more to the fore, and it will be much more advanced before you are long in your ministry.

We are living in probably the first human society to have so extensively prostituted the animal, the vegetable and the human kingdoms, so much so that we have almost destroyed the world in a greed-driven exploitation of everything that can be manipulated, the rivers, the oceans, the atmosphere, the forms of work and ways of life in which we must all exist.

Young people must be your concern. They have brought a breath of fresh air to many of life's institutions and formalised ways of life. Religion has to rise to that challenge, as many young people are finding it difficult to find God in the way he is too often preached. Society is in need of change, but the change that is coming is not often the kind that is desirable. Many young people today are ignoring their duties and responsibilities to themselves and to the Creator.

How are young people to be encouraged to become responsible members of society and to fulfil what they came for?

Firstly, remember it is in simplicity of life you will advance. Secondly, we have to become balanced and control our emotions. Realise there is always a reason for sickness and disease in the physical body. It is a barometer. The body is the temple of the spirit. Harmonise it with all around you. We have urgently to learn through meditation, concentration, and above all perfect inner balance, to control the body, dissolve sickness, eliminate the weaknesses of the flesh, and enjoy the fruits of the earth, without making food and drink our master. Thirdly, we need to harmonise with nature, to be aware of the gifts God has given us in the wind, the mountains, the rain and the trees. Fourthly, learn to communicate with yourself and with God, so that in times of crisis you will know better what to do than the person who has never had a profound and inward thought.

Achieving these four objectives will obviously mean leading a very different life from what society advocates today. But that is what you are enlisting for tonight. I am only elaborating on it a little for the needs of today. It is by leading such a life that this world will be changed, but it is a way of life that has to be seen by others ... on a lampstand where it can be seen. You have to work alongside those who do not understand, in order to teach them. How else can you influence those who are destroying present-day society through their political, financial and economic views, if you are not in a position to know them?

The choice is: do I subjugate the ego and look beyond the self to the common purpose of life or not? The world is faced with a choice about that right now. You can have a great role to play in this, because of the witness that the life you have chosen can give, if you live it well, and with generosity and gladness.

Spirit and Matter
St Mary's Oratory, 2 April 1994

In the past twenty years there has been a dramatic upsurge in a thirst for personal and spiritual growth among the mainstream of people. They are searching for a new meaning and purpose in their lives and are wakening up to their spiritual side. You can even see it in those who go so far astray as to reject the Church altogether; they are, deep down, seeking something more than they have been able to find.

It is of course true that in the modern North Atlantic world we have for a very long time been making ourselves into lop-sided beings – able to think, but not to feel – and I don't mean that in any facile sense, – to be productive, but not sensitive to anything deeper, to be rational, but not intuitive. We seem to have lost touch with a whole side of ourselves – that side we might call that of our real spirituality. And at the same time we have lived in a society that takes for granted that we expect things to be done for us, to an extent that was never expressed to that degree before in human history; one of the most obvious forms being the welfare state. But even in spiritual things, we have fallen into the trap of expecting things to be done for us.

So we give away our power to external things, to see if they can do things for us. We give away our power to others, to Kings,

Presidents, Prime Ministers, to lords, to priests, even to gurus, when people who frequent them feel they are being most spiritual. Most followers of gurus are simply into another and more exotic form of enslavement. Even to priests – it is not our purpose in the ministry of Orders in the Church to take away the spiritual confidence and power of others. That is not how you carve out a meaningful role for yourself as a priest, but rather by empowering people, by causing them to grow. It was this spirit that Christ stressed so often.

As we let the productive materialistic side of ourselves predominate we also formed a society that was unbalanced. The life of celibacy you are taking on is a challenge to that unchallenged philosophy of life, in which we all swim so unquestioningly today. The unbalanced society begins to produce and publicise an unbalanced picture of God that has little to do with the real thing – God being seen as a father-figure in the sky, fearsome, critical, punishing, but above all, separate from us. So heaven is no longer seen as here, but as out there; a place to which you must journey.

As we became more separate from God with the passage of time, he was gradually replaced by science, and we began to look to science and technology for solutions to questions and problems, as we once had turned to religion. This was why we have so unquestioningly come to believe in a world of separateness, of fear and of struggle, in which the physical world and its realities are the only things that count. This is why on some of the smarter chat shows in the Western world today some of the things which form the most precious part of what you and I believe, are actually laughed at if a person is temerarious enough to mention them under the harsh glare of the tinsel and the spotlight .

It was in this way that we began to separate matter and spirit, and why so many seem to have abandoned belief in spirit altogether. We began to accept that nothing exists or is real unless you can touch it, taste it, feel it, or subject it to repeated and sterile experimentation in the laboratory. And of course you can do none of these things with realities that belong to the world of the spirit. As deacons and as priests your primary task is to deal with the realities of the spirit, and some priests and deacons seem as tongue tied on the realities of the spirit as the unfortunate people they are sent to serve. They feel they are losing their relevance with people; to regain it they embark on a foolish keeping-up-with-the-Joneses in spiritual terms; accommodating themselves more and more to the secular to try to find an acceptability or respectability for their life and work among their secular peers.

So the unseen began to fade away from our awareness, and was slowly relegated to the realm of myth and fairy tale, and the God whose presence is within us was gently lulled to sleep, waiting for us to remember him again: to remember above all what Christ came to teach us, particularly in the Paschal Mystery of these three Easter days – that we are not just helpless creatures, the victims of blind fate and chance and evil and bad luck, but rather are children of God and heirs to the Kingdom of Heaven. If we have the conviction to truly believe it, we know that nothing can happen to us that the Father in heaven does not permit.

Do you remember that most chilling of all replies in the whole of the scriptures? Jesus was being questioned by Pilate, and refused to answer him. Pilate, exasperated by his silence said: 'Do you not know I have power to release you or to crucify you?' Christ said: 'You would have no power at all over me were it not given from above.' That protection of the Father is as real for you and me as it was for Christ, if we only have the confidence to know it. We ourselves create the world we experience; what we focus on is what comes to manifestation; whether it be joy or fear or guilt, it comes to us infallibly and with greatest objectivity. Why then are you so foolish as to feel a victim? It is absolutely all you will ever experience if that is the way you feel.

Since we became convinced that there was such a gulf, such a chasm between God and us, as there was between spirit and matter, it is no wonder that we came into such a mentality of feeling we are victims – victims of fate, of bad luck, of the ill will of others, you name it – that we came into such a mentality of victimhood that only doom and gloom could predominate in our limited minds, and from there it came into our lives.

As a result we fell into the trap of feeling that it was only through the difficult and the unpleasant that we could bridge the gap which we perceived as existing between God and us – bridging it through suffering, self-sacrifice, self-denial, martyrdom, or crawling painfully from one sacred place to another. All of these things have a very good and vital place in our search for God if they are done in the proper mentality. But the proper mentality is not one of victimhood, when we beseech God to look on our wretchedness. Christ taught us to pray, we all accept that. Did we ever see Christ pray in a spirit of victimhood? How long does it take to get the message?

What calamities come down on us because of this idea of separatedness that we have let take such a hold on us, especially in the way we present our faith as priests and deacons?

Look at the idea that we are separate and unrelated to God in any close way; the idea that the more we proclaim our unworthiness, and wretchedness, and sinfulness, the more pleasing we are in God's sight – that is close to blasphemy. That we are separate from each other, and from the planet; that the world is made up of separate and unrelated objects – this is at the root of our global crisis. If all other people and things that exist are separate from us then it is all right to exploit others and to subdue and ravage the earth in which we all live. Therefore it is all right to wage war, to torture, to wreak genocide, to perpetrate cruelty beyond imagination on each other and on the animal kingdom, which we conveniently feel cannot suffer because we are so limited in consciousness as to be unable to accept the full validity of any forms of life different from ourselves. It becomes all right to wreak havoc on the planet's ecosystem, to have the poorer nations exploited by the more powerful, to to practise science with no conscience or boundaries to its behaviour save the inability to go beyond the limits of its capacity to achieve. It leads to racism, sexism, and countless other 'isms' – all because we see them as separate from us, as other from us, and therefore as having no rights over us. Feeling separate leads to fear, fear to suffering, and suffering to exploitation and abuse.

The change of heart which the Gospel saw as the basis of repentance was *metanoia* – not guilt, not fear, but a change of heart. To wallow in guilt and fear is a very effective process, a great achiever, but what it achieves is separation from God in the most powerful way imaginable.

So the Western society at present in which you are going to minister seems to a large degree to be preoccupied with sexual matters, or, more accurately, with the abuse of sexuality. This too comes basically from separatedness. People have become confused by the mistakes and exaggerations which are so frequently spread around: that freedom of sexual expression is a solution to most difficulties, the only really healthy and normal way to live; the most significant means of freeing us from repression or of liberating us from spiritual and physical inhibitions. People then are often led to abuse their sexual energy, treating it more and more as a merely physical phenomenon.

There is a creative force in the human person which comes from the creative *Logos*, a term which comes to us from St John. In Western society, because most people are rarely made aware of this creative force except in its sexual form, it is normally known only by the label 'sexual energy'. But sexuality, and the Christ-like consciousness in the person (which is what we are aiming for in Christianity on our journey towards God), are simply two different forms in which the one creative force, the life of God's grace in us, is manifested.

Sexual energy is, in fact, simply the lowest and most dense form of this creative force; Christ-like consciousness is its highest focus. St Teresa of Avila spoke of our growth in likeness to Christ in terms of a journey through seven interior 'Castles', or stages, where we can focus our creative force. In a similar vein, St John of the Cross spoke of this ascending journey in his great spiritual treatise 'The Ascent of Mount Carmel'.

'Sexual' energy has, then, a relation to a secret which has nothing to do with the creation of new life. The secret is that just as this force helped the person into a body when he was conceived, so it can help him to return in full awareness to the original state of wholeness. There is, thus, a whole second purpose related to the creative force of grace within us, of which people in the celibate state may not be aware.

Normally people feel that this Christ-like consciousness is an illusion, attainable only by saints and mystics, but way beyond the reach of the average human being.

This path to the Kingdom of Heaven is very steep, but it is a goal which can be attained, a goal at which we must aim. The most effective way in which it can be attained, for the most part, has been lost sight of. To a great extent it is neglected even within religion itself, which so frequently now seems to have forgotten the importance of forwarding the spiritual growth of the human person, and can rely too much on the mere observance of rules, the reasons for which seem to have been forgotten or obscured.

In fact, even to many people who live ordered lives, sexuality is still a great mystery. We can understand it best in the following way. Even in God there are positive and negative polarities, but in him the positive and negative polarities rest within each other in perfect harmony and equilibrium. Creation was achieved when the negative pole was expelled from this unity, and the two poles drew apart, and became opposed to each other as force and resistance. But they belong to each other and can never be fully drawn apart. Unity continues to exist between them as a magical tension of infinite power which draws the two poles back towards each other. Without this tension there would be no creation, no life, for this very tension is what life is. So every living creature has these two poles within itself, else it could not live at all.

But the person does not realise in his physical consciousness that he bears within his spirit, which is his true self, these two poles. Instead he identifies himself with his body, which in the present order of nature at the level of materialism in which most live, manifests only one pole, and seeks completion from outside, from another person who manifests the opposite pole. Separateness at its most harmful.

In the primitive paradisal state both poles reposed in each other in everything that existed. The person yearns to be restored to this wholeness, but he does not realise that he can attain this primal state of consciousness, this wholeness, in his own physical earthly life.

It is by this transformation that our development towards God occurs, and that the spirit in which we do every other good work is transformed as well.

Celibacy has many, many meanings: it obviously signifies dedication, sacrifice, commitment to an ideal above and beyond the mentality of the material world, but the most basic and fundamental meaning of celibacy is the one of which I have been speaking.

We live in a world of separatedness; it exists at all levels, even in our inmost spiritual levels, most particularly in the area of our celibacy. The separatedness from God has to be bridged by prayer, not the mouthing of words, but in a true communion with him. That has to take precedence over everything else we do; and the quality of all else we do depends on how successfully we have done that. Separateness is the great curse of almost everything we know around us today – from relationships with others to our relation to God or to the earth. It is the most urgent thing that has to be overcome in any adequate presentation of the faith in our preaching and in the ministry of the sacraments. Let prayer be the foundation of your ministry, and let it lead on to greater awareness of these very fundamental truths of how we most effectively ascend back towards the God from whom we came.

CHAPTER 8

Daily Life of the Seminary

Cemetery Service
17 November 1984

We are here this morning to pray for the dead. It is something that is at the heart of the Catholic faith: it is also something that is at the heart of our feeling and sense as a people. The Irish people are a blend of many races, but the one which has left its stamp on all others is the Celtic. Unlike many other religions of the world the Celts saw God suffused in nature, close, near, relevant, interested in our lot, mirrored in the passage of the seasons.

The Celts were fascinated by in-between states – the time between darkness and dawn, dusk and twilight, from one day to another at midnight. The greatest in-between state of all of course is the moment of death when we pass from this world to another. But the Celts felt the dead remained close and interested in those left behind, and that they were especially close at one time of the year in particular, the great in-between time of the Celtic calendar, the Feast of Samhain, first day of the Celtic New Year.

When Patrick converted the Irish the transition from paganism to Christianity was a very smooth one with hardly any of the divisive battles against Druid practices, such as the cult of the dead, or the worship of trees or water, that tore asunder most of the area we now call France in the sixth and seventh centuries.

As a result, the feasts of the ancient Celtic religion were retained under new names in Irish Christianity. The feast of Samhain was also a harvest festival commemorating the belief that at this time of the year the souls of the dead returned to be close to the living. The night was alight with bonfires on the hills; candles were lighted, to welcome and guide the dead, but also to proclaim that the light and heat of the sun would return again and conquer the darkness and mists of the Winter which were now fast approaching.

November is our month to remember and pray for the dead. It

begins with the great feasts of All Saints and All Souls. These feasts are observed by the Western Church that came under the early Celtic missionary influences, but not by the Eastern or Orthodox Churches.

One of the central and most distinctive marks of the Catholic faith is the belief that we continue to grow and develop towards God after death. All the great religions of the world have realised that there is a gap between the level of life we have at death, and the level of life we need to have if the union of life we hope for in God is to be made possible. All the great religions have tried to show how that gap between where we are at death and where we will be in our final state, could be bridged. The Hindus spoke of re-incarnation through successive lifetimes, hopefully getting more and more perfect with each life experience. The Buddhists spoke of re-birth in the same vein. In Christianity based on the teaching of the scriptures, we have our belief in development after death: belief in purgatory. Unfortunately it is one of the beliefs in Christianity on which people seem to have grown silent recently. One detects even some type of unease about it. A lot of the trouble seems to come from the lurid images associated with it in the popular mind – images that comes not from the scriptures, or the Church's teaching, but from the medieval poems and sagas, but are not part of the Church's faith.

The Council of Trent summed up the Catholic faith on this issue of development after death, by saying that there is such a state, and that it is useful to pray for the dead who are there, especially through the Sacrifice of the Mass. This is the sum total of our official belief on purgatory. How are we to spell out our understanding in present-day terms?

At death, if our lives have been of the sort that will lead us towards God, we go into the vision of God. We see now with the clarity of the Spirit the glory, the beauty and the majesty of God. We see clearly in a review of our lives that all the things we treasured, sought or desired in this life, were attractive to us only because they were dim reflections of their creator. We see with equal clarity of the Spirit how poverty-stricken a condition we are in ourselves; how many chances we have missed, how many opportunities lost, as we assess the course of the life we have lived. We long with all our hearts and souls to be with this God of infinite, beauty, truth and love, but we cannot because of how imperfect we are. There is a suffering there, a great suffering, but it is not an arbitary punishment imposed by God, but rather the suffering of love in separation, a suffering which will diminish progressively as we advance closer to God in perfection.

We must try to help the dead in this state, by all our prayers and sacrifices, especially in the Mass. In the closing chapter of the Epistle to the Hebrews we have the beautiful vision of the whole of the human race, past and present, on its pilgrimage towards God – the Church militant, triumphant and suffering. The heart of this uplifting towards God is the system of the sacraments. The Eucharist/the Mass, is the chief sacrament, so it is no wonder the Council of Trent identified it as the most effective way of all of helping the dead.

During this month do not forget the dead in your own family above all. It was through their sacrifices that you were enabled to come here, and because of their faith the germ of vocation was passed on to you. Do not forget the dead of the College, both priests and students: people like Dr Montague, who built most of the Junior House, Dr Renehan to whom we owe St Patrick's and St Mary's, Dr Russell, who gave us the College Chapel; Monsignor McCaffrey who built Loftus House; and so on. There are many others who contributed equally important things to College life, but who are not associated with any great institutional monuments of this kind. We also owe a great debt to the quiet workers in every institution without whom nothing could carry on.

Remember your predecessors; those students in the years long gone by, who sat in those same seats as you, and who gave up their young lives when times were rough, indeed when conditions such as now ravage Africa were common in our own country. Of most we know little more than their names. Dr McCarthy left us in his diary a few snippets, for example, the death and burial of William O'Donnell of Raphoe on a cold wet day, 4 January 1858:

'Last night a little after 12 o'clock William O'Donnell, 2nd year's divine of the diocese of Raphoe – and brother of John Martin of Castleknock, my old classfellow – died in the Infirmary. I was with him to impart a plenary indulgence a little before High Mass on Sunday when he did not appear in any immediate danger. We had the requiem office in the College Chapel at 9 on the 5th and the body then removed to the Infirmary until 12 on the Epiphany. We had the usual procession to the grave – amidst rain – the poor mother following the body and the only friend near. We had no vespers.'

No Single Path
31 October 1990

Relationships with your parents, with your friends here, with those you know elsewhere, help to activate in you a sense of what you are and what you are here to do. The pains you suffer, the loneliness, the panic that you may encounter, the addictions, the pitfalls, all are doors to self-awareness; ways in which we can understand what we really are like, which is the path to spiritual maturity.

With each experience of pain like this comes the opportunity to challenge the fear or perception that lies behind it, and to choose to learn with wisdom. The fear will not vanish immediately, but it will disintegrate as you work with courage. When fear ceases to scare you it cannot stay. When you choose to learn through wisdom, your fears surface, one at a time, and you have the chance to exorcise them with inner faith. That is how it happens; you have to exorcise your own demons.

There is no single optimum path for any soul on this earth; no single optimum way towards the priesthood for you. With each choice you create numerous paths; and various ways of achieving your goal appear. It is important not to depend on your own judgment alone in determining what is best for you. Listen to others, especially those whose job it is to advise you. Above all listen to God or you may stand in the way of a richness that God has in store for you. If you are determined to have your life develop only in one rigid path, and none other, how can God help you in the same way as he can help you if you trust him? You may have your hand on a door which you insist on opening but it is going nowhere.

Let go occasionally. Trust. Be who you are and leave the rest to God. Be able to say. 'Thy will be done,' and know it within your intentions. Allow your life to rest in God's hands. What you are doing is releasing your own to a higher form of wisdom.

Remind yourself that you are supported; that you are not going it alone on this earth. Do not try to decide rigidly what it is appropriate that you should or should not ask for. Above all do not fear fear; so many weaken in their vocation because of fear, or because they fear the effort to overcome fear. And do not fear dependency. What is wrong with being dependent on God, without whose help we could not even draw a breath? God is there to assist your efforts. But he will not and cannot do things for you which you must do in free will. When you ask for guidance and assistance, assume that it is already beginning to pour forth, and try to relax your mind to receive it. How often we deafen God by too many words in our prayers! We deafen ourselves more often still by the same means. Allow yourself to really pray. So many times we pray like parrots; mumbling formulae whose meaning has become dulled in our minds through repetition.

Sometimes we are so hurt or so pained that on our own we can't forgive, and we cannot pray; it is enough to pray to be given the grace to allow you to do it. You cannot do that without prayer. It is not enough to want, or to intend, or to meditate. You must ask. You must believe. Never doubt; doubt corrodes faith. This is what the partnership with God means. When you pray you draw grace to you infallibly.

This trust in prayer allows you to give. As you give so it will be given to you. If you give with judgment, limitation and stinginess, that is precisely what will come into your life – judgment, limitation and stinginess. What you say to others shall be done exactly to you. Observe it sometime, if you don't believe me. If you radiate love and compassion, you will draw it to yourself. Haven't you noticed that people draw to them others who are like themselves? If you radiate fear and suspicion, and a sense of wishing to keep people at arm's length, then negativity comes to you because that is what you are asking for. This is why Christ taught that we must do to others as we would wish them to do to us.

As you discharge negative thoughts and refuse to entertain them, as you challenge and release your fears and choose to heal them, you align with your soul's desires for you and become fully empowered and inwardly secure. Humbleness, forgiveness, charity and love, all the gifts of the Spirit, take root and bloom, and you draw to you one of the greatest gifts which the universe has to offer, and your greatest gift to you in your ministry as a priest – human beings with open hearts.

Realise that you are not a soul in a body. You are a body in a soul, and act accordingly. That is how you will come of age spiritually.

Purgatory and Prayer for the Dead
7 November 1990

We are placed in the world to opt freely for God; to see him directly would mean that we would be overcome by his beauty and therefore would our free will be removed; so we see in a glass darkly, knowing him indirectly in the things he has made. We may make those created things into idols – when we substitute a creature for the Creator – in our adoration of power, money, possessions, sensuality. But if we see them as hints or lures of their Creator, then we are seeing them correctly, and our relationship with them will not be disordered.

At death we see with the clarity of the spirit that God was and is the source of all our longings, the origin of all that we have ever loved, enjoyed, and treasured, even though we may not have realised that while alive. We see with the same clarity that we cannot approach him, or be unified with him, because of our imperfection. That causes a great suffering, but it is not a suffering imposed by a vindictive God to achieve retribution; it is the suffering of love in separation from the goal of all its desires. All the greatest sufferings, even in this life, are sufferings of the spirit; betrayal, ingratitude. So do not worry about the fires so beloved by the poets of the hereafter; it has never been part of the Church's defined teaching, and, besides, the suffering of the spirit I have mentioned above would be a greater suffering than the suffering of fire, as indeed both Augustine and Aquinas have commented.

This is why we need to pray for the dead; especially through the Mass. The Council of Trent in speaking of this stage of our journey of salvation said that there was a post-mortem state of development, and it stressed the value of prayer for those in that state, especially the sacrifice of the Mass in which God's life is given to us for our absorbtion.

The closing chapters of the epistle to the Hebrews gives us a beautiful picture of the whole scheme of salvation. We have the Church suffering, the Church militant and the Church triumphant, in our more recent terms, all forming that magnificent communion of saints. This gives us a far more realistic picture of the place of purgatory in our salvation journey than the more usually cited texts such as 2 Maccabees 12.

'The glory of God is the fulfilment of the creature:' the age-old doctrine of the Church is so often forgotton or distorted in popular preaching about the hereafter. What God delights in is the true development and growth of those who bear his Spirit within them. This development may not be completed in this life. The true dignity of the human person, and the reality of the God with whom he seeks union, lay open the reality and perhaps even the necessity of a state of development which will continue in a dimension beyond the realm of material life.

The Nineties – A Decade of Polarisation?
28 November 1990

It took 7,000 years from the invention of the plough to the invention of the motor car; just over seventy years from the motor car to the space age. From iron age to space age in the span of a single lifetime. It tells you something of the acceleration of the rate of change that there has been in this century and the acceleration was never faster than right now; but now it's mostly in terms, not of scientific development, but in terms of consciousness, and that is where the real change comes as far as you and I as priests and seminarians are concerned.

For I believe we are entering one of the most momentous periods of change in this decade that there has ever been: it's a time that is going to be very volatile, the 90s will be the decade of the unpredictable. Two years ago who could have guessed at the total collapse of the Communist block and the greater uncertainties that are bound to follow it, the global uncertainty about the situation in the Gulf, the fall of Margaret Thatcher, the emergence of John Major almost out of nowhere to replace her; the very volatile circumstances surrounding our own Presidential election, not to speak of powerful movements affecting change in consciousness, such as the women's movement, the ecology movement, and the massive shift which is coming in the way people evaluate the role of the Churches in their lives. Nobody knows really where all this will lead us in the 1990s but it will certainly be a most volatile and unpredictable time. I believe we have seen nothing yet. And I further believe we are not prepared for it.

You will have noticed the dramatic and sudden shift in people's attitude to the Churches. It is not that they are drifting to godlessness, but that they feel the Churches do not have what they need to satisfy their thirst; again not perhaps something of which they are consciously aware in these precise terms. It is a drift away from any structure or form in religion, towards the fundamentalist sects, towards the New Age movements, towards the stand of the individual alone before God without any intermediaries. We in the Churches have to plead guilty to a lot of what we stand accused of. We just have not succeeded enough in showing people that the sacraments and teaching of Christ is a way to joy, enlightenment, freedom, and the uplifting of life on the way to our destiny. Instead the belief and moral system of Christianity is too often misunderstood only as a drudge and an imposition, a set of rules, the keeping of which is the price to be paid for belonging to a Church, or the price for avoiding the fires of hell. 'Have you got Mass yet? I must get Confession.' We are selling the faith short. The Churches have become so concerned with social justice, with the needs of the underprivileged and the poor, and with the conditions of society – all very legitimate concerns – that they have very little time left to say anything at all to the person who wants to grow spiritually. In fact it is nowadays almost something to be ashamed of in the mind of a lot of people, almost a sign of a dangerous level of spiritual pride, or of living in cloud cuckoo land.

But that is what the change of consciousness in the 90s is asking for. And that precisely was Christ's principal admonition to us: you are children of God and heirs to the Kingdom of Heaven; and this kingdom is within you. How else can you reach that kingdom then, except by growing spiritually? This precisely is what the greatest thirst of people is going to be in the very disturbed decade in whose boundaries we now stand. What will you, who will be priests right in the middle of this decade, have to offer them? You will need much more than being able to administer the sacraments, train a hurling team, run a youth club, or organise a credit union. What you need is what you will be personally, and you will need to be much more than a nice man, an attentive man, or a busy man.

For the last couple of weeks I have been trying to put before you some of the things that you need to do if you are going to be able to help those people in any real sense. I know a lot of you thought it was all very abstract, up in the air, too ethereal, something maybe for the enclosed Orders, but not for Maynooth, especially at eight in the morning. And even of those who didn't think that way quite a few misunderstood what I was talking about.

To some, however, it did get through. This is to be expected. Our upbringing, education, family circumstances, cast of character, and above all our level of personal development, all act as filters on what we see and hear. *You only hear what you are ready for, and it is you yourself who decides that.* But I would seriously ask you all, conveniently ready or not, to give the strongest consideration to what I am trying to put before you. I know how difficult it is; I too sat in those same seats as you do now, and I know the uncertainties, the difficulties, the joys and doubts, that you all face every day on your seven-year journey, without adding all this to it as well. Please don't be ostriches with your heads in the sand. It really is important that you try to open your mind to what I am trying to put before you, because the priesthood of Christ is about much, much more than being nice to people, helping the needy, administering the sacraments and being actively involved in the temporal well-being of the parish, no matter how important these are. I honour and respect the dedication of the many students who come here and after honest effort find the priesthood is not for them, but I must also in honesty say that far fewer would leave the seminary if they really realised that the work of the priest is first of all about this, and secondly about social concerns. Social concerns come second, and have no life in them if they aren't based on that foundation. You are not here in this oratory preparing to be social workers.

Shakespeare said that there is a tide in the affairs of men which taken at its height leads on to fortune, but if we miss the tide all our further ventures are bounded in shallow waters and of little significance. I believe we stand on the very verge of such a situation right now; it is of course up to you yourselves how you will respond, but realise that your future effectiveness as priests, as well as your personal well-being in the age of enormous uncertainty, if not chaos, that faces us, will depend on how you respond. It's a time when you need a strong sure anchor or foundation, right within yourself. It's not just a time of crisis – it's certainly that – but it's a time of unparalleled opportunity for you as well, when, if you have prepared yourself, your work will bear fruit to a degree unimaginable.

Bethlehem and Self-Centredness
19 December 1990

People's interests are often egotistical; everything starts and ends with them. We study, work, meet and marry, and even do good, in order to take and to gratify ourselves.

Egotism always has a pernicious effect on people. When you try to keep everything you receive for yourself the channels become blocked.

Have you ever wondered that after all the years of effort you still have not improved much? The reason usually is that while you have done a lot of things, you have not done the essential: the essential is the law of giving, self sacrifice. Most of what we do is for ourselves; even when we read, when we study, we are still taking. People work hard, often very hard, but they work to acquire, they develop themselves, to gain more power, to spread their tentacles.

Jesus spoke on this when he addressed the rich young man, who had kept all the commandments, and asked what further thing he should do to possess the Kingdom of God. Christ said: 'Leave all things and follow me, and then you will have treasure in heaven.' Christ knew the importance of the law of giving and taking. You give to become free; paradoxically you give in order to gain more, though you do not see it that way. You trade in old stock for something more fresh and new and incorruptible.

How foolish the young man was: he held on to what he thought would make him happy. Actually it was making him miserable – he did not see the difference between possession and happiness. Having things does not necessarily make you happy or unhappy; not having things doesn't necessarily make you happy or unhappy either. You are on the wrong track if you think Christ was talking about having or not having. He was talking about something entirely different. If you have divested yourself of almost everything it is fatally easy to fall into the oldest trap of all: being proud that you have become humble, glad that you are poor unlike the others, or that you are living in simplicity. All the time you enjoy the most delicious taste of the dagger of criticism in the back of those you feel may be less detached and less spiritual than you are now.

Many years ago a great wise man in the East – maybe a successor of the Magi who came to venerate the Christ child at Bethlehem – used to try to teach by demonstration. He used to publicly live what he was trying to teach to his disciples. One day a number of people came from afar to see him and they found this spiritual master sitting surrounded by every conceivable form of luxury. They were shocked and terribly disappointed at this display of materialism and they went off to a neighbouring teacher who had a great reputation as an ascetic. They met him in his single roomed house, where his only possessions were a jug of water and a mat. They were very pleased with this and said to the ascetic: 'Your simple manners and austere environment are much more impressive and encouraging for us to see than the shocking luxury and excesses of the Master whom we have just visited. He seems to have turned his back totally on the path of truth.'

The ascetic gave a great sigh and began to weep. 'Dear Friends,' he said, 'How can you be so shallow and so affected by the outward signs of things? It is one of the greatest barriers we have to overcome in our development towards God. The great Master is surrounded at this moment by every luxury because he is impervious to luxury. I am surrounded by simplicity because I am impervious to simplicity.'

We judge others nearly always by externals. The test is not whether we are in luxury or simplicity; the test is are we detached from both or not? To judge harshly is one of the most exquisite pleasures the materialist and the sensualist can enjoy. The most egotistical thing of all is how we judge and lacerate others so harshly. I have said to you before that other people mirror to us what we are ourselves. If you see something in another person that you simply cannot stand, then rest assured you yourself must have that fault in a high degree. If you simply can't accept that, or can't see how that could be, it just shows how deeply ingrained that fault has become in you; it has blended in to become a very part of yourself.

It was to divinise the world that Christ came down as man and was born in a stable at Bethlehem. He came into a sinful world, and he came because it was sinful. He dined with Pharisees and Scribes, and those whom the world called sinners. He never condemned anyone, unless their hearts were hard, but these he condemned most harshly, levelling, for instance, the most shocking criticism a Jew could offer when he called Herod a fox and the Pharisees a brood of vipers. But when they wanted to stone to death the woman taken in adultery he said to her: 'Woman, has no one condemned you? ... neither will I condemn you, go now and sin no more.' What was the difference? He did not see the sin; he saw the state of the heart that had sinned. This is the polar opposite of judging by externals.

The message of Christmas is to try to see into the heart of things. It was there at Bethlehem for the first time that we really saw how difficult it is to understand the ways of God; how he confounds the mighty and brings the expectations of the powerful and the superficial to nought. Who would have advised God to make his grand entrance into this world in a stable? The standards of the world are not the standards of heaven. To judge by the standards of heaven is very difficult, but it is the only way in which we can start to elevate the level of energy within us to where it can empower us to see, think, and love others, and probably the most difficult of all, to love ourselves, and to do it with the understanding and the mind of God himself.

In the stable at Bethlehem we have the supreme example of the most sinless, the most beautiful child the world has ever known; someone whose whole being was consumed with infinite love. Love cannot live in the egocentric man; it is one of the greatest barriers to our growth towards God. Egocentricity is the opposite to what being Christlike means. Reflect on this as you go home for Christmas; think about it a lot as you look at the infant in the crib, and make it your own. Nothing is of any use in these matters unless it is made your own.

The Seminarian and the Love of God
6 February 1991

The first business of any seminarian is to try to know and love God more and more. We cannot know God directly, we can't see him face to face, but only mirrored dimly in the things he has made. This is why the scriptures and we ourselves speak of him as father, as mother, as shepherd, as vinedresser, as a potter, as a lamb, as a king. I presume that at some stage in the past it must have dawned on you that God is none of these things in himself, but he has, to a degree unimaginable for us, the good qualities of all of these images – the love of a father, the care of a shepherd, the majesty and power of a king.

But nothing is more difficult to understand about God than what we call his love. Love, as it is spoken about nowadays in the films, on TV, or in the gutter press, is a very debased thing, quite frequently something crudely sensual and selfish. It was just the same when St John and St Paul lived – the two men who wrote most about God as love in the New Testament. If God's very nature is love, then to describe it they had to search for a word that wasn't debased in ordinary usage. In fact they went back three hundred years before the birth of Christ to find an antique word to do the job for them. The word was 'agape.' A word which is of course translated as 'love' in most of the English versions of the scriptures which you use. But agape is as different from love in the everyday sense as chalk is from cheese.

When we try to imagine what God's love means we can think of various things: the love of parent for a child, the love between husband and wife, the bond between friends. The OT used all of these in talking about God's love. If you have a friend to whom you are close here in the College I think you might find that your regard for him varies, depending on how he behaves. If he's good company, a good mixer, good at sports, cheerful, loyal, patient, tolerant, strong, you probably get on well, and feel that what you have must be a good friendship. But if your friend gets cranky, is moody, selfish, irritable, critical and unsympathetic, your friendship probably weakens, and may die altogether. In other words your friendship depends on conditions: it's a conditional friendship. The great difference between God's love and human love is precisely here; normally human love has quite a mixture of conditional love in it, whereas God's love has none.

His love for us is always the same, and makes no distinction between persons, no distinction between the good and the evil, the grateful and spiteful, the selfish or the generous. To all alike God always pours out his infinite love. The image of the sun can help us to understand better how God loves us; it can do that even better than images of father, mother and shepherd can. As the Old Testament says, God lets his sun shine on the good and the bad, on the just and the unjust.

You and I are like windows facing that sunlight. If we are clear and open and receptive, the sun pours in. People who are like sparkling clear windows are easily recognisable when we meet them; we often think that God must love them greatly. That isn't the whole story. God gives his love *to all equally*, just as the sun gives its rays without discrimination. What gets through to any individual is totally dependent on how they respond, on what *they allow* to come in. The really significant ways in which we prevent God's love from pouring in to us is not just by the traditionally recognised great sins, murder, adultery, fornication, great injustice, etc.. We can often think, like the Pharisees, that because we don't do these things, we must somehow or another be better than the average. But the other really great barriers to God's love coming into us is not only these, but above all the crippling attitudes we carry around inside us. These are the things that darken the windows. Doubts, insecurity, fears, lack of self-confidence, envy, or the weakness so often disguised behind arrogance, boasting and subtle bullying. These are the real things that cloud out God's love. This is why the sinner Magdalene was actually so much closer to God than those among the Jews of Christ's day who were considered most upright.

What are you doing about all this here in Maynooth? Are you too lazy to bother, even to think about these things a little? Your main business here is to learn more about God, to become more aware and to deepen that love you already have for him.

You are all generous and idealistic young men; you have great gifts, great promise, the ability to achieve great things for God and the neighbour. You came here to dedicate your lives to an ideal. That's a glorious thing, and rare in the world today. But what do you do when you come here ? After the first flush of enthusiasm is over? You are so busy doing so many things: class, games, study, skills, visits, making tea and socialising. All good things. But how little time you spend trying to deepen what's inside, and how you can even mock and make fun of what is being offered to you, being offered to you precisely because you are valued; when an effort is being made to try to help you. How sad to see ideals turn to cynicism so soon. You are judging yourself when you do that; the loudest laugh is on you.

This is why, despite your great gifts and promise, and the idealism and generosity with which you came, that so many of you leave the seminary who need not leave. Some will quite legitimately decide the priesthood is not for them. But many others who are very suited to the priesthood are content to drift on through the years here without ever making the effort to fundamentally change or deepen very much the relationship they had to God as a child or in secondary school. There can be other reasons of course why people leave who ought not leave, but that lack of spiritual maturity and the frustration and boredom it brings you here, is the basic one.

To help you to grow and to get control of yourself, and thereby to become free, there is a way of life asked of you in this house. It is a routine, I stress routine; a routine of attendance at Mass, meditation, spiritual reading, of study, of personal cleanliness, of care in keeping your room tidy, or participating in recreation, of giving up the small freedoms of being always able to go where you please. That routine is irksome and unpleasant, though some may actually wallow in it for the wrong reasons. That routine is not there to torture you, but to help you deepen, to help you become capable of loving God and your neighbour better; and you cannot do that without self-discipline; discipline I stress; not repression or time serving, as if you were an inmate in a low security prison. Self-discipline is, I assure you, the only way to become really happy or free.

I'm sure you often wonder if you are on the right path, or are making progress, or really have a vocation, or really love God? Do you want to know if you really love God, or if you are really making progress in Maynooth in the areas that matter? Then, look at how you behave when it is known that there is nobody supervising you.

That will tell you *infallibly* how much you have grown, how much you have deepened, and, most important of all, how much you really understand what the routine of life in the seminary is there for at all.

I have been trying to put before you a very simple but enormously important truth: that there is a power or energy in us that is poured down from above by the Holy Spirit, on which everything depends.

This power has to be elevated in us if the sun of God's love and freedom is to be able to pour into us and transform us. Unfortunately, for most people, that power is kept wandering all through life at the material and sensual levels.

If you really desire and value the things of the spirit – which demands so much purity of heart in every area – then that energy will automatically ascend and transform your outlook on life; your focus will change. Normally because of where your focus is, too much on the materialistic or the sensual, playing with the fire, you create ever more new problems which you have to battle against yourself in turn. Why not short circuit this whole tiresome process, and raise your focus beyond that customary level? But so many are not willing to do that; or perhaps cannot see how important it is. You are the ones happy to be social workers. Social work is a marvellous thing, but it is not the priesthood.

I said already that it is sad to see so many leave who ought not have left; who have squandered through laziness or immaturity, or lack of idealism or bravery, God's precious gift to them. That of course must legitimately be your choice (and I am not speaking of those who leave having given it their best). But if you are willing to do so little to acquire the things that really matter here, then, sadly, it is a very good thing that so many of you leave. If you are in that state and won't budge, then it really is God's will for you that you go, but it is a great loss for the Church, for all the people you could have been able to help, but the greatest loser is yourself. 'Where your heart lies,' Jesus said, 'here your treasure will be.' And the same holds true of your reward.

The Obscenity of War
20 February 1991

All animals kill; not necessarily for food or self-defence. Well fed cats will still mutilate a mouse. But there is something unique about human killing. It is not instinctual like animals' killing is. Some human beings love to hunt and kill, others abhor it, others couldn't care less one way or the other. Animals kill by instinct. Humans don't. In fact one of the most significant things about human beings is the lack of instincts we have. That is why our behaviour is so varied. Free choice in human beings replaces instinct in animals.

And if we can choose freely, we can choose evil as well as good.

Human killing is, then, a matter of choice. We can choose why, how, when and where we will kill. And this gives rise to enormous moral complexities. A person, for example, might become a vegetarian in order to avoid having animals killed. Yet to eat and live he still has to hack off plants from their roots and roast their corpses in ovens. Should the vegetarian eat eggs, the potentially unborn children of beautiful birds; or drink milk, which may have been taken from cows whose calves have been slaughtered for veal? Does a woman have the right to bear a child whom she doesn't want or won't care for? Does a woman have the right to kill her unborn child? Is it not strange that so many pacifists are advocates of abortion? Or that those who campaign against abortion are so often those who campaign for the restoration of capital punishment? We often think we are behaving ethically, but the odds are that our ethics may often be confined to parts of our awareness, so that our ethics are illogical and inconsistent when we examine them even a little. What ethical sense does it make to kill a murderer as an example to convince others that murder is morally wrong?

One of the big factors which makes us so illogical, is that we can't see beyond ourselves. Basically what Lent is about is trying to restore our ability to see a bit beyond ourselves. To get out of the rut, the rut our bodies are in, by bodily penance; the rut our minds and souls are in, by re-examining and evaluating afresh our basic attitudes.

We can't see beyond ourselves. We are far more likely to kill that which is different from us than we are to kill that which is like us. The vegetarian feels guilty about killing animals, but not about killing plants, because animals are more like us than plants. Some people will eat fish but not meat, because they don't believe fish can have feelings. There are fishermen who abhor the idea of hunting animals, and there are hunters who would shoot birds, but would baulk at killing a deer with its all too human eyes. The same is true when humans kill other humans. It's easier to kill a black person or an Oriental, if you are a European, than it is to kill another person who has a white skin and Caucasian features like ourselves. It's even easier when we call them niggers, or wogs, or rednecks, or kinks. It's easier for an Oriental to kill a European than it is to kill another Oriental. How have we let ourselves become so illogical, so blind in our ethics and basic convictions?

A century ago it required a week to get a message from the US to Europe, months to get in touch with China. The system of nation states made sense in those days. Now with global communication much of the system of nation states is obsolete and outmoded. But our narcissism makes us cling to these forms. And it is only in such a climate that war can flourish.

War is, unfortunately, a uniquely human form of behaviour. Some even feel that one of our few instincts is an instinct for war. But, as I have said earlier, one of the fundamental things about a human being is that his behaviour is mostly not instinctual. What we do someone decides on; and someone could change it too. So we have to face the fact that waging war is a choice for which someone is responsible. Whenever war is waged someone has lost their moorings. Whenever there is a war, someone is at fault, maybe both sides.

But it is usual these days for both sides in a war to proclaim themselves victims. In olden times, people weren't so squeamish, and you went to war to take what the other fellow had away from him. But nowadays we always have to have a pretence of higher motives. Even Hitler concocted reasons for his invasions. Each side now feels the other is the aggressor, and it the victim. So in the face of all of this we tend to throw up our hands and feel that nobody is really to blame for war. No one made the wrong choice; it simply happened, like spontaneous combustion.

This is rubbish; this ethical hopelessness; this throwing away of our capacity for moral judgment; this idea that it is impossible to identify evil. The ability to identify evil and change things is what Lent is about.

In the 1960s the war in Vietnam didn't just happen. It was started by the British in 1945, sustained afterwards by the French until they were defeated in 1954, and, with peace in sight it was revived by the Americans for another eighteen years.

Someone tried to find out what the troops on the way to battle in Vietnam knew about the history of that country, and how it had brought the war about. The enlisted men knew nothing. Ninety percent of the junior officers knew nothing. What little the senior officers knew had been taught in biased programmes in military school. In other words at least 90% of those going off to risk their lives in Vietnam hadn't the slightest idea of what the war was really about.

I wonder how many fighting now on both sides in the Gulf know the origins of Iraq and of those other countries that came out of Churchill's awkward solution to carving up the Ottoman empire in 1921? How can an entire people go to war without really knowing why? Assuredly Saddam Hussein is a tyrant, and he will be stopped in this battle; but how far away is the next and much more disastrous war that will inevitably arise from this humiliation of the Arab world and their even greater perception of the hatred of Israel? How can we go to war without really knowing why?

The answer is simple. As a group, people are too lazy to learn, and secondly, too arrogant to think they need to learn. They feel that whatever way they happen to see things is the right way, without the need for any further study. And whatever was done, they think was the right thing, without any further need for reflection. They were really badly wrong, because they could never entertain the slightest doubt that they might not be right. With laziness and narcissism feeding each other they all marched off to bloodshed with practically no idea of the real issues. How long more will the world tolerate this?

I am not criticising the Americans, the Vietcong, the Iraqis, the Israelis, the British, or indeed any others. In Ireland we are marvellous for pointing the finger at the great powers. But human nature is pretty much the same everywhere. We are lucky that we do not have the means and the power to commit these great acts of war and oppression. If we had we would be just as culpable as any others on which we might now like to lay the blame.

In fact I am not really talking about countries and waging war at all, and I am certainly not saying that we do not have the right to defend ourselves. There are some things so tiny that we need a magnifying glass to see them clearly. I am simply using as a magnifying glass, the great global conflicts between the mighty nations of the world. Why? To magnify what is in all our natures – yes, in yours and mine. You will find exactly the same features in yourself as the factors that have caused the present war in the Middle East, and every other war since the beginning of time. And until we uproot those attitudes there will never be peace.

The same arrogance is in us as is in the great warring powers; the same narcissism, the same inability to tolerate anything different from ourselves, like chickens pick to death one among them who happens to have suffered an injury or disfigurement. We have the same laziness in us, that prevents us making the effort to examine what we are doing. We are mini nations you and I. Don't point the finger at Saddam Hussein or George Bush or Gorbachev until we have rooted out the beam in our own eye. The only difference is that we have a smaller canvas to play on.

That is why there can never be any lasting peace until there is first peace in the hearts of men. And so many people in peace

marches and protests carry hatred in their hearts; and see no contradiction. Like the Oriental finding it easier to kill the European, they
imagine the war lords as different people from themselves. How
can you campaign for peace by hatred? How can you be at peace
with anyone else unless you are at peace with yourself? That is
what Lent is about, and that is the purpose of any mortification or
renewal that you set about in the blessed weeks of preparation for
the Resurrection of the Lord. The removal of blindness, moral ambiguity, illogicality, and narcissism. If you cannot see that we have at
this moment within ourselves precisely the same attitudes which
when magnified caused the Middle East War, then you really do
badly need this period of renewal and restoration and reflection
that Lent is. Lent is about renewal and preparation. 'Giving up' is
only a means of achieving that.

Penance and Salvation
19 March 1991

Lent, especially in its last few weeks, poses one of the great puzzles
of Christianity: why did Christ, the most sinless and the most holy,
have to suffer a death so inexpressibly shameful and cruel?

Of course we all know Christ could never have got away with
the things he did and taught in the corrupt Palestine of his day, but
there was a far deeper reason for his death than that.

The fact that he was willing to go through such dreadful sufferings gives us some dim clue of how immense God's love for us is.
His death was not necessary to redeem us (Augustine said one drop
of Christ's blood would have been sufficient) so there was more to
it than that.

Christ in his person was above all the negative feelings, fears
and limitations that plague us all, and prevent our ascent towards
God. These are the negative feelings about which I have been
speaking to you though the year up to now. Anger had no place in
him, nor pride nor arrogance, nor greed, malice, covetousness nor
revenge, nor the slightest form of any moral failing. In his life was
found nothing of the multitude of evils under which we all labour,
and that keep us separated from our destiny. All these he had conquered – why ? – to show us the way.

But there was one evil he had not yet faced and conquered– I
suppose the evil we all fear most – death. This, what St Paul called

'the last enemy,' was the supreme challenge he had to face and the supreme liberation that he could give to the world. Despite Christ's awful terror, which caused him to sweat blood when faced with his passion in Gethsemane, he held fast and went through it, and emerged into glory. So in his resurrection Christ had triumphed over every evil that mankind has to face. It is very difficult to be the Lord of Life, inexpressibly more difficult to be the Lord of Death. The Christ who rose from the dead and ascended was one who was perfectly free, who had triumphed over every human fear, danger and limitation.

In the Preface of the Mass it is said, 'by dying he destroyed our death.' He has liberated us from the terror of dying, and shown us that we ought not go around fearful, thinking of ourselves as victims. Our feelings act like magnets; if you are fearful, you will draw to you infallibly what will give you great reason to fear; if you are joyful and optimistic, you will draw that to you; if you feel you are unfairly treated, you will draw to you something that will cause that to be the case. We really do make our lives in this way; don't look too far outside yourself for the reasons why you are the way you are, why you have the troubles you have, why you have the joys that make your life so wonderful. We shape our own destinies, but we rarely realise that we do. We choose 95% of what we are ourselves, but we find that very hard to credit.

Christ suffered in order to show us the way and give us the means to triumph over suffering; if we see and understand God's design in this, then we can begin to see why it is we do penance, for it is done in imitation of Christ. Do we do penance to torture our bodies, to punish them, to batter them into submission? Do we do penance to suffer, so as to pay back what we owe because of some pleasure we took which we shouldn't have? If that is the spirit in your penance then you are wasting your time. Christ did not suffer to pay any ransom or price to an offended God; neither should our penance have that mentality. Christ suffered in order to triumph, and to show us the way precisely out of the vale of tears we are in. But so many Christians don't really want to leave the vale of tears; so many seem to believe that religion is a vale of tears, and if it isn't then something is wrong.

We only do penance to make us realise that our spirit is greater than our bodies, because for so much of the time, we have let our spirit be enslaved by our bodies, by too much of a love of comfort, or convenience, or by giving in to our evil inclinations when we gossip, or criticise, or act or speak unfairly about another. This is what bodily penance helps to rectify. It puts things back into shape. It tells us that we are not bodies only, that we are not even spirits imprisoned in a body, but that we are essentially a combination of body and spirit. Occasionally we have to do penance to keep the balance and put the body back in its proper place, and it's only then the body is truly happy. But be very careful that you do not do penance, any type of penance, simply and only to make your body suffer or feel uncomfortable. That has no value in the eyes of God, for when you are doing that you have strayed over the fine line between penance and masochism.

We do penance so that the spirit can be liberated, and be the one that directs our bodies; that is the only way in which real joy and real peace can be found. Have you ever looked at people who are dissipated, through the abuse of drink, or sexuality, or comfort or power? If we were to believe all the pop psychologists used to tell us, they should be the happiest of all, because they, we are told, have no repressions and no hang-ups.

But unfortunately they seem to be the most unhappy of all; because there can be no real happiness unless it is the spirit that is directing our lives, not the body.

When the spirit is directing our lives, then we are on the right track for our evolution towards God – which is another name for working out our salvation. This is when we are reaching for our fulfilment.

If you get the proper attitude and understanding of bodily penance, then try also to get a proper understanding of what we ourselve are. Some prophets of gloom never get tired of telling us we are sinners. Of course we have sinned, and of course we desperately need God's help, but there is a whale of a difference between recognising we are weak and that we sin, and actually defining ourselves in our very nature as sinners.

People who talk like that are on an entirely wrong track, and if you start off defining somebody as a sinner then you will never get out of that atmosphere of negativity. This is the same mentality that sees Christ's sufferings, by which he redeemed us, as some sort of awful penance demanded of him by a vengeful God as a reparation for the insults offered by the human race. These ways of thinking border on the heretical and are disastrous patterns on which to model ourselves, but you can often find them wandering around in some forms of pop spirituality; partners to the equally false view that we are not fallible or sinful at all. We are not to be defined as sinners; how far is such an understanding away from the teaching of Christ? We are actually, each of us, incarnations of God's almighty love; his children who are so inexpressibly dear to him, heirs to his Kingdom; that is where our real nature is, in glory, not in the gloom and blackness of sin.

What is it that pleases God in what we do? God does not want us to be unhappy or to suffer. God wants only that we should achieve our destiny. Those who think that God wants suffering are worshipping a monster and an idol, but not the true God.

St Thomas Aquinas put it well nearly 800 years ago: 'the glory of God is the fulfilment of the creature.' In short, being sad, morbid, torturing ourselves, being miserable, are not things pleasing to God. Penance and mortification should not produce any of these states in us; if they do they are being done in the wrong spirit. Our penances should be done freely and cheerfully in a light heart. If so they can be a part of our genuine evolution towards God. What pleases God is not our suffering, (nor what we may term our 'happiness'), but whether we are on the right track towards him. What's often called happiness, or what's often called suffering, today, is often quite far removed from the real thing. Penance or suffering is of no value in itself unless it sets us on the right track. God, and any true religion which claims to worship him, wants us to be truly happy and to be truly free. It is a great and necessary thing to do penance in Lent, especially bodily penance, but above all be sure to do it with the proper spirit; else we fall into the trap of the Scribes and Pharisees.

If you remember that the only thing that glorifies God is our fulfilment, and you are determind to follow out that fulfilment through joy or sorrow, then you will never go far wrong in anything you do for God our Creator either during this season of penance or indeed at any other time in your lives.

St Patrick's Day

Ní éarlamh an Choláiste seo agus na tíre seo amháin atá á chomóradh inniu againn, ach an t-aon réabhlóid amháin nár doirteadh fuil ann i stair challoideach na hÉireann. Dalta gach fear mór a mhair riamh, ba é a bheatha a shaothar.

Nuair a chuirtear sin san áireamh, cheapfadh duine uaireanta ar an lá seo gur mó de fhéile Mheiriceánach ná de fhéile Ghaelach atá san Fhéile Pádraig sa tslí ina dtéann sé i bhfeidhm ar aigne an phobail. Ar an ábhair sin, tá an baol ann go gcaillfí an fear agus an teachtaireacht san fhinscéal.

Today we keep the memory, not only of the patron saint of this College and of this land, but also of the only bloodless revolution that there was in the turbulent history of Ireland. And like all really great men his life summed up his work.

Sometimes one feels that St Patrick's Day is more an American than an Irish feast in the way in which it impinges on the popular imagination. There is a danger that we may lose both the man and the message in the legend, so let us look with a fresh eye at the lessons of his life.

Born in well-to-do circumstances, he was captured into slavery at the age of 16, agnostic then, and careless. He was at heart a lonely man and, even during his long years of later ministry in this country, he never really lost the feeling of being isolated and unwanted. Of course he had no friends or advisers to tide him over the customary storms of adolescence. He was forced to accept the drudgery of manual work, for which he had no aptitude. Later, when one would have expected more, he was unfairly and callously treated by both his fellow clerics and lay people. And yet he always managed to avoid despair and disillusionment, and his reception by the young as a hero spoke wonders of his determination to give them in guidance and formation what he had himself missed during the years of his youth.

Patrick, while no fool in dealing with the powers of this world, comes to us as a man of complete honesty who tried to hide nothing, and who always saw his vocation in life as a bigger thing than himself. He spoke out, when it was necessary, with such dignity and truth that there was never a suspicion of the conceit that can so often lurk behind the pose of campaigners who are self-righteous. Six years of captivity had made a man of him; for suffering is nearly always the best moulder of character. He found it hard to decide on important problems, but, once had had decided, then there was no turning back.

His converts in Ireland ranged over the whole social scale from Prince to slave girl. His real flair lay in the marvellous combination of enterprise and management he had in such a high degree. Due to his singular influence, in one single generation, the deeply ingrained native beliefs of the Irish were elevated into the bloom of the true faith, represented in the figure of the banishment of the snakes, the symbol of the matriarchal snake-goddesses of the Druids.

Many times he was tempted against his mission, against his friends, and, hard for us to credit, even against his faith. Sometimes this happened with a ferocity beyond belief. But he persevered, and despite the pain of exile felt 'in the deep heart's core' he transformed the religion of this land in his own lifetime.

He prayed constantly, worked unremittingly, all the time trying to be as sensitive as possible to those with whom he dealt. All in all, as Ireland's apostle, he was, and remains, the model for Ireland's priests and seminarians once the popular legends and misconceptions are stripped away. It was by no accident that this College named him as its patron, and dedicated itself to his ideals; ideals which, in the last analysis, cannot be achieved by human efforts that are not aligned to the power of God which comes through his grace.

Tríd is tríd, mar aspal na hÉireann eisiomláir a bhí agus atá ann do shagairt agus d'ábhair sagairt Éireann. Ní de thimpist a roghnaigh an Coláiste seo é mar éarlamh. Tá sé tiomnaithe dá chuid ídéal – ídéil nach bhféadfaí a bhaint amach sa deireadh le hiarracht daonna, ach amháin le cumhacht Dé tré thíolacadh a ghrásta.

So if all really great men are best known in the mirror of their lives, then we really have a lot to learn from the true Patrick, once the tinsel and plaster cast statues have been removed to reveal the real saint.

Being canonised a saint does not add to the saint's own glory, for being in the vision of God, it would obviously be impossible to increase a saint's joy and fulfilment. The Church in recognising someone as a saint places the life of that person before us as worthy of imitation; a true and exemplary Christian life. We need further, however, to be clear on the way in which the life of a saint acts on us as a model. As a model yes, but we are not followers; we follow only one, God, especially as revealed in Christ.

Our purpose here in this world, and afterwards, is to come to know and to be more like God, but we will never truly know God and never truly come to fully realise our potential as long as we set ourselves up to follow another, no matter how sanctified. We are to be inspired by their example, and to be helped by their prayers, but we are not the followers of the saints; if you go along that road all you will ever learn are the frustrations at being in the shadow of these ideals set out by another wondrous human being.

Our destiny is not to be like anyone else, but to bring out from ourselves the brilliance of the image of God which has already been placed in our souls. Learn to love, to accept, to forgive, and to develop into the paths of goodness, all that you are. Hold what you can be in high esteem, and move on into the joy and enlightenment that only true religion can bring, for your soul already desires it, and to go against it brings only disappointment. When we mistake the role that the example of others has for us we tend to give away all our power outside of ourselves, and reserve none. This is precisely why we have experience of great limitedness and furrows of sorrow, and why despite many fervent prayers we achieve so little.

In St Patrick we have a supreme example of what one man can do whose intention is strongly focused, whose political sense was highly developed, whose knowledge of the Fathers and of the Scriptures was profound, as recent scholarship has shown, and who worked unceasingly with enormous energy and drive as if everything depended on himself and yet his spirituality was so profound as to see everything as the result of that partnership of man and God our Father in which we are more closely united than the flesh is to the spirit.

At the end of his *Confessio* he wrote:

> This document was written in Ireland
> by Patrick, an uneducated sinner ...
> Do not attribute to my ignorance the
> little I achieved or pointed out, which
> pleased God. Let your conclusion be,
> and the general opinion rather be, the
> real truth, which is that my success
> was the gift of God.

Unconditional Agape
22 April 1991

Unconditional love is simply *being* love. That is all. When you *are* love you can never hate. When you love and are in a state of joy, you cannot find sadness. And when you are love, you cannot feel despair. When you are love you can only find happiness.

Love is *being* it, nothing more. Being it will be as versatile and unique as you are moment to moment. How do you know what it is to say 'I love you' to another person, and even more so to God? You do not even know the depth of what that means. It is only words. It is the emotion that creates life, and it is the emotion that the spirit records, not pictures or words: *emotions* or *feelings*.

It is a great truth that what you see in others is what you see in yourself. How can you recognise ugliness until you see it first in yourself? How can you recognise beauty until you know what beauty is within you? We see in others only what we really are in ourselves. And once we have become absolute or unconditional love, all we can see in others is love, or joy or beauty, irrespective of how they behave. You cannot have unconditional love for one person only. If you have reached the stage of having unconditional love, then you have it for every person. And it will be your love for them that will lift them into unlimitedness. To whom will you give thanks for this? Love yourself and the Father who dwells within you, for it is he who has done all these things. Love him for he dearly loves you with an unconditional love, and live in the present.

If God is unconditional love; every one of his actions ia a manifestation of love. It is impossible for God to be the author of any other type of action, even though at times the action may not appear loving in the short term.

How do you see forgiviness? Does God want to help us achieve a metanoia, or is he more interested in letting us know that we 'owe' him because he has forgiven us? How do you understand 'forgive and forget?' Most people who forgive do not want those they have forgiven to forget that they have forgiven.

We can fall into the trap of seeing God in that way.

Define wisdom. It is a learning from what you have experienced, from what you have done, even if that thing at the time did not help to advance your evolution. This helps us further to understand forgiveness.

So try to be unconditional love for yourself. When you fall from grace and then recapture it, you have been enriched and have learned from the experience. You have gained a pearl of wisdom.

What is the difference between learning and truth? You have a struggle with understanding this difference and the words you use give a clue to where you need to focus more in your process of growth. You have placed great stress on the intellect and on intellectual understanding, and for you truth is almost exclusively seen as an intellectual thing. You feel as a result that truth is something you should come to in an automatic way: that someone will sit there and speak it to you, and you will store it in the brain. But real truth is of a very different kind; it has to come through learning and experience. It is no use being told it, you have to come to know it personally.

This is why the intellect alone is not sufficient here.

You are judging yourself for having had the experience, but the only way to learn is through evolution, and to do this you must allow yourself to learn from the experience, otherwise it is impossible to learn.

You say you want to change, and that is true, but the matter is not as self-evident as you feel, and the case is not as open and shut as you say. The experiences you have had (car accident, etc.) are not things which you should continually keep before your mind, are not things that you have to have resolved. You have to learn from them and go on from them. You have to leave them behind having extracted the pearl of wisdom from them.

If you want to change, the first step on the road to change is to drop these worries you have and proceed on the path of change. If you are not willing to drop those worries once you have understood their significance, then it cannot be true that you really wish to change.

The Fool Says in His Heart
1 May 1993

Clouds bring rain and shade. They vaporize and pick up fresh water and carry it to places where it is needed. The snow sits on mountain tops, waiting patiently as a decoration until the warm sun of Spring melts it into rains needed for the streams far below. It melts just at the right time for the young crops to drink. The seeds buried in the ground stay dormant for years until the right conditions for their development appear; then they start to sprout. Defying the normal laws of nature, ice, which is heavier than water, does not sink as it should to the bottom of rivers and lakes, because it would kill the fish.

Without the magnetic poles we would have been unable for countless centuries to navigate the trackless oceans of water. Nobody quite knows what the poles are, but they just grew there, some say.

The earth is tilted on its axis at a precise twenty-three and a half degrees relative to the passage of the sun. Without it we would have no seasons. The earth spins on its axis at a speed of one thousand miles per hour. If it rotated in any noticeably faster way the force of gravity would be so counteracted as to make life very difficult, or else its slower speed would cause the land to be burned up by the long days of sun and to be frozen by the extended nights. But it turns at just the right speed to preserve the fertility of the fields.

The human heart never rests from the womb until death. How

does it get enough rest between beats? How does the kidney strain impurities from the blood and know what to allow through? Why do illnesses have particular characteristic resonances in the body which we call symptoms? Why do all illnesses not have the same indications in the body? – or perhaps none at all, just as radiation gives us no warning. How does the sugar-control mechanism below the pancreas maintain the level of sugar in the blood that is just right for energy, and yet make sure that it does not go too low or too high which would cause our deaths?

All the wonders we look on every day – are they accidental? Was there no almighty mind that made a thousand billion stars? They made themselves? No power keeps them on their steady course. Did a little flower invent itself so that we could have digitalis? Or a little snail that we could have the colour purple?

Did the marvellous complexity of the subatomic world invent itself? Did the marvellous proportions everywhere in nature and in abstract forms, which mathematics discovers just happen?

The fool says in his heart that all of these things, and countless others, happened by chance.

Raw Data of Religion
27 January 1994

The Christmas and Epiphany seasons tell us that to get at the core of God at his greatest, we have first to get into the core of ourselves, for no one who has not known himself first can hope to know God.

One of the most basic areas in this for the seminarian above all, is to get to know what he believes: if not, however good a worker you may be people will find you a sounding brass and a clanging symbol; an empty vessel. And you yourself will know that before anyone else; you will be the first to lose belief and confidence in yourself and in what you are doing.

Our world is full of people who think they believe in God but can't say why. Or people who don't believe in God, but only because they've never met an intelligent believer; even among those who are professional preachers of his word; preachers who only mouth pious platitudes. There was a time, perhaps, when that was enough, but that time is no more. In between there are a host of people who might like to believe in God, but haven't had the time to sit down and work out whether they do. Maybe we're all a bit in that category. If so, it's a very dangerous state for a priest or seminarian; is it any wonder so many leave the seminary or the priest-hood itself?

There is no such thing as a person who has no religious beliefs. We either have right opinions about ultimate reality, and the meaning of things and people, or we have wrong opinions. A person may have no formal instruction about religion, but he will have religious beliefs.

We live in a world containing ultimate mysteries such as birth and death, and free will and loneliness, and creative impulses, and community and conflict. These are the raw data of religion, and we all must react to them in some way. Our reactions reflect our basic assumptions about the nature of things, and these are our system of beliefs. These assumptions are either in accord with absolute reality or they are not. If they are not they will only increase our pain and suffering and our capacity to hurt others and destroy peace.

We are the heirs of a great, ancient and rich Christian civilisation, built up painfully by the labours and sacrifices of our ancestors in the faith. But we have taken it for granted for so long ; during that time it has been eroding and disappearing, and Christian beliefs and practices have been replaced by beliefs and practices which we, unconsciously and wrongly, suppose to be Christian, but are not.

Explaining Christianity is not the problem. If a person came among us from another planet he wouldn't first ask; 'Why do you believe in transubstantiation?' or 'Why do you believe in the Trinity,?or in the Chalcedonian formula for the person and natures of Christ?' These are important questions. But the prior questions are different. The visitor from outer space might ask: 'Why do the good die young? Why do 'the best laid schemes of mice and men gang aft agley'? Why do the wicked triumph; the just suffer; why does evil so often triumph over good? Why does a man's reach exceed his grasp? Why is there so much pain, sorrow, grief, misery and ugliness in human life and human society?

To take it a bit further; why should there be people on earth in the first place? Or for that matter why should there be an earth? Why should there be anything? These are the things that need explaining. These are the questions very ordinary young and not so young people are asking today. These are the types of questions that are beginning to feature more and more in even moderate TV programmes. Can you answer them? Very often it seems that the only people not asking these questions nowadays, are those involved in religion, the very people who ought to be asking them first of all!

There are answers to these questions, but they can only be approached by personal involvement, not by learning off by heart. These are the things that need explaining. Sooner or later people will make up their minds that the Christian religion is either true or false, not in terms of how persuasively we can explain the doctrine of the Trinity or the two natures of Christ (and these are also important questions), and not even in terms of whether the Christian religion makes sense, but whether or not the Christian religion can answer any of these questions, and what place the Church, of whom we are its ministers, has in this scheme?

Creation is the sacrament of the presence of God; a veil over his face. For what really terrifies people about God is not his wrath but his love. All that we see in the world reveals something about the Creator; the gentle water of baptism is the same water of chaos over which the Spirit of the Lord brooded at the moment of Creation (in that marvellous phrase of Genesis, *'Ruach Elohim...'*). It is the same water which parted to let the Israelites pass dryshod and returned to overwhelm the armies of Pharaoh; which drowned the world in the days of Noah, and which is added in the Mass to the chalice of the blood of Christ. You can see that in a sparkling drop of water on a leaf at dawn in Summertime dew. You can ask yourself is not the drop on the leaf terrible? It is terrible, because each drop of water, each grain of dust or sand, is a word, an utterance, a self-giving of God in the relentless outpouring of his love and power. We are allowed to listen to the child's singing, because the angel choirs would deafen us; we are given the beauty of the rose because the beauty of the face of God would strike us blind.

God's nature as truth confronts us in the fact that life is a series of problems to be solved and questions to be faced. God's nature as love confronts us in our situation as a communal creature, and we are forced to learn his way so as to avoid strife and conflict among us. God's nature as joy and beauty confronts us in the wonder and splendour of creation. Every choice we make, however, trivial, moves us closer to God or farther away from him. At our death we step out of space and time and into eternity and recognise God as that which we have been longing for all our lives, or that which we have been avoiding all our lives. If our faith is a set of platitudes, I am afraid we fall into the latter category.

At death we will be faced with only one question by God: 'Do you love me?' But we have to give an honest answer. To love him we have first to know him, and what he does and why. That is what people find most lacking in the way the Church's teaching is presented today: in homilies, in religion teaching, in counselling people who have difficulties with the faith. That sort of living understanding is what you do not unfortunately find in so many priests and seminarians today; that is why there is so much disillusionment; so much craving for false and extreme certitudes that have nothing in common with the truth of the Christian faith, as believers become more and more polarised; why so many people abandon their paths, as seminarians, as priests, as believers. To know God is the proper and basic study for all Christians, especially in your situation and mine. Everyone is confronted by the raw data of religion. What is made by way of reaction to them is the challenge.

Forgiveness
26 April 1994

What does it mean to forgive? It is the letting go of what would keep us imprisoned in imperfection. It is impossible to approach God without letting go the memory of those things that hold us in limitation. To pardon is to set the record straight – firstly, with others. To pardon is to blot out, to take away the imperfection that rests in our soul's memory. When we have grown enough to gain the pearl of wisdom from an experience we know why it came into our lives, and we can then readily forgive. It is before we reach that state of wisdom that the difficulty in pardoning arises. Love enters to take the place of imperfection when pardon is given.

But if the President or Sovereign of a country makes a mistake for which all of his people suffer, whom does he need to forgive? Not surely his people, but himself. In a similar way we too in a very real way are sovereign in our beings. We are the children of God, we have the divine indwelling in us. So even more basic than asking forgiveness of others is to ask forgiveness of ourselves.

What is truly accepted at the level of our deepest thought determines what we become. What we put out is what we will receive back in return. If we hate it will be brought back to us tenfold. If you send out goodness it also will return to you tenfold. This is why Jesus said it was so important that we forgive our enemies. Master your thoughts for they are creative – just as much when they are niggardly, victim-ridden or vicious, as when they are glorious, noble and loving. Unfortunately it is to the former condition that most of us habitually default.

The data stored in our souls is building the world in which we will live. Love can only begin to manifest for us in material reality when forgiveness replaces imperfection with love at the level of our deepest convictions. In this way, painfully slowly perhaps, because we find it so hard to accept that we are creating the life we experience, imbalance and negativity can be removed from our lives. The opposite, of course, can just as readily occur.

If we do harm to another then not only of course must you forgive yourself, but also ask forgiveness of the one you have injured. If they do not grant this to you, nevertheless bless them and love them, for the matter has already been made right in your soul. Those who refuse pardon are refusing the most humble offer of love that there is. And it will come back upon them in manifold ways, for their attitudes too will infallibly manifest in their lives.

To forgive is to pardon, and it forms the centre of the path by which we can grow towards God. For that reason it is surely obvious that nobody is worth the price to be paid for not loving and forgiving them.

Both kinds of forgiving should be done constantly. As regularly as we bathe or dust and clean our homes, so often should we scrutinise the collection of memories in our soul.

The evolving forth of the human being is a perilous process since our worlds of experience are formed not alone by the thoughts which we hold consciously, but also, if we buy into them, by those thoughts that form the social consciousness surrounding us. To grow we have to rise above mass consciousness, the lowest common denominator which constantly sounds the death knell for our hopes of advancement. This is the plane of judgmental attitudes, of spite, jealously, warring factions, hatred, envy and fear. It is by raising ourselves above these that we advance into the twilight of fresh understanding that beckons into new dimensions. But where there is no forgiveness there is no advance at all.

God is all that there is; he is all in all; nothing can add to or subtract from his being. But to him we do make known the unknown. God does not suffer from the negative side effects of what we see as mighty. He is not puffed up with pride and arrogance. That is the perpetual affliction awaiting to pounce on all who hold office and position in human affairs. God is not haughty; he does not try to intimidate those he loves. Nor has anyone to say to God that he is great, for he rests in a state that needs no affirmation. It is this state of being which guarantees that there can be no threat to what he is.

It is easy to see that the companion state to this must be infinite humility. In fact it seems that infinite humility is the first quality to derive from God's very being. The humility we show in asking for pardon is therefore latching on to something that is at the heart of the divine, into that splendour which is the source of the creation, the life giver and sustainer of all.

Forgiveness is not then the act of one weak in character, or of one less worldly wise. On the contrary it is that which offers us access to almost infinite power. It provides the fertile path along which love, kindness, joy, peace and truth can blossom in our journey towards God.

God and Joy
21 June 1994

God is not a serious Being; he is not a brooding Being, boring or restrictive. He is Magical, Movement, Contemplative. He is compulsive, drawing into himself from us as we make known the unknown. He is laughter and joy.

The greatest heights you will reach are in the midst of joy and laughter, and the loving of this wondrous life. When we have all learned to do that we will have reached the top of our potential, and from that vantage point we will be able to see many more pinnacles and greater valleys and more places than can be imagined at present.

Do not be afraid to be unlimited in your thinking, or to dare to think beyond restrictive thought, for there awaits a greater kingdom than you can imagine. What will bring you to this place has to be done in laughter and joy.

What is joy? It is not simply a state of happiness. It is a state of becoming. It is the ultimate, really, of becoming. In a state of joy you are in the 'flow' of what God is. And in there there is no room for hate or self-doubt, for war or jealousies or bitterness or differences. In a state of joy you are caught in a charisma of God-action. That is how the Father is. He is joy at all times.

The Father is the totality of joy. Unhappiness separates us. Fear separates us, war separates us, envy separates us, jealously separates us, sorrow separates us.

So the Father in his refined essence is complete joy. And the wonderful glue that holds all together is called Love.

When the Father burns within you, when that which is termed the Spirit is awakened within you, there will be joy and laughter, for you are free to express without the condemnation of anyone.

God is a happy entity. And the one desire the Father has for everyone, in accordance with the graces he pours out to them, indicating their greatest potential for happiness, is for them to be happy.

The more happy you become within your beauteous self, the greater you come to likeness and alignment with the Father.

What is joy? Joy is the freedom of movement without interruption. It is the freedom of expression without judgment. If is the freedom of being without guilt. Joy is sublime movement of Spirit allowed.

When you're in a state of joy you can hate no one. In a state of joy you love all things. In a state of joy, life becomes the fervour and intensity of a dawn when the sky becomes rose and the clouds are tinged in the most beautiful fiery red, and the birds are whistling in trees and the whole of heaven is set afire in a blaze of intense colour.

In joy you will cease to age and will live forever, for life is no longer a drudgery, but a victorious experience that you hunger for more of. When joy is apparent, you are at one in your Kingdom with Self.

CHAPTER 9

The Maynooth Union

Permanence in Change
The Maynooth Union, 11 June 1985

Six Presidents is almost a quarter of the entire number the College has had since its foundation; and over the twenty-three years of those six presidencies has stretched more momentous change than ever occurred in the College's history. Our College roll is now nearing its two thousand mark of which well over four hundred are seminarians.

Last night I had a privilege which was never given to any previous President of Maynooth, that of entertaining five of my predecessors; Monsignor Gerard Mitchell, Monsignor Patrick J. Corish, Bishop Jeremiah Newman, His Eminence Cardinal Ó Fiaich and Monsignor Michael Olden. I owe a great deal to them all; they cover between them the period of my entire adult life spent in this College. However, I know the others will forgive me if I single out one, Monsignor Mitchell.

His reputation for clarity, insight, and robust common sense in the lecture hall came to me, unfortunately, only at second hand. Our early years in Maynooth catch the imagination and memory when they are at their most fresh and never really lets them go again. For that reason Monsignor Mitchell will always for me be THE President of Maynooth. After he came here as a student, sixty two years ago, he never really left the College until his appointment as Parish Priest of Ballinrobe. He has made another bit of history today as well, for I think it is the first time in the life of the Maynooth Union that the Professor chosen for a Classpiece was here with the Golden Jubilarians to celebrate the fiftieth anniversary of their Ordination.

This past year has seen the opening of the magnificent John Paul II Library, which has been of very great benefit to the College. It has shelving for more than a quarter million volumes; seating for nearly six hundred students, and a full range of offices for library staff and services. Very many of you contributed generously to the erection of this fine facility and I want to pay tribute to your generosity and foresight now. Despite the success of our fund-raising efforts we still have a very long way to go on the road before the Library is paid for, and we hope we can continue to depend on your generosity and good will into the future.

The changes in Maynooth since most of you were ordained may, perhaps, appear to you to have been massive, but we cannot forget that they were probably not significantly greater than the changes in Irish and Western society in general over the same period. Some changes have been excellent and were overdue. Others were not so happy and did not further the good of Maynooth's traditional purpose as well as had been hoped

This does not spell disaster, but is simply a recognition that in all deep endeavours going through a significant cultural shift such as we have had since the Council, there are some things that do not admit of perfect wisdom in advance. It is something that has to be worked on continually.

The formation of youth (and that includes clerical youth as well as others), depends as much on the climate of an institution as on the content of the learning it dispenses. The stress in recent years has been almost exclusively on a culture that was technological, urbanised, and industrialised. Other values seem to appeal more to the youth of today – dignity as persons, freedom, personal identity, self-respect, and so on; values that are neither materialistic nor economic, but which must stand at the heart of all education and true formation. What I am talking about is the Christian vision. It is the basis of what we hope to be about in Maynooth, for both lay and cleric.

For the first time in human history major cultural changes now happen in less than the space of the human life-span, causing dramatic difficulties in self-understanding and appreciation, difficulties of identity, and, above all, difficulties in religious understanding and family relationships. In such a climate there is a great need for moral leadership and for instilling such leadership into candidates for the priesthood. We are at the cross-roads in Ireland today. We have the youngest population in Europe, the highest rate of unemployment, and the most expensive system of third level education in the European Community – a mix which gives even the most balanced educationalist great cause for worry. This is the situation which seminary training faces today. It is a major challenge, but just one aspect of the task facing the country as a whole. Have you noticed how difficult it is today to convey the necessity of continual effort and sacrifice if benefits are to be achieved, and if any nation or institution is to be worthwhile and remain really free? We forget the lessons of history that civilisations begin with religion and stoicism, they end with scepticism and unbelief and the undisciplined pursuit of individual pleasure. Civilisation is born stoic, it dies epicurean.

However, with all the attendant difficulties and with the educational opportunities in the widest sense available here, I think Maynooth retains the potential to be the best training ground for the Irish diocesan priesthood in today's world.

In last Sunday's second reading from 2 Corinthians you will find the direction of what I would like to say to you. It is the essential plan of Christian praxis, and the basic charter for positively moulding the mind and heart of the young, particularly of the seminarian. I quote: "No wonder we do not lose heart ... our troubles are slight and short-lived; and their outcome an eternal glory which outweighs them far. Meanwhile our eyes are fixed, not on the things that are seen, but on the things that lie beyond our gaze. What is seen passes away; what is unseen is eternal' (2 Cor 4:17-18).

Earth and all its achievements are horizontal. The perpendicular is the eternal, rooted in charity on earth. This is an essential vision we are in danger of losing today.

In the little renaissance of the early middle ages, the passion of the age was navigation, and the equivalent of the Nobel-prize winners then were compass-makers, cartographers, and the natural scientists of magnetism. On the old charts you will see the Windrose. It is the Polar Star, and it was dedicated to Our Lady, an observation that underlies the ancient hymn of our youth: *Ave Maris Stella*. Faith and technology were twins under the *felix coeli porta*. Faith and the supreme human ideals of the age were one. Today, as we are well aware, they are drifting far apart. This is neither necessary nor inevitable, but it is the headline at which all training of priests and leaders in the community of the Church must gaze today.

The National Seminary at Maynooth has constantly tried to move to one essential rhythm or beat – the training of priests to cherish the people, to live the sacramental life and to teach them the truths God gave us when he forsook the realms of everlasting day to come among us as a man. This programme has the solid predictability of essential things, but today it faces very new circumstances and challenges. We must make sure that it does not put on too much psychological war paint, sprout too many peacock feathers liturgically, and above all, make sure that it is more 'with Christ,' than 'with it.' The guiding spirit of all theological and pastoral formation must be rooted primarily not in the needs of the day (for assuredly he who marries the spirit of the age is soon a widower), but in the message of Christ which is handed down in the living stream of the Church's life. The needs of the day are very important, but we can easily start at the wrong end in trying to meet them, and thus pervert the Gospel. If we start from the revealed word we have the best guarantee of meeting today's needs. 'The glory of God is the fulfilment of the creature,' St Thomas Aquinas said a long time ago.

When Daniel Mannix was appointed to Melbourne in 1912, a very distinguished but somewhat forgotton man, Monsignor Michael O'Riordan, Rector of the Irish College, Rome, wrote to say he regretted the move. 'Maynooth,' he said, 'is more important than Melbourne; it is the *ecclesia docens* of Ireland.'

All the ways Maynooth followed, or will follow, are still present in your minds if you recall the strains on Sunday under Bewerunge, Michael Tracey, Charlie O'Callaghan, and the rest of *unam, sanctam, catholicam et apostolicam ecclesiam*. Two centuries ago the Catholic Church in Ireland was beginning its struggle to rise like the phoenix from the ashes of the Penal Days. Maynooth was its first significant achievement; and in Maynooth, in this wood and stone, was successively crystallised the ideals, efforts and the achievements of the Church in this land over the last two centuries. Not alone is Maynooth the incarnation of the spirit of the Irish Church but it is also one of the very few really native institutions we have in Ireland.

Through the accidents of history Maynooth and the Irish Church are joined in a very intimate bond. What happens to Maynooth, or in Maynooth, is a sign in advance of what will happen to the Church in Ireland. Your heritage is here. We have made this College what it is and it has made us all. This College needs your support and loyalty more than ever today if it is to do its job. Your presence here today is a sign that this loyalty will be generously given and it is in that spirit that I have the great honour to propose the toast of the Jubilarians, of each of the five year classes, of our guests, and of the Maynooth Union itself.

Jubilee: Assessment, Celebration, Renewal
Maynooth College Chapel, 16 June 1986

In the customs and religious practice of the Jews each week of years ended with a sabbatical year, in which it was obligatory to set slaves and debtors free and to let the earth lie fallow. As we read in the Book of Leviticus, at the end of seven weeks of years there was a provision for a jubilee year as the fiftieth. It was a year of liberation, of celebration, a year of renewal and thanksgiving and assessment above all.

Meeting one another again here in Maynooth after the lapse of years is bound to make us stand back, reflect and assess. It's a day when we chew the stalk of the sweet/bitter herb of memory. In that respect the Maynooth Jubilee Day, I think, is very close in spirit to the biblical idea.

So many different things strike us:

– Firstly, it is a milestone in life, a landmark we are always surprised to have reached so soon, having, it seems, accomplished so little on the way.

– Secondly, I remember that once someone divided the clergy into three groups: those who are obviously not very busy, those who are obviously very busy, and those who are very obviously busy. I suppose those three levels of deception abide in all human beings, not just priests, to a greater or lesser degree.

– Thirdly, we realise on a day like this that we are no longer young enough to know everything. It's been well said that every man over thirty tends to identify his youth with the worst fault he finds in himself. Be that as it may, I think, having weighed everything up, no really sane man laments the passing of the years. But the passing of the years has its dangers too. We know that intellectual blemishes, like physical ones, tend to grow more prominent with the passage of the years. This, I think, is why so many find it more profitable to circumvent older people rather than try to convert them to another point of view.

At times like today we might be more open to realise how Christianity, and our priesthood especially make us so ashamed of our own real feelings towards our fellow human beings, and how fatally easy it is to go wrong as a result of indulgence in a constant process of self-deception about our real feelings and motives.

Childhood reveals tendencies in us, youth, especially here in our Maynooth years, develops personality, but it is only maturity that establishes character, and of all the intellectual faculties judgement is the last to mature.

Jubilee in the Bible is a time of assessment, and when we reach these milestones we can always learn, no matter what age we are. Can we learn how to be more useful to others in the years ahead, or more fundamentally, how to be more at peace in mind and heart? The man who is too old to learn was probably always too old to learn.

But as well as a time of assessment and reform the biblical Jubilee was also a celebration. A Jubilee really is a monument to our faith and to our vocation. It is too easy in a false humility to under-value what we have done for God in our years of service, when we recall the lost opportunities and think of what we might have done. But nevertheless the contribution is very real, however much we may regret that it might have been more. The same is true in how we assess institutions, for even though the old Maynooth was prob-ably less 'Alma' than 'Mater', nevertheless it gave us much more than we will ever know.

This College is something of which to be very proud. In recent years it has gone, like almost all living institutions, 'through stirring times' – a phrase the Greeks used as a curse. The Church as a whole in Ireland has gone through the same process and there is no sign of any end. But I think we have had enough of using 'Vatican II' as a synonym for what is modern, new or radical. For those who know their theology, history or liturgy, or especially those who have good common sense, there was little that was startlingly new in the Council. As for being a term to describe the new and modern, it is time we realised that most of the clerical students now in the College were not born when it was summoned.

I emphasise these points because I think twenty years is ample time to absorb any impact, and it is time we stopped using the impact of the Council as some sort of excuse for lack of nerve, con-viction, and the energy that we believe characterised the Church in the past.

A few years ago when people used to ask me, 'What do you teach up there?' and I'd say 'Dogmatic Theology', I could feel behind their reaction sometimes that there was the unspoken opin-ion: 'That must be an easy job nowadays!' The only substantial dif-ference between the so-called old and the so-called new theologies is in method, not in content. The best thing as clergy that we can do is to have heart and to have courage, a courage and a vitality to which it is possible to set fire on this day, probably more than any other. The crisis after the Council was painful, but it was to some extent illusory, and also much less than the crisis there would have been if there had been no Council. Anybody who looks about him today with any perception will see that there is a much more real crisis ahead for the faith in Ireland. We can come through it with flying colours, but only if we have the nerve to meet the challenge.

Maynooth has changed, maybe a few of you today may even find the change a bit shockingly different from the time you yourself walked these halls. But the same truths, and the same values and the same ideals are at the heart of this institution now as they were then. Without a strong and vibrant Maynooth the unity, cohesion and sense of loyalty of the diocesan clergy will be dealt a fearsome blow. Gathered today as the members of the Maynooth Union, the College asks your support and your confidence. It is fatally easy and satisfying to criticise and do no more; no great enterprise can ever come from such a source. Let Maynooth of the past and present stand together. Hats off to the past; coats off to the future!

What I have tried to do is touch on the themes of biblical jubilee, and recall them to us today. It was above all a time of assessment, examination and renewal. It was a time to celebrate what had been achieved. It was a time to prepare to meet the new age with courage, energy and conviction. It was last of all a time for the renewal of vocation and faith. These are the themes of biblical Jubilee in Leviticus Chapter 25. There could be no better rallying call for the clergy of present-day Ireland. This is what will enable us to make sure that the heritage of our proud past is handed on undiminished to the future generations in this country who will largely depend on you and me for what they know of God. *Prospere procede!*

Maynooth: A Spiritual Odyssey
The Maynooth Union, 9 June 1987

A prominent Russian writer of our day has said that there is no use in building a road unless it leads to a church. Today I want to speak to you about a road to a seminary.

In a few years Maynooth College will be two centuries old. In the course of these two hundred years Maynooth has made only one public appeal for funding, 45 years ago – when the ancient buildings of Long Corridor and Stoyte House were almost completely rebuilt.

'*Ubi Petrus, ibi Ecclesia*' 'Peter and the Church are inseparable.'

This we all accept. A corol,lary is not so obvious: 'Ubi Ecclesia, ibi seminarium', 'Church and seminary go together' – at least since the Council of Trent.

I am very well aware that theologians rejoice quite frequently today in discourse about models and alternative models of the Church. No doubt we shall soon have a parallel discourse about alternative seminary dynamisms.

But my immediate task is more modest, in Ireland and now: to keep a roof over the heads of the foirm agus ábhar sagairt.

The fact is that large sections of the College, principally St Mary's and St Patrick's, are now almost the same age as Stoyte House and Long Corridor were 40 years ago at the time of the first and only collection Maynooth has had so far in its history. We now have a really major restoration task on hands as we approach our Bicentenary in 1995. And there is a further problem. While the Gospel urges us to spread fire on the earth, that is not a point of view shared by Kildare County Council, at least as far as this College is concerned. It will cost two and a half million pounds to restore our friendship with the local authorities in matters of fire.

I would like to stress some points that may need some clarification. As you know, the Hierarchy has approved a National Collection for Maynooth in order to raise funds for the refurbishment of the buildings of the Seminary, which I have just mentioned. Not a penny from this National collection will be spent on any other purpose in the College. The national collection is the Church's contribution to a partnership which some enlightened and far-seeing individuals in the Irish business community have launched for us.

We in the College are acutely aware that the success of the National Collection depends to a very large extent on the support given it at the local level by the priests in the parishes. Accordingly, I have made arrangements in practically all of the dioceses in the country now to have a member of staff come and address the priests personally at diocesan gatherings.

There have been many changes in Maynooth since the majority of us were ordained. We have now almost 2,200 students, and the number is growing.; more than 350 full-time staff, and a few hundred more on a part-time basis. These high-quality expanded National University of Ireland courses is something of which the College is very legitimately proud, and our lay graduates from them are now in the thousands. There are also nearly one hundred and fifty lay students in the Pontifical University, taking the combined Arts and Theology Degree. Changes like this strike the priest visitor who comes back very forcibly, nevertheless, because of the wide educational opportunities available, I think Maynooth offers an excellent training ground today for candidates for the Irish priesthood.

One of the most precious things in the human heart must surely be attachment to one's own and to one's own native place. I feel all of us to whom Maynooth was Alma Mater owe it a loyalty that is sufficiently deep to qualify for what St Paul called 'love without hypocrisy.' Love delights to show itself in excesses. Judged by external standards the widow's mite was too small a contribution to the Temple, just as the penitent's ointment was too much in the eyes of the money-grabbing Judas. But both had in them that inner generosity which is the essence of love's excess of the law. That is what I am asking you here today to accomplish for Maynooth.

Two centuries ago the Catholic Church in Ireland was beginning its struggle to rise like the phoenix from the ashes of the penal days. Maynooth was its first significant achievement, and so it remains today, founded only twenty years after the Catholic Archbishop of Dublin felt it was safe again to keep any records.

And in Maynooth, in this wood and stone, was successively crystallised the ideals, efforts and the achievements of the Church in this land over the last two centuries. It has supplied as well the vast majority of the priest staffs of the secondary schools, and of the other major seminaries in this country. It provides diploma qualification for the students of those seminaries too, so that there can be few diocesan priests in Ireland without strong links to Maynooth. Nine thousand people at local level have passed through its extramural courses in religious education since the beginning of the decade. An old Gaelic poet was glad that 50 kings were buried at Clonmacnois. More than 10,000 priests have left the halls and chapels of this College since 1795; 200 priests for every king. If we do not believe in ourselves we can hardly blame others for losing faith in us.

The best part of a century ago a distinguished predecessor of mine, Dr Daniel Mannix, was asked to give a reference for a student who was going to work abroad. He refused. 'To have been a student at Maynooth,' he said, 'is sufficient reference.' Those were high standards and they may not be attainable in all cases today, but it is a standard at which we must never cease to aim, and a standard which I know you must all hold precious. It is still accepted that the combined voice of the priests of Ireland on Sunday pulpits is the strongest voice in the land. Maynooth now asks that you keep faith and tap the wellsprings of generosity in every Church and parish next Autumn towards the renewal of Maynooth's historic and essential buildings, to enable it to carry on its work with dignity.

The late Philip Larkin once wrote of a church:

'A serious house on serious earth it is,
In whose blunt air all our compulsions meet,
Are recognised and robed with destinies.'

Maynooth is our serious house now. We must keep faith and 'gravitate to this ground, which, once we heard, was proper to grow wise in.'

The Greatest Flower of Faith
The Maynooth Union, 12 June 1990

I am delighted too see so many jubilarians here with us for this celebration today and too see so many faces who shared our joys and happinesses and sadnesses, here as students, so many years ago.

In particular I would single out the golden jubilarians, of whom we have thirty two with us, the biggest number that has ever been here for a meeting of the Maynooth Union.

Five years ago yesterday I said at this dinner that on the previous night, 10 June 1985, I had had a privilege never before given to a President of Maynooth, that of entertaining five of my predecessors. On 8 May we lost one of them, Cardinal Tomás Ó Fiaich; and on the day of his burial another, Monsignor Gerry Mitchell.

The Cardinal had spent most of his adult life here, as student, Professor, Registrar, Vice-President and President. He loved Maynooth in the truest sense of the word. It showed itself in the long hours of unremitting labour for its welfare, which so few knew about, but without which very little of significance can occur. More deep even than his love of people was his love of place, and he knew that Maynooth was the heart of the Irish Church, and that the future and well-being of the Irish Church was inextricably linked with the future and well being of Maynooth. As you know the College has been heavily involved in fund raising campaigns both here and abroad for several years, in order to carry out badly needed renovations. After the National Collection for the College three years ago, I wrote to all the priests in Ireland personally to thank them for their generosity and support in securing such a marvel-

lous response from the Irish people. I now take the opportunity to
thank you face to face today. That campaign was very much the
Cardinal's personal thing and its magnificent success gladdened
him greatly. I do not know how often he responded despite his
killing schedule, to requests from me to come to appear at 18-month
intervals all through the US to provide a focus and climax for our
ongoing daily efforts there; and he never refused. On his last visit
here he was enormously enthused when I outlined to him the
schedule for the £11,000,000 expansion of facilities on the new campus, which began a few weeks ago: the first phase of our new
Science Building under the European Structural Fund, student residences to accommodate 240 people, and a new student restaurant.
In fact on his last visit here just over a week before he died he was
planning with me his next visit to California in the Spring for another
event to culminate a fund-raising effort for Maynooth. He knew
what Maynooth meant to the Church in Ireland; and if our mourning for his generous soul is anything more than passing emotion, the
least we can do is to take up the torch he has passed to us and spare
no effort in bringing his ideals into practice within these walls.

Five years ago I remarked that, as the early years in Maynooth
catch the imagination and memory when they are at their most
fresh and never really lets them go again, Monsignor Mitchell
would always be for me THE President of Maynooth. He came here
as a student 67 years ago, and from his first day as a 'Chub' until his
appointment as Parish Priest of Ballinrobe he spent his whole life
here. His reputation for clarity, insight and robust common sense in
the lecture hall was a legend among the Irish clergy, more than
3,000 of whom had sat at his feet. Five years ago yesterday he was
last here; it was the first occasion in the College I think on which the
Professor chosen by the Golden Jubilarians for their classpiece was
here to celebrate it with them.

That evening he gave me a gift of five treasured volumes from
his library, which he had brought up from Ballinrobe: the famous *De
Ecclesia* of Dr Paddy Murray, Maynooth's great theologian of the era
of Vatican I. He ended his inscription by saying: '...with best wishes
for your success as President and theologian.' Whatever about
President, it was a wish that came too late for theology, because 1985
was the year I died as a theologian! However, in four years time, at
the end of my term as President, I hope for resurrection!

May God reward with his choicest blessing the Cardinal and
Monsignor Mitchell for all their labours and especially their labours
on behalf of Maynooth.

In the Old Testament jubilee was a time of assessment, examination and renewal. It was a time to celebrate what had been achieved, and a time to prepare for the new age with courage, energy and conviction. It was lastly, and most importantly a time for renewal of vocation and faith: these are the themes of biblical jubilee as you will find them in Chapter 25 of Leviticus.

Vocation is the greatest flower of faith. What we are celebrating today is above all God's gift of vocation to us. Like faith itself, as St Paul said, vocation can waver. It is always something that demands effort; it is no mystery how faith or vocation that are not maintained, will die. We should not preach the duty of Love to our people and urge it on ourselves. What we should preach is the duty of faith. To tell people in God's name that they should love one another, without any other preparation or foundation, is merely an amiable Gospel. And it is an impossible Gospel, for until faith gives the power to love it cannot be done. If we preach faith, the heart of vocation, the love will grow out of it on its own.

We have, thank God, still close to three hundred seminarians for the Irish dioceses here in Maynooth, and another seventy or eighty who come in from outside to attend lectures. By world standards it is excellent; by Irish standards it could be a lot better. Often I feel that one factor that impedes vocation to the priesthood in a young person is detecting a lack of nerve or confidence in the priests he knows. I really think few if any vocations to the priesthood arose without the encouragement and support which an individual priest took in a promising individual. Could I ask you to do that when you go home?

I am sure that combined with prayer the solution to a great many problems besetting the Church today lies there.

We have come from a time when for over twenty years incessantly the Church has been subjected to criticism. No doubt some of that was necessary, but equally true is it that it has gone too far. Whatever we say of the Church we have to remember that it was Christ's supreme gift to mankind, through which came the Spirit and his own Body.

A long time ago someone said:

'Trust the Church of God implicitly, even when your natural judgement would take a different course from hers, and would induce you to question her prudence and correctness. Recollect what a hard task she has; how sure she is to be criticised, whatever she does. Recollect how much she needs your loyal and tender devotion. Recollect too how long is the experience gained in so many centuries, and what a right she has to claim your assent to principles which have had so extended and triumphant a trial. Thank her that she has kept the faith safe for so many generations, and do your part in trying to transmit it to the generations that come after you.' (John Henry Newman to the medical students at Dublin in November 1858).

The ending of our century has had more than its fair share of predictions and omens. No other century has had such a wealth of apocalyptic prophecies surrounding its closing years. Never before has humankind faced so many crises all together. We stumble over critical threshold after critical threshold; the threshold of environmental pollution, destruction of the ozone layer, the tottering economies of the West, the flaring up of local wars that threaten to become conflagrations, the greenhouse effect; the technological thresholds which we overstep daily in atomic physics, communications, artificial intelligence, space technology, genetic engineering, solar energy, and revolutionary new conceptual models of science. We have all in all the most volatile mixture ever concocted in our little solar system.

From the sheer number and magnitude of all these accelerating lines of change, all converging in the closing years of this century, the indications are that settled times are not exactly around the corner. We know that Christ is the Lord of the Universe. Very hopeful things that were unsuspected have happened in the world this year; I am sure it will spread to a new religious awakening when the time is right, and above all when we have opened our eyes to see what these events are pointing out to us.

With a strengthened faith and optimism we can be sure that we will hand on the heritage of our proud past undiminished to the future generations in this country, who will largely depend on you and me for what they know of God.

Christ's Supreme Gift
The Maynooth Union, 16 June 1992

Three years from today, with God's help, we will celebrate the two hundredth anniversary of the College. Maynooth was one of the first really native institutions to have emerged in the history of modern Ireland, the first really official step towards the abolition of the Penal Laws. It grew rapidly to be synonymous with the Catholic

Church here, and no institution has contributed more to the Catholic Church in Ireland over these past two centuries.

Maynooth is best embodied in the Maynooth Union, in the flow of its graduates down the years. I am delighted to see so many back here today, who shared our joys, our sadnesses, our triumphs and our happinesses as students long ago.

There have been very many positive developments in the College over the past year, many of them perhaps quite different from what you knew here. But it is still doing the same work as it did when you knew it, and it is still one College under one administration. Many new courses have been introduced, including a very successful pastoral diploma course in Fourth Divinity, a new BA course in Local History, and a new BA in Finance. Next Autumn we will have a full time equivalent student body of almost four thousand. Four new buildings to house lay students in apartment-style accommodation and to house conferences in out of term time, were completed last year. A very badly needed student restaurant and sports facility were opened in October, and our new Science Building began a month ago. The Taoiseach will perform the foundation stone ceremony for it next week. This comes to a total of nearly £14,000,000 of construction in the present year, all of which should be either self-financing or from government or European funding, so that it will not be a cost to the College.

A great deal of renovation of the Seminary buildings in also under way, some of it very obvious, some less so. Last Summer the roof of St Patrick's House facing St Joseph Square was replaced, together with the dormer windows on that side. This Summer the three remaining sides of the roofs of St Mary's and St Patrick's will be replaced, with all the dormer windows on the main wings. This Refectory, recognised to be Pugin's finest hall, has just been restored, and this evening's dinner in the first function to be held in it. Because of a massive hot water mains leak underneath the floor, the floor had to be replaced, and the covering on the new cement cannot be put into position until August because of the time needed for drying the concrete.

I want to thank all of your most warmly for your support of the Collections for the College held in the dioceses five years ago and last year without which these renovations could not take place. Obviously no such collection could succeed without the warm support of both the bishops and priests in the parishes and we were very gratified with the response there was. All of this money goes to the seminary here alone, and we hope to have all of the fabric of the College in tip top shape before the bicentenary in three years time. The money needed for this is being raised in a partnership between the Irish Church at parish and diocesan level, and in a matching funds arrangement with the corporate community both here and in the United Sates.

A very warm word of welcome to the Golden Jubilarians: we have 23 of them back with us today. What a glorious thing to look back on half a century of dedication to the work of God; despite the faults and failings and regrets, which we so often let dominate our assessments, and of which we are always so powerfully aware, we can never forget how massive a record of dedication a Golden Jubilee of ordination is.

I used to think when I was a student that Silver Jubilarians were like creatures from another planet, and now, lo and behold, without any notable effort on our part, it has become the turn of our class to reach that august stage. At our private dinner here in the College last night we had a grand total of eighty five people, which included thirty five of the forty priests in our class. I am delighted so many were able to come. We have not, as a class, overburdened each other with many regular meetings, and the ones we have had, I think, were all the better for that. It was a very happy occasion last night, but tinged with sadness too, particularly for the times and people that are no more.

Maynooth in our student days is often described now as a closed environment. It was closed indeed in the sense that we were largely confined within the walls, but there was a very rich and active student life here; the plentifulness of games as well as opportunities for study; the myriad of student societies, for many of which Bishop Harty was responsible; the fact that we were thrust upon people of very different character, different customs, different ways of speech, all helped to smooth our corners and broaden our outlook, for to survive you had to change, and change for the better.

Looking around the tables at our classmates last night someone said to me, and I'm sure most of you feel the same, that the gestures, mannerisms and personalities, were the same ones we knew so well in the Junior Ref over thirty years ago. For people fundamentally never really change; but only grow more the same.

A lay member of our class leaving my room last night, or probably early this morning, spoke about how impressive a group the class was, and how dedicated and enthusiastic most people seemed to be. It would be impossible, he said, to find a similar spirit in any comparable secular grouping in a corporation or business. And I suspect their real strength comes from the fact that they do not realise how good they are. I thank you for the strong bonds we forged together here three decades ago, and which still can serve despite this passage of years, as such a powerful restoration for us all. What I have said of my own class, I am sure all of you can say as well of yours.

It took 7,000 years from the invention of the plough to the motor car; only 70 years from the motor car to the space age. In the years of our jubilee we have seen more change by far than the Church endured previously for centuries. The nineties show more and more the trend towards being a decade of polarisation, of the unpredictable, of violent change in environment, in culture, in social and political and above all, economic, structures, in ways of thought and understanding.

It is hardly any wonder that the Church, which of necessity has its roots in so many of these areas, should be feeling the pressures of change very strongly; the problems that face and preoccupy us all are not just problems facing the Church, they are the problems of a society in a massive world-wide shift, unprecedented in its suddenness.

Faced with such a panorama, and with such an uncertain future ahead, it is all too easy to panic, or to take refuge in that rigidity and authoritarianism behind which fear and insecurities always and so infallibly hide. Or to take refuge in the naïve and futile optimism of the new age beliefs. When we fear something we only empower it more.

Christ warned us of the dangers of fear and the guilt which it spawns. Guilt is a natural and necessary thing; but a guilt which is brooded over or over-emphasised is a dangerous and unwelcome thing.

The heart of the message of Christ was that the Kingdom of God was within us, and it is our business here on earth to get in touch with it more and to let it grow and permeate us. Everything in the Church was meant to serve that process. The scriptures, creeds, councils, the teaching office, the sacraments, were all given to help that growth of the kingdom within us. Often in the Church we have not kept that sufficiently to the fore, and that is why so many of the fundamentalist sects and new age groupings are making such inroads on us now, fomenting a form of religion that is facile and short term. Too often in a time of great crisis such as we now face we stress the rules and regulations all the more, and tend to forget the reason why they are there. Rules and regulations are indispensable, and the farther a person or society drifts from God the more necessary they are. But they were there for a purpose, and to stress the rules without the illumination of their purpose is not an effective way to meet the challenge of our times.

The Church was Christ's supreme gift to mankind; the sacrament of his body, it was through it his Spirit came to be with us for endless ages. We are not entering an age of unbelief; but an age of polarisation and volatile change, when people are thirsting for what we would call the awareness of the Kingdom within them. The fortunes of the Church in the years ahead are infallibly tied to how well it can respond to and develop that awareness that is in the hearts of so many today. Therein lie the fortunes of this College, and the fortunes of all of us at these tables here this evening.

It gives me the greatest pleasure, in that spirit, to propose the toast of the Maynooth Union, of the Jubilarians and of our guests and to wish them well in that enterprise in the years ahead.

Signs of the Times
The Maynooth Union, 15 June 1993

The establishment of Maynooth College well before Catholic Emancipation by Grattan's Parliament was the phoenix of the Irish Church rising from the ashes of the Penal Days. The future and well-being of the Irish Church is inextricably linked with the future and well being of Maynooth; what the Irish Church thinks of Maynooth reflects what it thinks of itself, and what happens to Maynooth is a preview of what will happen to the Irish Church as a whole. Our forefathers left us this magnificent College, one of the most beautiful in the world, as our heritage. The College Chapel, built from the pennies of the poor at one of the most dismal economic periods in our history, is an eloquent testimony of the regard in which the priesthood was held in the hearts of the Irish people.

As you know the College has been heavily involved in fund raising campaigns for several years, in order to carry out badly needed renovations. After the National Collections for the College I wrote to all the priests in Ireland personally to thank them for their generosity and support in securing such a marvellous response from the Irish people. I now take the opportunity to thank you face to face today. Since the new John Paul II Library, built at a cost of over £8,000,000, was paid off five years ago our efforts have been almost totally dedicated to the renovation of the seminary buildings and the building up of endowment. If restoration is well done it will not be glaringly obvious, and I think this magnificent Refectory in which we are gathered this evening is a fine example of a massive restoration well done. All of the roofs and dormer windows in the Gothic Square in St Patrick's and St Mary's Houses were replaced last Summer and the previous Summer, and a major restoration work will commence on the interior of St Mary's in a few weeks time. Extensive fire precaution work has been done and a substantial amount has been restored to the College endowment which had been depleted by various emergencies over the years.

All in all these works on the seminary buildings today will come close to three million pounds over the past four years. Decline in student numbers makes education and formation less economical and there is a serious need to rebuild endowment for the seminary now as total income from fees, whether contributed by the student personally, plus what comes from the dioceses, covers only about 60% of the cost of educating each seminarian. The other 40% has to be found by the College by some means or other above and beyond fees, and it is becoming a crippling burden. We are enormously grateful to you for the outstanding support which so many of the clergy have so dramatically shown towards their *alma mater* in recent years, and we hope you will be very proud of what has been accomplished that is visible, and also proud of the far less visible and far less apparent things, such as the improved ways of formation and education that have been put in place in recent years.

Today we are well into the brave new world forecast by people like George Orwell and Huxley. But instead of the massive enslavement of the individual which they foresaw, the massive communications explosions have in fact curbed the power of dictators, as we have seen so dramatically over the last three or four years. A new situation has begun to dawn. Down through history power has tended to be associated with institutions, with physical and military power; kings, governments and God were powerful. But individuals were not. The only way the individual could assert himself or herself was by opposing tradition, by tearing down, by rebelling.

Today there is a new possibility, which I think we have not here in our society sufficiently realised as yet, for we still cling fast to the idea that the only way to achieve change is to rebel; this is probably because of our past; but I think we have long had the opportunity to get past our past by now. I have often been amused by people using the catch cry 'Vatican II' as a shorthand for all that was new and progressive when most of the people to whom they were talking hadn't even been born when Vatican II closed.

Today there is a new possibility. The individual can influence reality by identifying the directions in which society is heading. Knowledge is power; and even if you do not approve of the way things are heading you're empowered by your understanding of trends.

I feel biology is at the stage today where computer science was in the early sixties, and we are set to see an explosive change occur in this field. Things like transgenesis, intruding genes from one species into another, are now becoming fairly commonplace in the laboratory

The implications of genetic engineering at this level are enormous. If genes can be transplanted between species, even at the present relatively undeveloped stage of this science, it is obvious that the neat divisions between species cannot any longer hold. The lines of demarcation become vague, or may even disappear. Genetic engineering is the root development in biology today, for when the DNA life code is fully mapped and understood, and the technology to make use of it is developed, the possibilities that will become feasible are literally mind-boggling, and will shake to the foundations any philosophical view or theory that has not already tried to wrestle with the questions these issues propose, principally about the very nature of life itself.

Are we ready for such an advance? The ethical problems of surrogacy, biotechnology and other biomedical issues, with which we are already familiar, will only increase as we approach the end of the decade. We have to try to anticipate the future of biotechnology to prepare us for the spiritual dilemmas we will face. These ethical questions are related to our need to understand what it mans to be human, especially as we reject the notion that science and technology have all the answers. The chaos which the debate about natural selection raised nearly a century and a half ago will be regarded as mild compared to the debate about unnatural selection which has already begun.

At the dawn of the third millennium there are unmistakable signs that a world-wide multidenominational religious revival is on foot, but it is not of the kind to give solace to organised religion. By now we well know that science and technology do not tell us what life means. We learn that through things such as literature, the arts, and spirituality. As we approach the date of the third millennium people are already 'tuned' to expect fundamental change; and it is usually regarded as threatening. At times like this people typically group into small clusters usually at the unorthodox end of the religious spectrum. It is a field-day for preachers of extreme points of view; fundamentalism at one end, replacing God with the unconscious, at the other.

When people are buffeted by change, the need for spiritual support intensifies. Most seek reassurance in one of two ways: either through inner-directed, 'trust the feeling inside' movements, or through outer-directed 'this is the way it is' authoritarian style religions. Both are now flourishing. This is an age which has little time, firstly, for institutions, and secondly, for ideologies (which are, I suppose, institutions of the mind).

Unfortunately, when the Churches are threatened, they tend by react in a defensive way by emphasising precisely both of these aspects of themselves, institution and ideology, thereby setting themselves up for demolition by the rising generation. I feel this is what is at the back of most of the decline in institutional religious practice, for we are by no means living in an irreligious age.

Assuredly, it will not be by condemning what are perceived as threats from these newer and less familiar religious movements, that the Church will fulfil its mission and retain its followers more effectively. It would be much better if the Churches would ask what is it that these groupings are offering which people find lacking in the Churches? Please note I am miles away here from suggesting that we pander to the lowest common denominator to retain congregations, which has happened in some cases. What I am talking about is regaining a sensitivity to those things once so central in our own traditions, which may have become obscured and forgotton, and for which there is now a thirst in people's hearts.

The Crisis of Vocations
The Maynooth Union, 21 June 1994

The Maynooth Union is one of the oldest such gatherings in the world. It came out of the Maynooth Centenary celebrations and in many ways it is a memorial built of living stones to the College's first centenary of 1895, and one that has never lost its vigour over the intervening years. Next year, with God's help, we will celebrate the College's two hundredth anniversary. The actual date for marking the central celebration is hard to pin down. The Royal Assent was given to the Act of the old Irish Parliament on 5 June 1795,

George III reputedly saying this gave him more pain than the loss of the American Colonies!

However, even a moderately careful reading of the Act will show it did not establish a College at Maynooth, or indeed anywhere, but established Trustees who had the purpose of establishing'one Academy for the education only of persons professing the Roman Catholic Religion.' The submissions by the bishops over the preceding few years to the Lord Lieutenant and to Henry Grattan do clarify the issue to some extent, since it was obvious that the purpose of the institution (originally they sought to have four) was for the education of clerical students, four hundred of whom had normally been studying in France before the upheavals of the revolution. It should also be apparent that the motive of the government, or the bishops, could not have been to have students educated at home rather than in France, where they would be exposed to pernicious revolutionsary principles, since these students were already barred from France before the submissions about establishing the new College in Ireland were ever made.

Such is the stuff of which legends are made.

In any event the Royal assent to establish Trustees for one College was given on 5 June; over the course of that Summer various sites were contemplated, but it was due to the initiative of the Duke of Leinster that the College eventually landed in Maynooth, and that 'Maynooth' came to acquire the resonance it has today. Nobody knows when the College opened for sure; but it is generally accepted to have been in September. The Trustees themselves, however, when the Long Corridor extension was constructed at the back of Stoyte House, chose to regard the date of the laying of the Foundation Stone of the new Buildings by the Lord Lieutenant – 20 April 1796 – as the College's 'Foundation Day,' and as such it has been observed in the College's Calendar ever since. So do we celebrate the Centenary of this College in June or September 1995, or in April 1996, or when? I leave it to wiser men to resolve!

This is my tenth and last time to have the honour to address the Maynooth Union. There have been dramatic developments in the College over that decade, possibly more than at any other comparable period in its history. The most obvious of course has been the expansion of the National University of Ireland part of the College; staff numbers have doubled and student numbers trebled during the past decade. Eight new buildings have been constructed on the North Campus to cope with the demands which this dramatic increase in numbers make. The main range of Gothic Buildings, including the seminarians's rooms in St Mary's and St Patrick's, have been re-roofed and extensively restored and renovated. New lighting is being installed in the College Chapel, and two years ago this Great Refectory – in Pugin's phrase – and the finest Hall he designed anywhere – certainly the finest formal dining room in this country – was extensively restored. If restoration is well done it will not be glaringly obvious; I think we have succeeded in that here, but the downside often is that there may seem to be little of a dramatic kind to show for your money! That at least is not the case with this refectory.

There has been a significant expansion in the number and extent of courses offered, both in the Pontifical University and the National University here, and the major debts of ten years ago have been dealt with. I am most grateful to all who made this decade of considerable expansion possible, particularly to the Trustees and Visitors, who have had to listen to me for more than sixty of their meetings, and to all of you, and your brother clergy throughout Ireland, who have supported us in so many ways, ranging from the vacation placements of seminarians, to the magnificent support in the National Collections held for the renewal of the seminary buildings. I greatly appreciate the very generous words which Cardinal Daly has just now spoken in my regard concerning what has been achieved here during my two terms of office, and I warmly thank him and his fellow Trustees for the courage and dedication which they have shown in embarking on many of these projects, and particularly last month in approving the appointment for the first time of a separate Head for the National University courses here.

The Presidency here over the past ten years has certainly been a very onerous office to hold, but I would not wish to have missed the experience. The division of labours between the President, who will now guide the Pontifical University and seminary, and the new and temporary post of Master, who will be Head of the National University here, will greatly reduce the burdens, and will prepare for the situation when the new University legislation comes. This will provide a new Governing Body for the National University at Maynooth. There have, of course, been many false dawns and false hopes about new University legislation appearing, but while it will not appear during this coming summer as we thought earlier this year, it is probably realistic to hope that the College's bicentenary year will not pass without the implementation of the new legislation, as the White Paper on Education is expected within a few months.

If I were asked what was the single greatest regret I had during my time as President, I would have to say it was the fact that seminarian numbers are only seventy percent of what they were when I began ten years ago. Unfortunately, from all the evidence to hand, and realising how risky prophecy is, it seem as if this situation is something that will continue for the foreseeable future, and most likely will worsen, perhaps to a considerable degree.

This poses enormous problems for the future of the seminary, not just for the future of any individual institution such as Maynooth. But the fortunes of Maynooth are of course of paramount concern, for, as I have repeatedly said over the years, the seminary at Maynooth was the visible face and symbol of the Irish Church, and whatever happens to Maynooth is a powerful signal of what is due to happen to the Church in Ireland as a whole.

Every conceivable effort has been made here in recent years to promote vocations and to encourage and properly train those seminarians who come here. But I am convinced that the crisis we face in terms of numbers is not something that any amount of techniques and strategies focused on the issue itself will do much to solve.

It is obvious that the hostility and negative publicity to which we have been subject for quite a while now can cause a decline in the attraction which this dedicated life can have for a young person, as well as greatly reduce the nourishment and support for a vocation which the family normally provided so significantly in the past. But there are deeper reasons.

I have heard the view advanced that the priesthood has not been sufficiently appreciated by the Church, and that God may wish to remedy this by calling fewer people to the ministry. This is a point of view that does deserve serious consideration, but personally, apart from the normal hazards attendant on deciding what is God's will in detail, I think it might be difficult to harmonise with what we know of the character of God's actions as revealed in Christ.

Another question that can be posed is to ask whether we in the Church have been successful in presenting the revealed word of God in a way that meets that for which people deep in their hearts are searching? I know this is a pathway strewn with minefields. However, we are not living in an irreligious age, far from it. But we are entering an age of polarisation and volatile change, when people are thirsting for what one might call an awareness of the kingdom within them. Why is it that so many of our contemporaries find God attractive, but the Church , his instrument of salvation, lacking in meaning or even irrelevant? Why is it that so many find solace in the many New Age style movements, or in the many mystical-style forms of religion or quasi-religion that are growing so rapidly today? The Church in the richness of its tradition has far more to offer in this line than any of the above-mentioned groupings, but it does not offer it to any significant degree. As a result many people are finding their desire for a real spiritual growth into Christ not met in the Church. To so many we appear to offer only a religion of rules and regulations, with little understanding of why those rules and regulations are there in the first place. Some retreat to try to find a remedy in a rigid authoritarianism, but far more, at the opposite extreme, in the movements of the New Age. Undoubtedly the New-Age-style movements, with so little place for the effort and self-transformation necessary for our growth into Christ, do offer a deceptive and false security, but they are proving fatally attractive, and one of the main reasons for that is that we are not any longer offering those aspects of the Catholic Faith for which there is such a thirst in so many today. So we would be better served to ask what it is they have to offer which we are not offering, than to begin to level warnings and condemnations.

Vocation is the flower of faith. Or to use another analogy, the state of vocations is the tip of the iceberg, if the iceberg be taken as representing the state of the faith as a whole.

If there is a shortage of vocations it will not be remedied by techniques and remedies that dance only on the peripheries. It will not be remedied by engaging in the trendy issues of the day, by which some have hoped to regain some relevance, but only by a fundamental re-appraisal of the whole presentation of the faith.

When that has happened, despite all the powerful counter-forces in our society to which I referred earlier, the crisis of vocations will solve itself. But until that happens in the Western world at large, I fear there cannot be much improvement for which we can hope.

I warmly thank you all again for coming back to celebrate your anniversaries with us today, and particularly I thank Cardinal Daly for his very generous tribute to the work that was accomplished here during my time as President.

Maynooth has come through many difficult times in the past. Those who will read Monsignor Corish's new history will see that very clearly. Likewise the Church itself has come through many more crises and many more centuries. Difficulties have to be seen as opportunities; opportunities which often bring out the finest qualities both in persons and institutions. It has been that way here in the past on many occasions; I am confident it will be so again. In that spirit I propose now the Toast of our Guests, the Toast of the Jubiliarians and that of the Maynooth Union itself, as it completes one hundred years.

CHAPTER 10

Moments of History

Retirement of President of University College, Dublin Dr Thomas Murphy
20 November 1985

When the Royal University was disappearing into the sunset the Colleges which were linked with it began to look around for new forms and structures. At the establishment of the National University of Ireland there was considerable debate about what status would best suit the purposes of Maynooth, and eventually the status of Recognised College was agreed, even though considerable discussion had taken place between the officials of the University and Dr Mannix, as to whether the Arts and Science students from Maynooth would travel in to Earlsfort Terrace (University College, Dublin), for their lectures each day.

Fortunately that did not happen, or I would not be able to host this function tonight for President Tom Murphy. The links between Maynooth and the NUI have grown very strong over the intervening years. Dr Whitaker, the Chancellor, is of course, the first Chancellor not to have been a member of the Maynooth staff! My distinguished predecessor, William Walsh, was the NUI's first Chancellor, and the second Chancellor, Eamon De Valera, stands in no need of my words to bring him to remembrance. Dr Mannix was the first Pro-Vice-Chancellor in Maynooth, and his portrait hangs side by side with that of William Walsh here in this room tonight. We are delighted to have with us tonight the Provost and officials of Trinity College as well as the Presidents and officials of the National University Colleges, to join in this tribute to Tom.

'Let us praise famous men,' says the Book of Ecclesiasticus. I would not dare to do such, except all of us in principle, and President Tom Murphy in particular.

Of Tom Murphy I can say, hand on heart, that he needs no speech of mine to praise him on the eve of his retirement. Words in any case always fail to match reality, even in the hands of the most skilled manipulators of language.

In my poor grasp of words let me say this: I am his county man. He is a traditional man, and when I say this I am not referring to those fluttering pennants called Liberal and Conservative. I mean rooted, gracious, aware of ambiguities, at ease with the fall of man, and more so, with his redemption and glorification.

To Maynooth, my Alma Mater, he has been brother, father, and friend in ways more deep than we can ever be aware. For that we owe him a profound debt of gratitude.

I go back now to University College, Dublin, and its tradition of Celtic scholarship, to find a verse to praise our guest. 'Ó Murchú of the dark brow, I will resume your first name. Much more is due to your praise, but gold is never refined by a single heating' (Irish Bardic Poetry).

Now to the rest of us in principle. *Is leor nod don eolach.*

As Macauley's schoolboy, the public names that I knew in Wexford were Cabinet Ministers, distinguished University figures, Bishops, Judges. To twist the meaning of the phrase a little, without such an *altum dominium* of leadership the paradox is that democracy is footloose and directionless.

Professor Lee of Cork said in *The Listener* recently, that we should develop a talent to develop our talent. For the time being that's a signal challenge to us.

As Heads of the Universities in Ireland gathered here tonight, we should reflect on Tom Murphy's proto-patron – Hypocrates, who said, *'ars longa, vita brevis.'* Yes, skill, depth, sanity, balance and insight, are slowly acquired. Like all the precious things of life, hard to attain, more difficult still to retain. We should release them reluctantly. We should watch out for the lure of the catch-phrase: Conscience as cosmetic for the permissive: or for everything slapdash; ponder the force of Kant's question: What can we know? What should we do? What may we hope for?

They are lineal descendants of the first University, the ramblings of Socrates through the streets of Athens saying, 'The unexamined life is not worth human living.' For better or worse the joys and sorrows of the President of Maynooth do not begin or end with the NUI connection. The College is nearing its second centenary – the second centenary of a foundation on the same site, and under the same patronage as the foundation of the first College of Maynooth in 1518. The whole College in all its parts here, not alone the NUI, owes a great debt to Tom Murphy. In that spirit I thank you on behalf of us all and I have no doubt that your 'retirement' will be every bit as varied, productive and exciting as the full life you have already lived, which has been of such enormous benefit to medicine, and to third level education at large in this country.

Dedication of Renehan Hall
and Formal Opening of Philbin Art Collection
11 October 1988

One of the most precious things in the human heart must surely be attachment to one's own and to one's own native place. I feel all of us to whom Maynooth was Alma Mater owe it a loyalty sufficiently deep to transform with the passage of the years into what St Paul called 'love without hypocrisy.' And love delights to show itself in excesses. Judged by external standards the widow's mite was too small a contribution to the Temple, just as the penitent's ointment was too much in the eyes of the money-grabbing Judas. But both had in them that inner generosity which is the essence of love's excess of the law.

The result of just such an inner generosity is what we're gathered here this evening to celebrate. In the little brochure for this evening's event, I called attention to the similarity which struck me between Laurence Renehan, in whose memory this Hall was recently named, and Bishop William Philbin. Though separated by one hundred and thirty years, their gifts were in the same order, and had the same motivation. Renehan's manuscript collection, assembled with love over so many years of labour, was the most significant addition to the Maynooth Library that it has ever had up to this day, and it preserved many MSS that probably would not have survived had they, through some mistaken loyalty, been retained locally. Bishop Philbin's art collection, assembled with love and care over half a century, falls into the same category of significance. Gifts of this kind have been rare in the history of the College. It is very fitting that this Collection, which began in Maynooth more than half a century ago, should find now here its permanent home.

The formation of youth depends as much on the general climate of an institution as on the content of the learning it dispenses. The stress in public affairs in recent years has been almost exclusively on a culture that was technological, urbanised and industrialised. Obviously an university education in these difficult days has to

have a very strong regard for establishing or increasing your earn-
ing power. But it is not so obvious that an education which merely
did that could ever be described with justice as a true university
education. For true university education also has to deepen and
widen the mind. It was well said by Adlai Stevenson that what a
man knows at fifty that he did not know at twenty is, for the most
part, incommunicable. All the observations about life which admit
of ready communication are as well known early on, to an attentive
person as they are in middle age. All these things have been heard;
much has been read about them, but they have not yet been lived.
What we know at fifty that we did not know in our early years is
not the knowledge of formulae, or collections of philosophical
descriptions, but the knowledge of people, of what they did in certain circumstances that challenged, of places, of sights, sounds, of
victories, sleeplessness, failures, devotion and selfless service, and
so on. What we are talking about here is the human experiences and
emotions of this earth, and not least in addition, a faith and reverence for the things that cannot be seen.

The point of education is to ensure that people are so guided
that in the middle years they do not have to go back and fill in the
spaces in their living which were left blank when growing up.
Many values will always appeal to young people – dignity as persons, integrity, disinterestedness, personal identity, self-respect,
and so on. These values are not economic or materialistic, even in
the widest sense, but they constitute a quest which is at the heart of
all education and all formation. What I am talking about is the
Christian vision. It is the basis of what we are about in Maynooth.

Bishop Philbin, I know how much of your heart and soul has
gone into this collection over that period of half a century from the
early years of your friendship with Evie Hone. You will well
remember this room in which we are gathered; in the last century it
served as a lecture hall, and you yourself knew it as such in your
student days; since the 1930s it had been a dingy and gloomy store-
room for back numbers of newspapers and periodicals. This year
we restored it as a new board room since many of the College bodies are now too large to meet in the old Board Room in Stoyte
House. The restoration has been very successful. Your art collection
seems to have been designed for it. The bronze bust of yourself
which was presented to you by Marjorie Fitzgibbon, you have
asked me not to display until after your death. The other thirty six
works are here.

I asked the Trustees to name this beautifully restored room for

President Laurence Renehan. It was through his genius that one of the greatest nineteenth century architects, A.W. Pugin, was retained. It took courage to depart from the Georgian-style architecture that formed the other three sides of St Joseph's Square. Pugin and Renehan gave us our beautiful Gothic buidlings, and whatever dis-advantages accrue from the tendency of most architects to sacrifice internal convenience to an impressive façade, we cannot deny the magnificence of the old Library, of the Great Refectory, the ground-work for the College Chapel, undoubtedly the most outstanding of its kind in the world, and of course the façade by which Maynooth is best known world-wide – St Patrick's House. It was largely through Renehan's efforts that the Parliamentary grant from 1845 came in. When the funding for the Pugin buildings came through it was of such an unsatisfactory scale that St Mary's Square would have resembled more a small yard than a quadrangle had not Dr Renehan scraped together enough funds from private sources to extend it to what we know today. He it was too, when all is said and done, who really first established our library.

Bishop Philbin, Pugin's timbered ceilings, cut stone fireplaces and windows, your art collection, the name of Renehan – in whom the love of Maynooth ran as deep as it does with you – all go to pro-duce this most civilised meeting room in the College. It will serve powerfully in the appreciation of the incommunicable for many long years but serve also as a monument to your own life-long ded-ication to Maynooth. Love's excess of the law is rare, but if it did not appear occasionally most of the world's great institutions would be significantly the poorer.

Opening of the Irish Parliament
Assembly of the 26th Dáil Eireann
29 June 1989

A Uachtaráin na hÉireann, a Thaoisigh, A Ardeaspaig, A Cheann Comhairle, agus a Theachtaí Dála uilig: Beatha agus Sláinte! Agus fáilte róimh anseo inniú chuig Aifreann Cheiliúradh na Dála.

It is certain that no one with the name of Sallust is a member of this: The Dáil. He was an ancient Roman writer, very much a politi-cal observer, and a chronicler of what should be in the life of a State.

He quotes, or imagines, the steely Cato as saying, 'Do not think that it was by force of arms that our ancestors made a great nation out of a small community. What made us great is energy in our own land, a rule of justice outside our borders; informing policy, a mind that is free because not at the mercy of criminal passions' (Sallust, Cat 52,1 Qff). He goes on to say that Rome's greatness was won by the exceptional qualities of a small minority, and that this minority was responsible for the 'victory of poverty over riches' (ibid, 53, 2-5).

These echoes resound for us, since the original words describe a perennial political programme.

You politicans are 'a small minority' in our population. But you are elected to show 'exceptional qualities.' We are not speaking of genius but of constant dedication, decency and selflessness for love of country.

It is time on this sacred occasion to give thanks for our State. First, we are a democracy. A Church can live, and often must live, with many regimes. But, I venture to say, that a democracy serves best the image of God in which man is made. Man is made to be just and loving in freedom, and I feel that vocation gets its greatest scope in democracy.

We must give our nation due praise. In what is now almost three score years and ten we have emerged from a burdened colonial past, one of the longest in history, to create a country which is not without respect on earth.

Our missionaries, first in time, made our name known. Our Army and now our Police work for peace in many places. I have seen them 'on location' and felt proud of their humanity and humour. The unfussy way of being just, and nothing arrogant.

I even remember young experts from *Bórd na Móna* helping to analyse tropical bogland in Burundi, in central Africa. You may add to the list yourselves. In recent years, the country has, in spite of now obvious problems, a colourful and lithesome air. Comhaltas Ceoltóirí Éireann has disciples from Kiev to Iceland. We have enlightened legislation in artistic matters. For the poor and the old we have as sensitive a soul as anywhere. These fires you must stoke more.

I stress with small examples what has been achieved. It is never enough. But I stress acknowledgement of what is, and hope.

A European statesman once referred to us as 'Europe's most theocratic state.' It is not a description I value, but I do want us to be aware of spirit, of a plus, of the hidden mystery, music, poetry, and universally prayer, try to touch and body forth.

You get the fragrance of it in Patrick Kavanagh's 'A Christmas Childhood':

> The tracks of cattle to a drinking-place,
> A green stone lying sideways in a ditch,
> Or any common sight, the transfigured face
> Of a beauty that the world did not touch.

The State is not theocratic. In the State God is best served by the decency, justice and charity of the legislator. This will not always be without debate, but decisions must spring from reflective conscience, not from short-lived anarchies.

'The State' said Hegel, is 'the Divine idea as it exists on earth.' That led to catastrophe and horror in our time.

No religion tells man to be bad. Ours is Judaeo-Christian, and Islam has considerable stakes here. Our morality comes from the Synagogue and the Greek thinkers, all under the mantle of the life of Christ. Some of us may claim to be agnostic, but I have often found in such, a surplus of justice, but agnosticism, or difficulties with belief, stem often not from the beliefs themselves, but from distortions and caricatures for which they are often mistaken. The identification tags may differ, the justice always remains the same.

As you legislate, I suggest you keep the melodic line of these reflections before you. *Is leor nod don eolach.*

The welfare of mankind in Ireland and on earth, the face of God in Paradise, is the Christian *Summa*.

The Mass rose from one man's justice and love. Even those who do not call him God, would not dispute a vocation of going around 'doing good.' You are empowered makers of the public good: work, health, education, the arts, the environment.

And give your hearts to a green universe. Make sure those who follow us can quote Kavanagh:

> I can remember seeing something of the gay
> garden that was childhood's...

It may interest you to know that St Paul uses the same Greek word for Christ (Hebrews 8:2), for himself, (Romans 15:16), and for the pagan government officials (Romans 13:6). The word is *leitourgos*. It means, literally, a person who does a holy work. The wealthy men who sponsored the classical Greek dramas were called such.

Without putting too fine a point on it, God is honoured and human beings are served, at Mass, in prayer, by a better teacher of French, a new cardiac unit, a kinder pension scheme, or a re-designed inner city.

Your task is vast but profoundly human. You have chosen a high-risk vocation. You have real courage. May God give you his spirit to carry it out with integrity.

A Dhia do mo stiúradh, a Dhia do mo mhúineadh,
A Dhia do mo theagasc;
A Dhia do mo shabháil, ar gach áit a mbíonn an peaca.
A Iósa grámhair, a fuair grásta ó d'Athair,
Do mo sheoladh i ngach áit i mbearna mo leasa.

European Community Eclair Grant
of £1,000,000 to Maynooth College
Mary O'Rourke, Minister for Education
13 September 1989

Minister, distinguished guests, and members of the College Staff, I am honoured to welcome you here for this extremely significant occasion, and in particular to be able to welcome the Minister for Education, Mary O'Rourke. In her case the word 'welcome' has a special significance, because this College is her Alma Mater, and she is one of its most distinguished graduates. We are very proud of her achievements, and delighted she could come here this evening to make this announcement for our scientific research at the College.

The life and vigour of any university stems above all other considerations, from the standard of its teaching and the quality of its research, because it is research that gives life and vigour to all education and formation, and it is research which forges the basic link between universities and the societies which they serve.

The Minister's announcement this evening highlights the fact that Maynooth is at the forefront in scientific, technological and environmental research, which is interfacing with and contributing to industrial development. In fact, for all of us here I think one of the most significant aspects of this occasion and this discovery, is its enormous impact for good on the environment.

The research which we are dealing with here tonight is an early response on the part of Maynooth to what the government has been calling for as part of the National Plan to be supported by European Community Structural Funds.

The two partners in this project which Maynooth has in the academic and business world are major international institutions and corporations who have modern facilities and large financial resources.

Science is not the first thing that the man or woman in the street associates with Maynooth. In fact, however, Maynooth has always had a strong scientific stream in its education. This goes back to the very beginnings of the College when a French Professor of Physics came here and established a very worthy tradition. It was at Maynooth, in this tradition, over one hundred and fifty years ago, that the Induction Coil was invented by Dr Nicholas Callan. This formed an essential link in all future developments of electricity. This pioneering work has continued over the intervening years although mainly in the field of the theoretical sciences, and I am proud to say that in the last twenty years, during the rapid expansion of the College, the progress of our Science Faculty has been one of which we are very proud. The quality of its research and of its postgraduate students is one that speaks for itself, and all of this has been accomplished with very limited resources and facilities. We have now close to six hundred science students, and unfortunately the majority of them are housed in temporary prefabricated buildings. The very high quality research leading to the project which the Minister will this evening announce, was itself largely carried out in pre-fabricated buildings.

This underlines once again how urgently our long-awaited Science Building is needed in the College. I think probably nowhere else does such a disparity exist between the high standard of teaching and research and the facilities within which it is carried out. In that respect I am glad to be able to thank the Minister publicly here this evening for her warm words of support for this project which she expressed in Dáil Éireann in the early part of the Summer, saying that the Maynooth Science building was one of the projects which she hoped would be considered worthy to include in the Government's submission to Europe. I would like to compliment the Government on the success of the partnership concept, which is close to our hearts in all we do, and have pleasure now in introducing the Minister who will make the formal announcement of the Eclair Grant of one million pounds for our Department of Biology.

Presentation of Festschrift to
Monsignor Patrick J. Corish
'Religion, Conflict and Coexistence in Ireland'
Renehan Hall, St Patrick's College, Maynooth, 28 March 1990

Prophecy and history are generally considered not to mix too well. In fact historians are often thought of as prophets in reverse, charting the safe regions of accomplished fact, while prophets, in the strict Biblical sense, engage in the much more perilous task of trying to read the signs of the times and to speak out the truth fearlessly in charting a course for the future. Too often, history is seen as little more than how Edward Gibbon described it: 'the register of the crimes, follies and misfortunes of mankind.' And about the only thing we learn from history is that men never seem to learn from history.

The man we are honouring this evening is a living witness that most of the opprobrium, which historians seem often to have attracted to themselves, is badly placed and undeserved. Because in the mind and mouth of Dr Paddy Corish history was made vivid and alive, as the more than four thousand students who have sat at his feet can testify; he was that very rare combination of prophet and historian, in whom the search for knowledge of the past was never allowed to issue in a mere dusty record, but was transformed into a charter for the present and future.

He comes from 'the bright May meadows of Shelmalier' which gives me an added pride in what he continues to accomplish. I am delighted that we have so many of his relatives and friends here with us tonight; and especially so many of his colleagues in the Arts and Humanities Departments of the Irish universities who have come to express both their good wishes and their professional admiration.

The main achievement of any lecturer is something that cannot be determined with precision: the spirit he has imparted to the mind of his students; but we are at least sure that his record here in that respect is one that is almost impossible to surpass. He has also greatly enriched the historical sources of the College, editing the *Archivium Hibernicum* and the fasicules of the *History of Irish Catholicism*. Since 1956 he has been a member of the Royal Irish Academy, and has worked extensively on its committees and those of the Irish Manuscripts Commission and of the Catholic Record Society. The list of his publications in this Festschrift is a *res ipsa loquitur* for the range and depth of his scholarship. It began forty three years ago with his publication on Bishop Nicholas French of Ferns, mirroring that attachment to one's own and one's own native place, which must surely be one of the most endearing and noble features of the human spirit. His latest book, *The Irish Catholic Experience*, is a gem of rare and mature scholarship, expressed with great beauty and economy of language.   *

On his retirement, Scott Elledge of Cornell said, 'It is time I stepped aside for a less experienced and less able man.' Dr Corish did not have to make such a choice. The test of any person is, I suppose, the preparation he has made for his succession, and Professor Vincent Comerford was a scholar who had come to full bloom under the benign guidance of Paddy Corish. I congratulate Professor Comerford and his Department of Modern History on this excellent production, *Religion, Conflict and Coexistence in Ireland*, which through the greatest dedication and hard work they have produced. I do not think any more fitting or deserved tribute could have been paid to this man who transformed the study of Church history in Ireland in his own lifetime, and became in the process one of the major Irish historians, while building up the Department of Modern History here to its present strong and vigorous state.

He has made his mark not only on the academic life of the College, but was also a pioneer of its development in the sixties. I think it is safe to say that for him it was all a labour of love. He knows the history of every stone in Maynooth, and for a quarter of the life of the College he has lived within its walls. Recently our Trustees recognised his standing by appointing him the College's first archivist.

Winston Churchill said once that history would be very kind to him because he intended to write it. I am sure that was not Dr Corish's motive in accepting recently one of his greatest challenges to date: that of writing the Bicentenary History of Maynooth, even though he has a quarter share in it! And I am equally sure that no other person, in terms of his life's experience here, as well as his qualities as a professional historian, could come near matching his suitability for this immense task. I think it will be his greatest work, and the one above all by which he will be best remembered. They say God cannot alter the past; only historians can do that, but we trust in Dr Corish's integrity that the colours will be true!

For all these reasons, and many others, it gives me the greatest possible pleasure to present to Monsignor Corish this specially bound first copy of *Religion, Conflict and Co-Existence in Ireland*, on behalf of the Department of Modern History, and on behalf of all his friends, colleagues and admirers in this College and throughout the land.

Opening of New Centre for Dublin Travellers Education and Development Group Programmes
2 April 1990

Your Grace, Minister Ahern, dear friends:

I am delighted to be here on this historic occasion for the formal transfer of the Free Church for use as the new Centre for the Dublin Travellers Group.

The Group has had very important links with Maynooth since its foundation in the early 1980s, two of the original group being from the College. Links have been maintained and developed, particularly through our Department of Social Studies and the Community and Youth Work Courses. Three project workers in the Travellers Education and Development Group (Niall Crowley, Ronnie Fay and Gearóid Ó Riain) are past students of the College, and two staff members from the College are already deeply involved in the voluntary management group – Anastasia Crickley and Enda McDonagh. It is my hope, through these associations and the Pastoral Theology Department of Maynooth, that a strong link will continue to be maintained with this centre by the staff and students of Maynooth, both clerical and lay.

The first Traveller student on the professional Community and Youth Work Course at Maynooth did his preliminary training with the DTEDG (Thomas McCann). We are glad to say that both he and Michael McDonagh, who attended the next course, graduated with high acclaim, and we are enormously gratified at the quality of the work they have done since leaving the College. I am sure that an equally fulfiling role awaits the first Traveller woman, Helen McDonagh, who is at present a student with us on the Community and Youth Work Course.

The DTEDG has also facilitated the training of other youth and community workers from the College, by providing placements for students and supervising them during their initial experience in the field. The innovative and alternative approaches to work with Travellers being developed by DTEDG provide an ideal environment for the students on placement who are interested in participating in an organisation working with marginalised groups. The role of the DTEDG to date provides lessons for other voluntary groups working to bring about a society based on respect for all, especially the oppressed.

We are grateful to the DTEDG for offering us the benefits of experience of direct work with Travellers. They have also given us insights on how to develop an inter-cultural society. DTEDG staff have been available to share these insights with third level students at Maynooth and elsewhere through modules on education and other departmental courses.

We are delighted to be associated with the work and commitment of this organisation, and are profoundly impressed by the work and commitment of this organisation, and by its dedication and professionalism. I wish it every success in reaching the high goals it has set.

In particular I wish DTEDG and PAVEE POINT (The group set up to fundraise and act as trustees for the Centre), every success with this beautiful building. The grouping of interests that have come together – the corporate sector, statutory and community groups, the Church of Ireland, and groups in the Catholic Church – is truly unique. I want to commemorate the contribution of the Church of Ireland in particular. No doubt many members will have fond memories and feelings of this building today. It is always very sad to see a church close, for we always lose something of our culture, and of those precious things in the human heart that lie close to God, when it happens. But I am sure that those who have had to witness that loss will be enormously encouraged by the excellent purpose to which their building is now being put.

I want to acknowledge the involvement of the other groups that contributed to this; the Jesuit Solidarity Fund which contributed £10,000, the Columban Fathers who contributed £3,000, while Maynooth itself contributed £25,000, in addition to many other donations for which we are immensely grateful.

Buildings are a start, in this case a very great and noble start. I am pleased to present this cheque for £25,000 to you to help with it. In it there is a signpost and a pledge of hope for the resolution of the problems faced by the Travellers. We hope there will be many who will follow that lead in the years ahead.

Guím gach ráth ar an obair anois agus i gcónaí.

Cardinal Newman Centenary Celebrations
6 August 1990

The liturgy forbids us to commemorate anyone below the blessed, unless by way of a lesson for our own spiritual growth. Newman wrote so much, over such a wide field, and has been commented on so extensively, that it is enormously difficult to pick out one salient characteristic that might define his heart for us.

At the end of Newman's life, his sister Harriet, a Protestant, and her grandson, came to visit Newman at Birmingham; and the child asked him: 'Sir, What is the difference between a Cardinal and a Saint?' Newman said: 'Cardinals belong to this earth.'

This sums up well his view; no matter how much he valued the achievements and honours of this life what summed him up was the *primacy of the spiritual*. And in that it is again difficult to isolate what he regarded as its root. I've searched for a single adjective, and the best I can come up with, for all its imperfections, is 'impeccable.' This I think could well be said to be the heart of Newman's attitude in all things, from the height of his philosophy of religion in the *Grammar of Assent*, to the ideals of a gentleman, to the theory of the University, to the transcendent spirit of his hymns, to the high dignity of the Cardinalate conferred on him at the end of his life by Pope Leo.

To be impeccable means trying to be flawless, to be who you are in terms of your destiny; not to be weak in the understanding of your truth, which is the grand treasure that is you.

Many of us are not impeccable; we squander the richness that we have been endowed with by God in social consciousness; we sacrifice it to others' opinion of us; we gravitate to them so as to present ourselves in a favourable light. So many of us are under the auspices of being someone's else's character, and are not aware of what we are. If we were aware of what we are we would not be in the troubles into which we descend so often, and which are created by ourselves.

The person who is impeccable would die for his word, and would turn his back on the world rather than prostitute his truth to satisfy the multitude. He who knows himself believes in himself. But every time we give away our conviction and our freedom in order to satisfy the opinions and demands of others we lose the power with which God has endowed us. And then we become saddened and confused on our way. But to appreciate oneself as a child of God is to live in wisdom, and to abide in its sublime truth, joy, understanding and unwavering perseverance.

But we are still frightened in the depths of our being as much as on the surface. We are frightened to die, we are frightened of our own condemnation by society. If these and so many other fears are there, then we are not impeccable in Newman's sense. It is very rare to find someone who is honourable and noble (they are the same), and who in the face of death can forgive and understand others, and yet never give away their own truth in the process. This is what it takes to make another Christ.

If we cannot accept responsibility for our own lives but lay the blame on teachers, parents, the environment, the times, then we are not impeccable. The problems and illusions in which we get lost, it is we ourselves who have created them, and no one else forced them on to us. If we can accept who we are and what, and know where the blame lies, squarely on our own shoulders, then we are on the way to being impeccable. A person who knows this creates a vortex of spiritual power that gives him strength to love what he can be, to find the presence of God within, and it will inspire us to become greater than that which we are, and help us to know why we are the way we are. Then the power will come and free us from those connections to others that has enslaved us, which we have allowed to happen.

When we look inside and know ourselves and are true to ourselves, we know also for certain that the truth will make us free: to live that is to be impeccable.

Such virtue is a rare, rare, jewel to find in the course of history. It is what it is to know who you are, and the power you possess as a child of God, to feel a kinship with the stars and the earth, the river, the seasons, the wildfowl, the glistening dawn and the magical twilight, with all that exists. It takes only one person who has come to terms with himself to find that relationship. Unfortunately to come to terms with oneself is normally only done in the face of the opposition of one's friends, one's colleagues, or of one's family, as Newman knew to his cost, because the world does not take easily to the primacy of the spiritual. But a person who has reached to this has touched God, truth, and Kindly Light, and such people are exalted, unfortunately often through suffering; they are risen above the murk and mire and the requests they make to God lie beyond the backdrop of forever.

This was Newman's legacy; this striving was at the heart of all his achievement, spiritual, practical or academic; that our life should not be one of folly, but of impeccable existence, lived on the basis of our dignity as children of God. The world we face today is far indeed removed from the one in which Newman wrote and worked; it is so easy to lose his message if our admiration remains only at the level of slavish copying.

Many people today are pointing to the conditions the Church is experiencing, in both East and West, and in both First and Third Worlds, and they point to them with some considerable alarm

(Thirty Days, July-August 1990). They point out, for example, that in the first free elections in 40 years in Czechoslovakia the Catholic party, explicitly supported by the Bishops in a pastoral letter, won fewer votes than the old Communist party; they point out that Cardinal Glemp cannot secure the re-introduction of religious instruction in the schools from a government headed by a man who calls himself a 'Christian Democrat.' It is often difficult to know what to make of such facts which we hear only at second-hand, but it hardly unambiguously supports the view we often hear that the Church in Eastern Europe was strengthened by the forty years of persecution, and it certainly does give us all great cause for worry. And in the West we seem to be entering more and more into a situation where the Church is no longer greatly opposed, but often neither greatly regarded, and where men 'have forgotton all gods except Usury, Lust and Power' (ibid, quoting L. Guissani: *The Religious Conscience of Modern Man*).

Ten years ago the Orthodox theologian Olivier Clement, in his book *The Revolt of the Spirit*, said that the good fortune of Marxism was that it met a Christianity 'empty of any transfiguring energy.' The same, I am afraid, could be said of so many versions of Christianity in the Western and Third Worlds today; where Christianity has been weakened and crippled, very often from within; the transcendent message diluted or almost eliminated. What is needed is 'a renewal of the faith in which the unity between faith and life, and between God's grace and human initiative is placed at the heart of things'; it is only something on this level that can really hope to meet the need; for in the last analysis it is only the heart that can speak to the heart. It is precisely what Newman tried to do in his own time, for on the level of spiritual longing things tend to remain perennial. To carry on his message and his methods, to revive his insight, to place the primacy of the spiritual at the head, and so be impeccable, and to long for and achieve a transfiguration, must be the best way to keep the memory of that blessed man who was the prophet of the Second Spring, and who has so much to offer to the Catholic Church in its mission to the thirsty spirit of the world today.

European Social Policy Analysis
New Master's Degree
Office of the European Community Commission,
Dublin, 10 October 1990

Distinguished Guests:

I am delighted to have this opportunity of speaking a few words to you at the launch of this very new experiment in inter-European education. Maynooth College has joined with the University of Bath and the University of Tilburg in the Netherlands to provide this one year post-graduate course.

It is very encouraging to see the European Community, now that the progress of economic and political integration has been accelerated under the terms of the Single European Act, turn itself to wider issues, which, I hope, will be a prelude to recovering the cultural riches of Christendom, which is the underlying bond of European unity from our richly endowed past. Our post-graduate degree is intended to prepare students for the new environment of the European labour market when Europe-wide problems and proper responses to them have to be considered.

In addition to Bath and Tilburg, Maynooth is also joining with the Universty of Crete, the Technical University of Lisbon, and the Computense University of Madrid. These six Universities form an 'Inter-University Cooperation Programme' which is supported by the ERASMUS Programme. The fact that there are nineteen students from seven countries shows the promise that this venture holds.

This course represents a very considerable commitment by the Institutions involved as the ERASMUS funds cover only the expenses connected with staff and student travel, language learning and the presenting of course materials. The course being started requires a great deal of energy and time from academic and secretarial staff as well as the College administrative staff.

This is difficult, particularly in Ireland, where provision for postgraduate studies is still far from ideal, and I hope that we can look forward to an amelioration of this situation in the near future when the value of ventures such as this becomes more widely recognised.

In particular I hope we will be able to attract students from the Public Service to this course, as that particular sector has now increasingly to take account of European Community developments, even in the social policy field.

I would like to register, on behalf of our College, our gratitude to the European Commission for their support of this exciting project, and particularly for welcoming us to their building this evening. I would also like to thank our colleagues in Bath and Tilburg and in the three other Universities at Crete, Lisbon and Madrid, all of whom have put a great deal into the planning of this course. All of us will see our best thanks in the success and value which the course will have for its forthcoming graduates.

Pontifical Academy of Sciences
Renehan Hall, 20 March 1991

I am joined by the Director of the School of Theoretical Physics of the Dublin Institute for Advanced Studies in welcoming you here for this very special occasion to mark the appointment of Professor James R. McConnell to the Pontifical Academy of Sciences. It is only the second time an Irishman has received this honour, the previous member being Dr Arthur Conway of University College, Dublin, whose insignia we have the honour of holding in our museum.

The Pontifical Academy of Sciences is regarded a the only international academy of this kind that there is. It was founded in 1603, and flourished under various titles until given its present designation in 1936. It is also unique in being based in the beautiful Casino of Pope Pius IV in the Vatican Gardens, and has numbered among its eighty members some of the world's most distinguished scientists, many of whom the casual observer might find strange to discover under Papal patronage.

At the present day I suppose the most obvious example of this is the distinguished Cambridge cosmologist and theoretical physicist, Stephen Hawking, whose modest goal is to have a complete, consistent and unified theory of physical interactions, which would embrace all possible observations! I wish him well in that challenging quest: he has certainly gone far farther along that path than any of his predecessors.

The membership of Stephen Hawking and several others in the Pontifical Academy came as somewhat of a surprise, especially to those not familiar with the unprecedented interest in the relationship between modern quantum mechanics and what is often loosely called mystical awareness, over the past decade or two, and the surprising quasi-mystical character of some writings of very distinguished scientists involved in quantum physics and relativity, such as Heisenberg, Schrödinger, Einstein, Pauil, Planck and Eddington.

I remain to be thoroughly convinced that the fringes of modern physics support the insights of mysticism and certain forms of religious awareness, but I certainly do welcome the far greater openness towards the nature of fundamental reality which characterises so many of the researches in the fundamental areas of contemporary science, and which probably would also serve to enrich much of the fundamental quest of contemporary fundamental theology had it not so often blatantly and frequently appeared to surrender most questions of the transcendent to the scientists!

However, such complimentarity between these disciplines was the motivation behind the foundation of thie Pontifical Academy, and there has never been such promise that that ideal would be justified than there is today. If the Christian witness in the sciences was a large, but not the only part, of the Academy's aim, it was, nevertheless, rare that a man who would combine both the scientific and religious in his own person, such as Professor James R. McConnell, was successfully nominated for membership.

This gives us all the more reason for celebration at the very signal distinction he has been given, and the Institute for Advanced Studies and Maynooth, who have both been Alma Mater to him, are equal in celebration here tonight.

Foundation Stone of New Students'
Restaurant and Sports Centre
24 May 1991

It is difficult to predict the vagaries of weather in Ireland at any time, and on the plains of north Kildare in particular. The clouds and mists that cling to these lands are slow to release their hold in the mornings, so when the Minister for Education, Mary O'Rourke, selected 8.00 a.m. as the hour for laying this Foundation Stone, I really thought we had tempted providence too far this time. However this magnificent sunny morning has very effectively banished all scepticism!

Last year the Government under its programme for Increased Student Intake in the Universities, made available additional monies for the improvement of the physical infrastructures of the Colleges. This College has been very poorly endowed in terms of indoor sports facilities and the original dining provision in the Arts Building has grown very inadequate with the growth in student numbers.

This new building under construction will have an area of over 2200 square metres. Six hundred and forty square metres is devoted to the Sports Hall and 420 square metres to the ancillary areas. The Sports Hall will be big enough to host inter-varsity basketball, netball, volleyball and indoor football. In addition a large room will be provided for weight lifting. Offices for the Student Union officers, sports officer, travel shop and a small general shop will also be included.

A very generous foyer will be located between the Sports Hall and the restaurant. The large restaurant of six hundred and forty square metres will be divided into two sections, one for main meals and one for lighter snacks, and it will have a fully serviced kitchen and self-service area.

The government has made available a sum of £600,000 towards the two million pounds cost of this building and the refurbishment of the dining area in the Arts Building. The balance of the funding will be provided through private arrangements within the College.

Construction began on site here on 19 March last and we are assured the building will be handed over to the College on 30 September next. Obviously this will be a record for a building of this nature and we look forward greatly to having this fine new facility for the new academic year.

I warmly thank the Minister for coming to formally lay the Foundation Stone today and also for her support through which the government funding aid was received. Recalling that she was one of the first lay students to enter the newly-opened up Maynooth in the mid-nineteen sixties, when in fact she and I were contemporaries here, we assure her always of the warmest of welcomes, and also of our gratitude for the positive support she has always shown not only to the various capital projects from Maynooth submitted to her, but also for her strong encouragement of the new university legislation which will alter Maynooth's position within the National University of Ireland.

The Social Question One Hundred Years After
Rerum Novarum.
12 June 1991
To open the Conference and introduce the Opening Lecture by
Archbishop Cahal B. Daly

I am delighted as President of the College to welcome you here for the opening of this major International Conference to mark the Centenary of *Rerum Novarum* by focusing on the social issues of to-day in the light of the past achievements of the century in Catholic social statements. In a particular way I want to welcome the Golden Jubiliarians, the Ordination Class of 1941, who were pioneers in their foundation of the Christus Rex Society, which was a significant forum for the discussion of social issues since that time.

Pope Leo focused on the condemnation of socialism and the class struggle, while strongly affirming the right of workers to a just wage, and the obligation of the state to protect the poor and the weak. A century later Pope John Paul's *Centesimus Annus*, which some, I think perhaps a little inaccurately, would regard as his first social encyclical, covers many of the same themes.

Particularly noteworthy is the promotion by the Church today of those aspects of human behaviour which favour a true culture of peace, as opposed to systems in which the individual is lost sight of, his freedom and creativity is neglected, and in which his greatness is usually posited in the arts of conflict and war.

Any move forward may mean making important changes in our lifestyles, to limit the waste and the colossal damage to the environment, which may unfortunately be already in some cases too far gone for remedy, so enabling every individual and all the peoples of the earth to have a sufficient share of its resources, which is their right as beings made in the image of God. Certainly new spiritual and material resources are unrgently needed today to face the new types of social issues, so as to obtain for our times a new and overall enrichment of the family of nations.

I have great pleasure in introducing the opening speaker of the Conference, His Grace Most Rev Cahal B. Daly, Cardinal elect. The Archbishop has been the outstanding figure in the Irish Church for very many years who has been a pathfinder in his comment and direction on Irish Social Questions.

Opening of University Village Apartments
3 October 1991

Over the past six or seven years the College has been greatly strengthened by the suppport and encouragement of many friends in the United States. We are assembled here this morning in our new University Village which has been constructed on a site which had lain vacant since the North Campus was first developed in the early 1970s.

These four buildings, which are a model of tasteful design and landscaping, were made possible by Section 27 of the Finance Act, whereby relief can be obtained by writing off some construction costs against rental income. Construction of these four residences began in April 1990, and they were handed over to the College on 29 May last. They will house two hundred and forty students in forty eight apartments, which will greatly relieve the acute accommodation shortage for students in Maynooth town itself and the surrounding areas. The total cost was approximately four million pounds repayable by the College over a twenty year period under the above-mentioned financial scheme.

One of the very earliest sources of support for the College's programme in the United States came from two staunch friends, Charles and Angela Hargadon of Louisville, Kentucky. Although they have visited the College and take a very personal interest in its development, unfortunately they are unable to be with us today because of illness. The College proposes to commemorate their pioneering support by naming the first of these buildings in their honour.

Los Angeles is a vibrant city and full of the vitality that belongs to the new and the strong, with a great richness of culture. It is the capital of the Pacific rim, and the world's leading producer of aircraft and military ordnance, as well as being a great world centre for communications, and the shipping, financial and distribution industries.

It is easy to forget that Los Angeles has six world-class universities. Many Irish emigrants flocked there, and California at large was one of the two great centres to which Irish priests have continued to come in significant numbers right since the beginnings with Bishop Francis Diego y Moreno and Fray Junipero Serra.

It was into this wonderful setting that the Maynooth campaign for the restoration of its seminary buildings came in the mid-1980s. It represented a partnership here in Ireland of the Church and the corporate sector and it was hoped that those of Irish descent in the USA would lend their efforts to this very worthy cause. That project was adopted enthusiastically by Peter and Pamela Mullin and later by stalwart friends of Maynooth such as Richard Riordan and the Leavey and McCarthy families.

By naming the other three magnificent residences after these families, Mullin Hall, Leavey Hall and Riordan Hall, the College wishes to commemorate their support and generosity in perpetuity.

We are honoured to have with us a very large number of the Friends of the College from the United States and all over Ireland today, particularly Cardinal Roger Mahony, Archbishop of Los Angeles, and the Chairman of the Maynooth Trustees, Cardinal Cahal B. Daly. I have the great honour to ask their Eminences to dedicate these buildings in honour of Charles and Angela Hargadon, Peter and Pamela Mullin, Thomas and Kathleen Leavey McCarthy, and Richard Riordan, and to ask them to accept in this commemoration a gratitude from all of us here in Maynooth which it is not possible to put into words. The realisation of the fine accommodation which so many generations of Maynooth students will enjoy here will best register the significance of what their guidance and support has meant to this institution.

Our Lady of the Angels
Unveiling of the Los Angeles Memorial Statue
by the Archbishop of Los Angeles
3 October 1991

Since the days when Fray Junipero Serra walked the length and breath of California Irish priests have travelled across the six thousand miles that separates Ireland from the Pacific shores, to minister all across the state of California. That number was of most significance during the first half of the twentieth century.

Today we are honoured to have with us Cardinal Roger Mahony, Archbishop of Los Angeles, together with a distinguished lay group from his diocese ,which was at the heart of the Maynooth endeavour in California. Thanks to their generosity a very great number of projects in the College that will be of lasting value have come to fruition.

To mark the outstanding contribution which Irish priests have made to the City of the Angels over the years members of this group visiting us today resolved to commemorate their dedicated work. They commissioned the renowned Mexican sculptor, Victor Gutierrez of Mexico City, to create this beautiful bronze of the Patron of Los Angeles. The work of Victor Gutierrez is well known and highly admired in California as much as it is in Mexico, and we are delighted to have this very fine specimen of his work here at Maynooth.

I warmly thank all those associated with this inspired project for their generosity and assure them that this statue will long be treasured and venerated here at the heart of the Catholic Church in Ireland.

I have pleasure now in inviting Cardinal Mahony to bless and dedicate this statue and garden.

The Royal College of Surgeons in Ireland
Charter Day Dinner
Proposal of Toast of the College
8 February 1992

My pleasant duty tonight is to propose the toast of the Royal College of Surgeons in Ireland on this occasion of the Charter Day Dinner.

I have doubts that I am qualified for this task. I did have the honour last November of conferring the degrees of the National University on the *alumni* of this College, and I may perhaps mischievously claim another link, ancient and weak this time, with the denizens of this venerable institution. It's told of the Battle of Moytura, near Cong, in the year 487 BC, that the leader, Nuadhat, lost his hand there, and had a silver replacement made: the first reference to an artificial limb in Western literature. It's now the well-known emblem of the Irish Army Medical Corps as Colonel Clune will vouch, and of course it features prominently in the crest of the Royal College of Surgeons. The College I come from in Irish is 'Magh Nuadhat;' the plain or clearing of Nuadhat, and perhaps Mr Hederman felt that the bond of the silver hand might engender a silver tongue for tonight's requirements.

But still I have doubts that I am qualified for this task. Traditionally, in the Universities, the toast was put into a cup called the bishop, the cardinal, or the *copus*. Bishop or Cardinal I am not, and if anyone calls me a *copus* I shall have to challenge him to a duel.

But before the toast I should express my pleasure at the presence of their Excellencies the Ambassadors of the United States, of the United Kingdom, and of Germany; His Grace Most Rev Donal Caird, Archbishop of Dublin; Sir Terence English of the Royal College of Surgeons (England); and last, but not least, of Mr F.A. Duff, Fellow of fifty years.

To mention any more would simply be to introduce household names to household names.

In Evelyn Waugh's novel *The Loved One* , one of the characters is an ex-RAF Squadron Leader called Denis Barlow. He makes a kind of living in Hollywood as a master-dispenser of literary quotations. My generation grew up in the same culture, and we are now veterans of the hardy regimen of the Greek and Latin classics before it disappeared into the computer wonderland.

From that time I have a gruesome medical souvenir, courtesy of Plutarch.

Alexander the Great had summoned three thousand actors and artists from Greece to Ecbatana in Media. The imperial carnival was cut short however when Alexander's bosom friend, Hephaestion, got a fever. Being a young man and a soldier, Plutarch says, he could not confine himself to the strict diet his physician prescribed. In any case his physician, Glaucus, had gone to the theatre. Hephaestion ate a fowl, drank a generous draft of wine, and died.

Alexander was, the phrase has it, 'transported beyond reason.' He had the physician crucified, banned all music, had the tails of all his horses and mules cut, and then threw down the battlements of the neighbouring cities. So however poorly done by by his patients a surgeon may occasionally feel today, things have improved.

We are not in church, nor on a psychiatrist's couch, but we should still give a thought to what we are.

There is a favourite doctor in the memory of every family, because the medical profession is at the very heart of existence. There is nothing of the random or of chance about it. The word *consilium* in the motto of this College has a multiple battery of meaning: deliberation, decision, stratagem, wisdom, good sense. You are an order of humanity, chastened by the reality of pain and suffering. You are modestly jubilant in your gifts of consolation and healing. You are the perennial response to the antiphon of Hippocrates: 'Life is short, but art is long.'

The Irish proverb says that we dine more easily with neighbours. The distinguished guests I singled out at the start may wish to take with them a few souvenirs from the not-so-secret history of the College.

The College, these guests will be glad to know, has *alumni* everywhere. The name of the President of the Students' Union, here present, is Bassam Nasr. He will know the great names in Arab medicine from the Middle Ages.

Had our guests been around in 1797 they might have met our President Hartigan marching around Dublin with a pair of kittens in his greatcoat pocket.

In 1916, they would have seen the friend of W. B. Yeats, Lady Constance Markiewicz, who commanded the College 'garrison', surrender her sword to an embarrassed young English officer. There is a street named for her in Warsaw.

Should our guests look under 'fascia' and 'ligament' in a medical dictionary they will find the name of President Colles.

'Jacob's membrane' was baptised here.

Preventive medicine was born here. Adams McConnell pioneered brain surgery in Ireland, and, in 1885, Agnes Shannon became the first woman medical student in Britain and Ireland. There are other proud *etceteras*.

Haec olim meminisse juvabit. It will always be sweet to recall such things.

As I ask you to rise for the toast – I will adapt a line from a Dubliner, Sheridan, in the *School for Scandal*:

'Let the toast pass, drink to the Royal College of Surgeons.'

International Conference on the Life and Theology of Hans Urs Von Balthasar: Christ, Beauty and the Third Millennium
Maynooth 1 May 1992

Your Excellencies, fathers, sisters, ladies and gentlemen:

I am delighted to welcome you here this evening for the formal opening of the international conference on the life and theology of Urs Von Balthasar and I want to extend a particular word of welcome to His Excellency Archbishop Gerada, Apostolic Nuncio, and to His Excellency, the Australian Ambassador, Mr Terence McCarthy and Mrs Margaret McCarthy. We are very honoured indeed to have them with us here tonight.

Urs Von Balthasar's first published work appeared 67 years ago and right up to the time of his most unexpected death his output continued to present the most stimulating and relevant ideas so badly needed today by both the Church and individual members of it. Great theological works are normally rooted in the times in which they appeared but Urs Von Balthasar's work, probably from the highly unusual roots from which it sprung, has in fact grown more relevant to the needs of the time than when it first appeared; a very eloquent witness to his prophetic role in the Church through most of this century.

I had the great privilege of knowing him well for most of a decade, when I joined him on the International Theological Commission, and also when we worked closely together helping with the extraordinary Synod of Bishops to commemorate the 20th anniversary of Vatican II in 1985; the Synod from which came the historic proposal for a new universal catechism from Cardinal Bernard Law. About ten years ago we had shared a taxi together to Fiumicino airport, but because of a sudden strike at the airport we were left together for most of a day, which was I suppose when I first got to know him well, and which later led him to involve me as a member of the editorial board for the launch of the British and Irish edition of *Communio*. One of my greatest regrets at the time of his death was that he had agreed to come here to give the main student's retreat the following year. One of my most cherished memories of him was at a piano recital of some of his favourite pieces, and a reception, given by Cardinal Ratzinger, in the Castel Sant' Angelo, on 29 September 1985, to mark his 80th Birthday.

Urs Von Balthasar was a most civilised and urbane man, a cheerful and delightful companion, with a wry sense of humour. He could put down those who disagreed with him in the most polite, concerned, but devastating way. On one occasion when Fr Yves Congar, the legendary Dominican theologian, had been holding forth at great length, and with great passion, as was his custom, on something with which Von Balthasar did not agree, Von Balthasar said at the end: 'You have made some very fine points, Fr Congar. In fact I held similar opinions when I was a young man!'

I remember at the first meeting of the International Theological Commission which I attended, Cardinal Seper, who was then Prefect of the Congregation for the Doctrine of the Faith, and therefore *ex officio* President of the Theological Commission, asked us all to introduce ourselves, as there were quite a few new members then. As each man's turn came some very impressive titles were announced; Dr X, Professor of Dogmatic Theology, Dr Y, Professor of Moral Theology, Professor of Systematic Theology, Professor of New Testament, Professor of Church Dogmatics, etc.. When it came to Von Balthasar's turn he said: 'Urs Von Balthasar, never a Professor.'

His favourite story was one told us by the Holy Father himself. A Polish lay brother towards the end of his life in the monastery decided he would like to become a priest, and was given permission to begin his studies with the help of some learned men in the monastery. Unfortunately the brother, who, at the best of times never had much aptitude for study, found the going increasingly difficult, his headed buzzing and confused with reams of dogmatic theology, moral theology, church history, scripture, and canon law. Just before his final examination he had been studying canon law, with particular reference to dispensations. Eventually the day came when he went in for his final, oral, examination, before the Abbot and the chief people of the monastery. The Abbot thought that to be kind he would start him off with an easy question so as to set him at his ease, and said: 'How many Gods are there, brother?' After a lot of thought, because he suspected a trap, the brother answered: 'One, Lord Abbot.' The Abbot was amused at the amount of thought that had gone into the answer, and said: 'But could there not be more?' And quick as a flash this time, and suddenly remembering his Canon Law, the brother said: 'Only with the special permission of the Holy See.'

I tell these little humorous incidents not simply for enjoyment's sake only, but more to illustrate some significant aspects of Von Balthasar's approach to life and his method in theology which surfaced all through his works. He was undoubtedly for quite some years, the greatest living theologian, always profound, but always absolutely down to earth, totally against all impressive-sounding theological statements that could be regarded as woolly or meaningless, utterly and completely loyal to the Holy See, yet trenchantly against what he would regard as forms of exaggerated loyalty which he regarded as positively harmful. He was always a man of the Church and a man of the civilised world. His post-graduate students were often treated to a recital of Mozart at the opening of an interview.

He was enormously concerned with the Church and world in the post-Vatican II period, and with exposing the hidden ambiguities and inclinations of many trends in theology over the past twenty years; the trend to the Bible, while neglecting the subsequent tradition; the trend to the liturgy which so often lost the core and degenerated into spiritual managing and the self-satisfaction of the community; the trend towards the form of ecumenical movement which aimed at levelling ones own traditions totally; the trend to the secular world for what was termed 'relevance' while devaluing or forgetting the mystical and the sacred, where he felt God was primarily met; or against the trend for a fashionable theological pluralism.

It is almost impossible to survey Von Balthasar's theology, but it has been described as as an unfolding in the unity of experienced event and reflective thought. This appears clearly in his major work since 1961 which is the theme of this Conference. It is arranged as a trilogy, which intends to unfold the centre of the Christian faith. The three guiding points of view are taken from the medieval transcendentals according to which the fundamental qualities of the true, the good, and the beautiful, belong to being as such, and which apply analogously to the revelation event itself. Theology, then, has to be set forth within these three perimeters of the good, the true, and the beautiful, as theological 'aesthetic', as theological 'dramatic' and as theological 'logic;' the three hinges of this Conference.

Within this task tonight's topic, theological aesthetics, forms the fundamental access to the mystery of revelation. It is where the trilogy begins. Revelation does not depend on the spontaneity of the one receiving it, who can grasp what is hidden within himself; revelation instead comes from being receptive to what is showing itself, and to be as it is in itself. Only in this way can the love of God in Christ begin to be perceived as the infinite fullness of the goodness and truth of God's goodness and truth, present in a hidden way in finite human form and yet being still revealed therein.

Such an experience of revelation does not happen to the uninvolved observer, who considers what is being offered to him in a detached and clinical way, or who persist in a pleasurable aestheticism. The act of perceiving is only the first step; one has then to proceed to being enraptured, to being carried away, away from our own preoccupations with self and joined into the event of the love between Father, Son and Spirit.

May I pay a warm tribute to Frs Bede McGregor and Tom Norris, and their helpers, who were inspired to organise this conference on such an important and critical theological area. Your attendance in such numbers is an ample vindication of the enormous efforts they put into this event.

I have great pleasure in introducing the Rev Noel Dermot O Donoghue, formerly professor in this College and in Edinburgh, to speak to us on the first aspect of this Conference: Theological aesthetics in Von Balthasar.

International Conference on
Pastores Dabo Vobis
14 May 1993

You Eminences, Your Excellencies, My Lords, Fathers and Sisters, Ladies and Gentlemen:

I am delighted to welcome so many people here today for our International Conference on the Post-Synod Exhortation of our Holy Father Pope John Paul II. *Pastores Dabo Vobis* was issued by the Holy Father not yet fourteen months ago. A year and a half ago when I first proposed to the Trustees of the College that we hold a Conference on the theme of the 1990 Synod of Bishops, it was greeted with enthusiasm, and after the publication of *Pastores Dabo Vobis* we began straight away to make concrete plans.

I want to express our gratitude to Cardinal Daly for the strong support and leadership which he has given to this Conference since it was first proposed. I know how much he shares with us here at Maynooth our deep concern for the best possible training and formation of priests in the circumstances of today, and we value his presence here despite very many other pressing pastoral commitments which he has this weekend. Fathers Bede McGregor and Thomas Norris and their helpers have done a marvellous work in bringing this Conference to fruition; the fact that we have more than 250 participants is ample warrant of how worthy a project this is.

We are deeply honoured indeed to have as our opening speaker His Eminence Cardinal Pio Laghi, Prefect of the Congregation for Catholic Education. It is nine years since we were honoured by the visit of his predecessor Cardinal William Baum, when he blessed our magnificent new John Paul II Library on its opening day in 1984. You are all aware of the central role which Cardinal Laghi had in the preparation of the Synod and in the elaboration of *Pastores Dabo Vobis* itself, so it is especially appropriate to have him deliver the keynote address. Again, I know very well the many commitments he has this week and deeply appreciate the effort which he has made to be with us today.

In the perspective of history I suppose the 1990s will go down as a period of exceptional volatility. Many positive, many negative things are appearing. We have recently seen the re-integration of Europe with all the challenges, opportunities and problems which it brings. Last week here at Maynooth we had a meeting of 146 of the Rectors and Presidents of the universities in Europe; Civil universities, obviously, as well as Catholic and Pontifical. It was one of the largest working meetings of university Heads ever held in Europe and it was a great privilege for the College to host it. I suppose university and third level institutions in general are excellent barometers of the state of evolution of society and it was particularly interesting to hear the views of the 26 Rectors we had here from Eastern European universities, especially in relation to their attempts to restore theology once again to its rightful place in their curriculum.

There are many parts of the world today in which there is a magnificent flowering of vocations; there are other areas of the world, unfortunately the ones with which we are more familiar, where there is an equally dramatic shortage. Many priests who have been ordained for some time have grown discouraged by the demands of a society which had radically mutated from that into which they were ordained. I think the day is long gone when any system of seminary formation no matter how perfect, could produce a priest at the end of seven years, fitted *ab initio* for a life-long ministry. The question of on-going formation of priests and their support, especially in the early years of the ministry is something which must concern us all. At the end of the Synod the Holy Father said that in the face of the crisis which the Church in the Western countries especially is facing, the first answer of the Church must be a total act of faith in the Holy Spirit, and he assured us that this 'trusting abandonment will not disappoint if we remain faithful to the graces we have received.'

This Conference should be seen as one fairly significant attempt to remain faithful to the graces we have received. The Church has constantly returned to the subject of the life, ministry and formation of priests, from the Synod of 1967, and the Synods of 1971 and 1974. It has often been unfairly said that the Vatican Council was the Council that said a very great deal about every part of the Church except the priest. In the years since the Council there was no subject treated by the Magisterium which did not have some direct or indirect relationship to the role of the priest in the life of the Church and the world.

Pastores Dabo Vobis has changed the focus of those earlier treatments to the process of formation itself and the quality of priestly life. We are all very conscious of the very different background from which the majority of candidates for the priestly ministry now tend to come. One can no longer automatically presume a family background of the same Catholic stability, of the same understanding of Church, as was there in the past. One must also face the fact of what avenues in the Church have attracted many of our new candidates to the path of preparation for the priesthood. A significant minority now come from the prayer group movements, some express in their lives the same thirst that inspires so many of the disparate movements of the so-called New Age. There are areas which we must face, not so much to condemn or disapprove, but to become sensitive to the issues in the hearts of people which are causing these popular movements to arise in the world. Despite all its very obvious materialism of outlook, even unfortunately in some religious forms today, we are not living in a non-religious age, but quite the opposite. It is an era of immense challenge to the Church, especially in the West, to rise in an inspired way to these issues; to find language and approaches which will reach the hearts of so many today and assuage the thirst they have for something that transcends the level of the horizontal and material which so pervades our culture.

The Church's work in the formation of priests is a continuation of Christ's own work. I think it is very worthy of note that the image which the Synod and our Document puts before us is that of the Shepherd; one of the most profound and moving images of leadership in the whole tradition of both covenants. In the East the shepherd leads, he does not drive, and he leads not by force or fear, but because of the love and attachment for him which the flock has. It is a beautiful and inspired image for the formation of priests today; that we should be shepherds after his own heart.

There are many desert area in the world, harsh and barren; however, after even a brief shower of rain the desert explodes in a rainbow of colourful blooms. It's another way of saying the darkest hour is often just before the dawn. It is our hope that our reflections on *Pastores Dabo Vobis*, inspired by this Conference, will help us to cause that shower of life-giving water to descend on so much of what is barren today. There are enormous problems facing the world at large today, but there are also very hopeful trends beginning to appear in the consciousness of humanity, that perhaps were never there to the same extent before. Is it too much to dare to hope that the age that will come will be one of incredible blessing, of restored ecological balance, international co-operation and of more universal harmony? There are some evidences that that view of the world that is coming may not be too utopian, but a realistic if difficult possibility. Let us hope that in being faithful to the graces we have received, we in the seminaries and universities will play a proud role in preparation for that new world.

I am honoured to present to you Cardinal Cahal Daly, Primate of All Ireland, and Chairman of our Trustees, who will introdue our speaker.

Dedication of the Heritage Wall
23 May 1993

This is an historic moment when so many distinguished Irish-Americans are gathered here with us this morning for the dedication of the Heritage Wall. All of their Irish ancestors left this country to cross what John Boyle O'Reilly called 'that bowl of bitter tears' in search of freedom and opportunity in the new world. They have returned here to Maynooth today to see the names of their Irish forebears carved into the granite slabs of this monument. The names of the three Patrons are carved across the top of the monument: Cardinal John O'Connor of New York, Cardinal Bernard Law of Boston, and Governor Robert P. Casey of Pennsylvania.

The Heritage Wall stands directly across from the main door of the John Paul Library, in the construction of which so many Irish Americans had a significant hand. It encircles the monumental bronze of Imogen Stuart which depicts the Holy Father and two children during the Papal Mass in Phoenix Park, Dublin in October 1979. The Pope blessed the foundation stone of this library on his visit here in 1979. The bronze was unveiled here in 1985 to commemorate the generosity of all those people here in Ireland and in the United States who contributed to the erection of this magnificient new Library. The structure and landscaping of the Heritage Wall complements that bronze extremely well.

The circling mound of earth brings up the memory of the ancient Irish earthen forts that can still be seen dotted so plentifully around the Irish hillsides today. These ancient dwelling sites were regarded as sacred places in rural Ireland. Frequently such sites wre given by prominent individuals as sites for churches in the early years of Christianity in Ireland. This is why many of the very ancient churches in Ireland are located in circular sites.

The Heritage Wall itself is carved from Wicklow granite. Grantie is very different in its origin from sedimentary stones like limestone, because it wells up from the molten centre of the earth itself; part of the very innermost nature of the land on which we stand. The enclosed circular area of the monument is paved in granite sets also.

So we have here a very special form of monument deliberately designed to recall what is central in our heritage and in the bonds of filial piety that bind this country and the North Eastern United States. The molten bronze from which the figures were created has always been taken as a symbol of persistence and durability; something which has always been characteristic of the bonds between our nations. The earthen mound and the granite call our minds back to beginnings, and it is about beginnings and the most precious things in the human heart that this monument is concerned to perpetuate. It was from here at Maynooth that so many Irish priests went out to follow the paths of the emigrants all through the last century and the early part of this. As we proceed to today's dedication we keep green in our memories the noble qualities of mind and spirit which has been their heritage to us, and we trust that it will be their qualities even more than their names which will be recalled here, and inspire us to imitate the paths which their lives laid down.

Dedication of The Lady Chapel Altar
24 May 1993

A few weeks ago in this College Chapel Cardinal Daly ordained twenty eight young men for the Diaconate, in the age old ceremony of the laying on of hands in silence, and the prayer for the giving of the Holy Spirit, as we read of in today's first reading

Nearly eleven thousand priests have gone out from this College to serve as priests in every parish in Ireland, all over the English speaking world, and all over the third world, to India (in a mission from here in 1838), the Far East in the Mission founded from Maynooth in 1917 (Columban fathers), Africa, and more recently in South America. In the New York area a rota of six new Maynooth priests are now kept to help with the new influx of Irish emigrants, and the same holds true to a lesser extent in many other areas of the continental US.

The Cardinal is offering this Mass for Mrs Casey's grandmother, from whom she first knew of Maynooth College, a memory going back into the 1870s. If she and her father came to the College and visited this church, she would have found it the same as it is for Mass this morning. This church, such an architectural gem in itself, is in another sense a symbol of the things that are unchanging in the Church, and that must pass unaltered from generation to generation in very different times and circumstances: things primarily to which this College is dedicated; the 'care/cure of souls', in the ancient medieval phrase; which is the heart of the work of the priest, the heart of the work of this College.

To those who know a little of Christian history, probably the most moving of all the reflections it brings is not the thought of the great events and the well-remembered saints, but of those innumerable millions of obscure people, every one with his or her own individual hopes and fears and joys, sorrows and loves, sins temptations and prayers. They may have left very little trace in the normal sense in the world today, maybe not even a name, but have passed to God entirely forgotton by the human race. Yet each of them believed and prayed, as you and I now believe and pray, and found the journey hard, grew slack, repented and started again. Each of them worshipped at the Eucharist, and found their thoughts wandering and tried again.

There is a little badly spelled rustic epitaph of the fourth century in Asia Minor: 'Here sleeps the blessed Chione, who has found the new Jerusalem, for she prayed much.'

Not another word is known of Chione, some peasant woman who lived in that vanished world of Christian Anatolia. But how wonderful if all that should survive of us after sixteen centuries was that one had prayed so much that the neighbours who saw all ones life were sure one must have found the new Jerusalem? What did the Sunday Eucharist in her village church every week for a lifetime mean to the blessed Chione – and to the millions like her then and every year since? The sheer, stupendous quantity of the love of God which this ever-repeated action has drawn from the obscure Christian multitudes through the centuries is an overwhelming thought.

This love of the Eucharist became embedded deep down in the life of Christian peoples, colouring all the *via vitae* of the ordinary man and woman, marking its personal turning points, around which the life of this College is based; marriage, sickness, death, the beginning of adulthood, taking up a role of leadership in the community. The seven sacraments, symbolised in the seven standing stones at the Heritage Wall which the Cardinal dedicated yesterday, are the heart of the Christian life, the heart of the Catholic Church, the heart of the work of Maynooth.

The heart of the seven sacraments is of course the eucharistic action, which we offer this morning for the soul of Mary Farrell McCadden. It is deeply embedded in the life of Christian peoples, running through them year by year, with the feasts and the fasts, and the rhythm of the Sundays; thus the Eucharistic action became inextricably woven in to the public history of the Western world. The thought of it is inseparable from its great turning points also; Pope Leo did this on the morning before he went out to confront Attila, on the day that saw the continuity of Europe saved. Another Leo did it three and a half centuries later, when he crowned Charlemagne Holy Roman Emperor on that great circular disc of blood red stone that stands inside the main door of St Peter's Basilica. Laurence O' Toole celebrated it on the morning he daunted the Normans outside Dublin. It was what consoled and strengthened the great Oliver Plunket, Saint-Archbishop of Armagh and predecessor of Cardinal Daly; martyred at Tyburn. It was at a time when there were only 38 priests left in the whole of Ireland, and when the Mass had to be celebrated by hunted men in the remote recesses of wild hill country and marshy bogland.

Because Maynooth was the phoenix of the Irish Church, rising from the ashes of the Penal Days, its fortunes, problems, hopes and opportunities must always remain inextricably bound up with the course of the Catholic Church in Ireland. Maynooth has now two proud centuries of passing on the faith behind it; we prepare for a new century and a new millennium, something for which the Holy Father has so often called.

This morning as we offer the Mass for Mary Farrell McCadden, we are using the same words and gestures as they did in pagan Rome, as they did at Constantinople while the silver trumpets of the Basileus still called across the Bosphorus in what seems to us now the fabled land of the Empire of Byzantium; the same rite used by Charles de Foucauld in the desert, by Killian, by Gaul, by Romuald, by Columban; we do it this morning with texts that have not changed more than a few syllables since Patrick used these very words at Slane and Armagh fifteen and a half centuries ago. Let us give thanks as we offer this Mass for another blessed Chione, Mary Farrell McCadden. We ask that God will crown her with the fruits of her labours, which we see so evidently in the strong faith of her grandchild and great grandchild here with us today, and in the family and friends we are so privileged to have with us for these memorable days at Maynooth.

We face volatile and unpredictable times in which the Church will have much to suffer. We are strengthened by the outpouring of the Spirit that has been promised in the sacraments; and consoled by the words of Our Lord in the Gospel today: 'I have overcome the world.'

Callan Science Building
At the Opening by An Taoiseach, Mr Albert Reynolds
28 September 1993

Taoiseach, Your Eminence, Guests, Members of Staff and Students:

This is a landmark day in the history of Maynooth; this new building will accommodate 730 students, 280 in Computer Science, and 450 in Biology, at all levels ranging from first year undergraduate to doctoral level. The new facilities will provide our biology students with experience in handling the most modern scientific equipment, and an in-depth exposure to advanced laboratory procedures.

The Callan Building will also provide key facilities for advanced research programmes in its designated laboratories. These research programmes represent the interface between the university world and industrial work: the continuum of a research agenda, in which applied and basic research are intrinsically linked. This research infrastructure will have long term implications for national development in the rapidly growing areas of computer software and biotechnological industries.

This magnificent new building, and it truly is magnificent, has been funded with assistance from the EC Structural Funds Programme, 1990-93. This European contribution to the infrastructure of Maynooth calls to mind an earlier contribution of human capital which came to Maynooth in 1795 when Professors from the Sorbonne at the University of Paris, and some other prestigious French universities, arrived to staff the newly founded College, particularly in Physics and Theology. From those very early beginnings Maynooth has naturally always treasured its European connections, and even further afield, for the College has always looked to the world rather than to Ireland alone. Our students today avail of the Erasmus mobility scheme, our history Department is part of the ECTS programme, and Maynooth academics are represented in all the major ECLAIR, Inter-Reg, Horizon, and the Human Capital and Mobility Programmes.

This new Science Building represents not only an additional facility, but also constitutes an important element in shaping the evolution of the north campus of the University. Together with the new restaurant and sports facility funded by a mixture of private and public funds, this building defines and creates an ambience of collegiate life and a display of all that is best in modern Irish architecture. The Callan Building itself is a sensitive treatment of a brief which required large scale laboratory facilities, and consequently required a deep and massive building. But by the inclusion of the internal courtyard, landscaped with plants chosen with an eye to their pedagogical value in the Biology teaching programme, and by the provision of this extensive concourse, the design team have created a building that is first class in a professional sense, but which never succumbed to the sacrifice of a human scale and aesthetic ambience which so often has to happen in modern buildings.

At Maynooth, in terms of its older buildings and grounds, we are fortunate to have a College campus that must be reckoned as one of the most attractive in the world. It's no harm to remember occasionally that those beautiful quadrangles and gracious buildings have come to us, not from a period of full and plenty, but from one of the most economically deprived periods in the history of our land, and in the history of this College. Of all the arts I often think that architecture is one of the most slow to make an impression, but one of the most lasting in its effects once that impression is made. Despite the very necessary rigid constraints on all funding today, the design team have managed to combine utility and beauty in this building and its environs in a remarkable way. Up to four or five years ago this north campus used to impress me as the approximate equivalent of Shakespeare's blasted heath on the plains of north Kildare. With the addition of the six new buildings here over the past three years, and seventh in progress, the design teams have begun to leave a campus of which future generations will be as proud as we are of our nineteenth century architectural heritage.

So for this, as well as for many other reasons I want to warmly thank the design team for what they have given us.

Lastly, I come to a man whose name in justice should be writ large across all of this building: Professor Seamus Smyth, Vice-President, under whose chairmanship the Callan Building was designed and built to such a high standard. When I was Vice-President I chaired only one Design Team; that involved with the construction of the new Library a decade ago, and I know very well what such a task entails. Professor Smyth however had the misfortune to be Vice-President at a time when the President decided to try and build four large new apartment buildings, a sports centre, a restaurant, a major science building, and a new students' union, all of which have gone up in the space of the last three years. Seamus Smyth has borne an enormous burden in bringing all of these new projects into realisation, and everyone can tell of the patience, imagination, dedication and fortitude, which he brought to these, as he does to every task in which he is involved. All of us, and all who will use this building owe him an immense debt, as indeed we do to his wife Rosemary and family who bore the long and necessary absences from home which all of this work entailed.

I have great pleasure in welcoming An Taoiseach, Mr Albert Reynolds, TD, to speak to us now. I know personally of his interest in this College which has manifested itself in so many ways. He laid the Foundation Stone of this building in June of last year – it stands in the landscaped garden outside – and made time in a very hectic schedule to come to perform today's opening.

Last May when for the first time in Ireland 146 of the Presidents of the Universities of Europe met here at Maynooth, the Taoiseach took the unprecedented step of inviting all those present to a reception and dinner in the State Apartments of Dublin Castle, which he hosted himself. It left an impression on all the participants which will be long remembered. Taoiseach, thank you for coming to day; thank you for being the staunch friend to the College which you so truly have been. I have pleasure now in inviting you to speak to our guests, and the staff and students.

New Student Centre
16 January 1994

Within a few weeks of my appointment as President nine years ago I did an interview for a staff magazine. One of the questions asked what my priorities would be during my time in office. I remember replying then that I thought it a shame that the North Campus of the College seemed so bare, uninviting and windswept, in comparison to the ivy-covered and gracious walls of the old College squares to the south across the Galway road. People seemed always to want to flee from here when their work was done. It was a pity as the site had great potential for an expansion of the university buildings.

Since 1989 we have been very fortunate through several extremely creative projects to have built four new student residences, a sports centre, student restaurant, the Callan Science Building, and now this new student centre. Three days ago the Minister for Education, Ms Niamh Bhreathnach, announced that £5m would be awarded to Maynooth for a second new Science building and while I will not see this built in my own time as

President I am enormously enthused by this further vote of confidence in the future of the science departments in the College.

The North Campus has been transformed over the last five years with a warmer motif than the more severe original architectural styles used here. I think we now have a very inviting campus here in which the interplay of buildings and landscaping has been superbly done, despite the inevitable shortage of funding, and a very attractive ambience in modern form to complement the beautiful Georgian and Gothic styles of the South Campus. While outside appearances are important naturally they are not to be compared with the facilities they house, and in this respect we have done well also.

In that interview back in 1985 I said that one of the things which most concerned me was the provision of facilities for students over and above the academic. For that reason it has been very gratifying to me that we have been able to provide the four new apartment buildings as well as the Sports Centre, Restaurant and now this fine new Student Centre. While the old Student Union Building was a welcome addition in the 1970s, the seemingly endless additions and adaptations to what was essentially a prefabricated structure over the intervening years, led to a building probably rich in character, but deficient in every other way. It was felt that the only rational decision would be to demolish the old building, but due to problems with timing it would not be possible to have the new building in service until close to Christmas of the present academic year. I want to register the thanks of Professor Smyth and myself to the students for bearing with the lack of a building since last Summer and I know the new one will well compensate for the inconvenience.

The situation reminded me of the story of the Quaker Meeting House of bygone days in Pennsylvania. The Meeting decided that a new Meeting House should be built; that as far as possible the material of the old Meeting House should be used in the construction of the new; and that the old Meeting House should continue in use until the new one was ready. We didn't quite get to that stage here, but at times the resemblance threatened to be uncomfortable.

Plans for this new Centre evolved through a series of discussions with the Student Union Executive during 1992-93, and the idea was approved in principle by the Trustees at their meeting last March. The building has a capacity for 1,000 students and consists of a fine function room and servery, a glazed atrium, a bar, three committee rooms, a green room and stores and toilets. The overall impression is one of light, spaciousness and comfortable fitted seating, and it will provide the students with a very necessary and long-awaited social facility. By common agreement it represents the most salubrious Student Centre on any Irish Campus at present.

I warmly congratulate all concerned and have great pleasure in declaring this new Student Centre open.

Knighthood of St Gregory
15 May 1994
Presentation of Mr William E. McCann
for Knighthood of the Order of St Gregory

The Knighthood of the Order of St Gergory was instituted by Pope Gregory XVI, and was reformed by Pope St Pius X. It is one of the highest honours that the Church bestows on a layman who is not a Head of State.

The significance of this Knighthood is underlined by the patronage it was given by Pope Gregory XVI: The Order of Pope St Gregory the Great. Gregory the Great died in 604, and the qualities of that saintly Pope who so finely balanced the temporal and the spiritual, are the qualities the Church wishes to discern in those selected for this high honour. Born into a wealthy patrician family, and at the age of 30 given Rome's highest civil office, Prefect of the City, Gregory was declared a Doctor of the Church after his death, distinguished as much for spiritual as for temporal leadership.

Despite his material success he felt a vocation to Monasticism, and he converted his home into a Benedictine Abbey. For seven years he was ambassador at Constantinople, and then was chief adviser to Pelagius II. It was he who was the significant exponent of the doctrine of divided powers: the emperor was God's vicar in things temporal, the Pope in matters spiritual. He was a prolific author in liturgy and theology, and he made a lasting contribution to the development of the Plainsong which bears his name today, Gregorian Chant.

In ancient Roman society the Knights or Equites ranked just below the senatorial class. In medieval history the Knight became an armed warrior who belonged to the nobility, and by the 10th Century the institution of Knighthood was well established generally.

Military tenure was generally subject to the law of promogeniture, which resulted in a class of landless knights, and at the time of the Crusades these landless knights formed the great military orders of knighthood: great military as well as religious bodies. Important among these were the Knights Templars, the Knights Hospitallers, the Teutonic Knights, the Knights of Calatrava, and the Knights of Aviz.

It was into this tradition that Pope Gregory introduced the Knighthood of the Order of St Gregory the Great for truly outstanding services to the Church. The Church in Ireland through its Primate has sought and received this honour for Mr William McCann. He has been married for twenty five years to Virginia Ann Blouin and they have two children, Tiffany and Nevins. William McCann is President and Chief Executive Officer of Allied Junction Corporation. He did graduate studies at Boston University, served in the United States Navy during the Korean conflict and was a guest Lecturer on management matters at Louisiana State University.

He is a board member of several significant corporations and has been a distinguished lay leader in many ecclesiastical and civil endeavours.

In January 1981 he was invested into the Knights of Malta by his close friend Terence Cardinal Cooke, in recognition of his philanthropic work for the Archdiocese of New York, and became a Knight of the Holy Sepulchre in 1993.

William McCann was financial advisor and close friend of President Reagan, and to Presidential Candidate General Alexander Haig.

He is a man of deep personal faith, which he learned from his Irish born father and mother, and has a deep love for all things Irish, especially for the Irish Church, and for Maynooth which is so central to it.

Last October he hosted a marvellous function for Maynooth in the Immigration Museum on Ellis Island in New York Harbour when more than 500 people rallied to the cause for a night that will be long remembered. Just weeks ago he hosted an attendance of 1200 people for the Right to Life organisation in the United States. He has done significant work for the Vatican Delegation to the United Nations and is a friend and advisor to Cardinal O'Connor of New York and Archbishop McCarrick of his native Newark Diocese.

CHAPTER 11

Life Changed, not Ended

Archbishop Dermot Ryan
Pro-Prefect of the Congregation for the Evangelisation of Peoples
Former Archbishop of Dublin
Maynooth College Chapel, 28 February 1985

The preacher must never speak for himself. On this occasion he must try to speak for the sorrow and sympathy of this community.

There is no need to rehearse the biography of Archbishop Dermot Ryan. The media have done it well.

All I will mention is that he was a student of this College, and loved it in the truest sense of the word. It showed itself in the hours of unremitting labour which he devoted to its interest over many years. He was the Archbishop of the diocese in which Maynooth College is placed, and was one of its leading Trustees. Last year he was called to be the Church's chief evangelist after the Pope. And, perhaps uniquely, instead of being a Cardinal *in petto*, that is in the affectionate intentions of the Pope, he was a Cardinal for a morning only, during his obsequies, dressed up for what ancient piety called 'his birthday to heaven.' One suspects he would be, and is, captivated by the logic of it all.

The preacher represents the congregation, but he has to make his points as he sees them, and the liturgy of the Church never countenances the mere memorial of an individual, without also drawing lessons from that life for our own.

For most of his life Dr Ryan was a Professor in the area of Old Testament studies, the book of the young Jesus, and of all the Jews. There, and in the pages of the New Testament, which was so close to his heart, I shall try to find something for our inspiration and example, to serve as a portrait of how he appeared to me.

He was a man of the biblical text, and appropriately there are some central scriptural terms that sum up the man as I knew him.

An old Irish bardic poem says: 'The Prince should have a steady eye.' Dermot Ryan did. His logical turn of mind and directness of approach could at times be off-putting, and were often mistaken for something approaching cold-heartedness or lack of care. In fact it was simply the marshalling of a noble, open-hearted, and warm character, in the interest of efficient administration. He ploughed his way relentlessly through prodigious amounts of work, always keeping his eye firmly fixed on some goal. The Greek for the 'steady gaze' is *apoblepein*. It was this, Xenophon said, that the fatherland looked for in a patriot. Dr Ryan would not fail the secular test for he held Ireland and all he looked at in a steady gaze.

But – *a fortiori* – a phrase he used often, when Hebrews 11:26 speaks of 'steadfast gaze' it is Moses it has in mind. Moses left the luxury of Egypt for the sake of his people. Not earth, but Heaven in the end. Archbishop Ryan had a steady eye for perspective.

He was well-known for his insistence on the rudiments and even on rote learning. Sometimes this was mistaken for intransigence or extreme conservatism, but of course, it was not that. He was a schoolmaster. And what may seem a stubborn pedantry is in fact well rooted in the New Testament. 1 Peter 2:21 says this: Christ left us a 'perfect pattern' that we should follow in his footsteps. The word it uses for 'perfect pattern' is *hypogrammos*. It was a word used for Christ, and it was taken wholly from Greek schoolmastering. In Plato's *Protagoras* the schoolmaster wrote the headline for the pupil to copy – an *hypogrammos*. So there is and has to be a need for a Christian pedantry while we stumble onwards towards the full *logos*.

Finally, a word to bind the Testaments in a common attitude. It is a work that says 'worship,' 'piety,' 'reverence,' all together, and oddly its most striking use in the New Testament is in 1 Timothy 5:4, where the word *eusebeia* means 'filial piety in the home.' That kind of mind, a constancy to the truth in a simple setting, was very much Dr Ryan's thing.

But on a larger canvas, *eusebeia* in Isaiah 11.2 means simply 'fear of the Lord.' It is basically 'true religion'. Reverence, prayer, obedience: these things he served, and for that reason we are buoyed up with hope in our prayer this evening that the man of steadfast gaze sees now no longer in a glass darkly, but face to face.

Sheila Byrne
Student of First Science Class
St Joseph's Oratory, Maynooth, 7 March 1986

Deep within our hearts we suspect that grief for those we have lost in death must largely be a grief for ourselves. This could not be any other way, and it is perfectly natural and correct. The Liturgy of the Church reaches down to support us in this grief. We are here in this world to work out our salvation – it's a phrase so familiar and over-used that maybe we can often forget what it means or forget at least that it means something incredibly wonderful. It means that just as the life of an animal is above that of a plant, and the life of a human being above that of an animal, what our salvation means is that we have to rise above the level of human life to a share in the Divine, the life of God. If we fail to do this during our time of opportunity in this world, then we will lack the means to live at the level that is to come afterwards. When Christ our Lord was transformed in the resurrection he left his glorified life available to us in this world, principally in the seven Sacraments (which are the Church), each one of them beamed in on the great high points of human life – the 'passages' as some often call them now in modern psychology – birth, the foundation of a new family, adulthood, the role of leader-ship in the Christian community, the falling away from the path of true growth and development through sin, and death itself. Really there is only one great sacrament, the eucharist, the other six chan-nel that one sacrament into the various areas of significance in life, the Passages. The eucharist is the principal way in which we take God's life into us, so as to evolve painfully towards our destiny. Through it we can help those beyond the grave as much as those still in this world. It is the Church's belief that it is the most effective way of helping those who have died to continue their growth and development more and more in the likeness of God. The closing chapters of the Epistle to the Hebrews expresses this very beautifully.

So we are praying this evening for Sheila in the Mass and we are praying also for her family and friends, that God will help and con-sole them in their most bitter loss, until we meet again when there shall be no more weeping, or crying or sorrow. She had started out in the Science Faculty here; studying the veiled works of the creator in his creation. Given what we can know of God from his creation, it is a pity that we usually speak of our destiny in heaven in such deplorably inadequate, childish and even unattractive terms. For everything that we have known, loved, cherished and enjoyed in this world, is attractive to us only because it is a dim reflection of the God who made it; and it was left here in this world to give us a clue in some inadequate way to what he is really like. Everything we know love, cherish and enjoy in this life, is what we will see in God when we reach our salvation, except that it will be seen and enjoyed in an incredibly higher way in him than in the things in which we see his reflection now. It is a destiny beyond our wildest dreams, of which St Paul said: 'Eye has not seen, nor has ear heard, nor has it entered into the heart of man to imagine what God has prepared for those who love him.'

Looked at in this way many of the great tragedies and sorrows of this life are put in a very different setting. They are brief and passing and not worthy to be compared to what will be ours for endless ages. This should be our consolation. St Augustine said 'God is closer to us than we are to ourselves,' but if there is ever a time when that closeness is at its most intense, surely it must be in times of tragedy and intense grief – very often when we labour under the illusion in our loneliness and sorrow that we have been abandoned even by him.

The greatest cross to be borne by the human race is death. St Paul called it the last great enemy. It was this above all that Christ came to overcome, to make it merely a transition to glory. St Paul said: 'O death, where is your victory? O grave, where is your sting? Death is swallowed up in victory.' This is our faith, our hope and our confidence, and this is the spirit in which we now offer the Mass for Sheila, with you, Liam and May, Dermot and Fergal. Knowing that the flower that bloomed for such a brief time, but so beautifully, is transformed in the vision of God, and awaits a glorious reunion in the fullness of hope, where to us God will be all in all.

Terence P. Cunningham
Professor of Canon Law
Maynooth College Chapel, 23 September 1986

Only saints and fools have no fear of death: the majority of us fall somewhere in between. No matter how strong our faith the thought of death brings great apprehension; we face the great unknown about so many things, and what we do know probably fills us even more with anxiety. We know we must render an account of our stewardship to God, and part from all the familiar people and things of this world.

Christ's teaching has been reiterated so often by wise men down the ages: that the whole of our life is to be lived as a preparation for death and that the quality of our life is shown by the way in which we face death.

Dr Terence Cunningham was a sublime example in this regard. When he told me last March that he was going into hospital I did not realise the sad news that was to come a few days later: that his case was beyond hope. Long ago one of the great saints was asked what he would do if he were to be told he would die tomorrow: 'I would carry on with what I was at.' And this is what Dr Cunningham did. Very few knew his life was to be so short. Certainly his colleagues never heard from him that it was to be so. He told me he would continue to lecture as long as he could, and in fact refused offers of help to finish his course of lectures for the year. Through his long and slow deterioration over the Summer no one heard him complain even though he was suffering a great deal.

He came here to Maynooth after a distinguished secondary school course in St Patrick's College, Cavan. His course here was of the same quality and he became a distinguished graduate of the Dunboyne Establishment. He was a man of duty, faithful to the letter in the subject he taught as well as in all other things. He was quiet and shy, but of strong convictions, too intelligent to be hypnotised by the newer techniques of mass appeal often demanded of men in his situation over the last few decades.

One of the most precious things in the human heart must surely be attachment to one's own and to one's own native place. Fr Terry Cunningham was absolutely devoted to and intrigued by the history of Maynooth and of the Diocese of Kilmore. His painstaking research and scholarship made many significant contributions to the history of the priests and people of Kilmore. But he also took great delight in discovering the interesting trivia that can so often be the added bonus of local history. He was delighted to discover that the last Abbot of Bangor was the first Sacristan of Maynooth. He had a deep interest in the life of Dr James Browne of the diocese of Ferns, who was Professor of Sacred Scripture and Hebrew at Maynooth, and who went down to Kilmore as its Bishop in the early decades of the last century. He had one favourite letter of Bishop Browne which he came across, and which he quoted to me often as I was also from the diocese of Ferns. It was a letter in which Dr Browne very unflatteringly compared Cavan town in size and significance to my native village of Taghmon in Co Wexford, and he lamented in the difficult circumstances of the 1830s how much he missed Maynooth and the support of all his friends there.

And I know that Dr Cunningham too would have missed Maynooth. He came here in his youth, and apart from a few short absences handed back his life to the Lord in the closing days of his thirtieth year on the College staff. To me he was successively respected teacher, valued colleague and trusted friend. He had the interests of the College at heart. I suppose having said that you have said it all, and most of what follows must be mere embroidery.

What a symmetry there is to the life of a priest when his requiem is sung at the altar where he was ordained! This church, probably the most beautiful of its kind in the world, was built from the pennies of the poor at one of the lowest periods in the history of Ireland. It was the gift of the Irish people to their priests and a statement of what the priesthood meant to them. I feel that Dr Cunningham in his quiet way lived up to these expectations. We will miss him greatly, but I know that his memory will remain green here long after those of us who were privileged to know him will have passed on into the fullness of hope.

May I offer you, his relatives and friends, on behalf of all the staff and students of Maynooth, our very deepest sympathy in your sad loss. You know that he will always be remembered in our prayers, as he will in the prayers of the fifteen thousand priests over the years who sat at his feet to be taught the laws of God and his Church.

Séamus V. O Súilleabháin, CFC
Professor of Education
Junior Chapel, Maynooth, 16 October 1986

Our late colleague was probably the most highly regarded of Irish educationalists. He was the longest serving Professor of Education in Ireland, serving on our staff in that capacity for over twenty years, right up to his death, in the afternoon of 7 June last.

Brother Séamus was by birth a US citizen, born in New York in 1921, but of course his upbringing from childhood was in his beloved West Clare. His affections were also spread through Roscommon and Belfast, where he spent long and fruitful years in teaching. Before he came to Maynooth he had a distinguished career as Head of St Mary's Teacher Training College in Marino.

His arrival in Maynooth coincided with the opening of the College to lay students – twenty years ago. And the dramatic expansion of the Higher Diploma Course here was one of the pioneering aspects of the College's expansion in its early years. His insight, determination, and hard work, built up the highly respected department and the increasingly large numbers of graduates which our Higher Diploma Course has to its credit today. That tradition and the staff which he influenced and encouraged, are his lasting and precious legacy to us. The work of the Irish Educational Studies Association was very close to his heart, and he retired as its President only two years ago. He constantly stressed the need for those who were professionally involved in education to keep in touch with research and to contribute to the educational debate. And this was his attitude right to the end.

But leaving aside his outstanding professional qualities, there were many other things in him as an individual by which those who knew him well were inspired. We admired his efficiency – his ability to steadily plod through incredible amounts of work, very necessary work, but often repetitious and boring. He was a man of duty, punctilious in everything he undertook. He was correct and upright, but above all courteous. His only concession to the magnitude of examination scripts which he had to correct after examinations each Summer was to sit out under the ancient yew trees in front of Long Corridor where Silken Thomas is reputed to have played his harp four and a half centuries ago. It was said of the philosopher Immanuel Kant, that people could set their watches by the regular time at which he set out on his walk every day. When Brother Séamus appeared at the end of May each year, sitting under the yew trees, it was a more reliable sign that Summer was nigh than the uncertain weather itself could often provide.

'Faith is the beginning and the end is love, and God is the two brought into unity. After that what comes next in importance for a Christian is whatever else that makes up a Christian gentleman.' The whole way of following Christ is well summed up in these words of Ignatius of Antioch, disciple of John the Evangelist, and the first to use the term 'Catholic,' as he was on his way to Rome to be martyred by the wild beasts in the amphitheatre. Devotion to work and duty however distasteful it may be at times, and a cultivation of the ordinary virtues of care, concern, and respect for others, form the basis of any good Christian home – this is what real spirituality is in the mind of Ignatius. And I think this idea of perfection in the ordinary things of duty is what Séamus excelled in and left us as a towering example. Despite his relentless efficiency and devotion to duty, he always cared for those who were about him and those who assisted him in his work.

Séamus was about to enter his Golden Year with the Christian Brothers. He was coming to the end of a very fruitful teaching career. Retirement would not have suited him. Very often when we see a person snatched away by sudden death at the height of their powers and achievement, it seems to us a great tragedy. But I have often thought, contrary to this, that one of the greatest blessings that God can give us is to take us to himself at the time of our greatest happiness. None of us can plan the time, and certainly not the circumstances of our death. But I think that if Séamus had his wish he would have chosen these circumstances of his passing.

Despite the many problems that teachers face in their work, I have always felt it is one of the most significant of all human vocations. Very often the results and the rewards seem non-existent or intangible. But the influence of a teacher can be very profound and it is one of the really lasting things in human life. The influence and inspiration that a committed teacher can impart is the closest thing to something eternal that can be accomplished in this life. For its influence can percolate down through the generations, helping to uplift the heart of man for countless years. That's a frightening vocation and at the same time a great consolation to all who have tried to impart knowledge and values to others. Seamus was one of those few teachers whose influence spread far beyond any individual school or county.

The new circumstances of the 19th century allowed the emergence of more significant Irishmen than had appeared together in such a brief time-span for many centuries. But a giant among the giants must surely have been Edmund Ignatius Rice. Aquinas said that compassion was love moved by the sight of misery. That was the crowning factor in that charism which helped Brother Rice and his followers in the Christian Brothers, in Philip Larkin's words, 'To robe with destinies the naked of the earth.' This living tradition was one we were privileged to see in the life of Séamus V. O Suilleabháin. As we meet this evening to offer Christ's sacrifice for him, we know that God will not be outdone in either punctiliousness or generosity. May his great and generous soul harvest the pearls of wisdom his long and full life brought to him.

Peter R. Connolly
Professor of English Language and Literature
Maynooth College Chapel, 10 February 1987

Father Peter Connolly read everything and watched television with great selectivity. The last things we remember him talking about animatedly at lunch on Monday, the day he died, was a BBC programme on Sunday night concerning the apparitions at Medjugorje. 'He spoke about it,' said a man who had been his colleague for forty years, 'as usual with penetration and lucidity.'

Peter had a splendid critical mind. Our Lady of Medjugorje, it is claimed, says that Russia will come to glorify the Lord. Russia, too, fascinated him, but I do not know if he had a comment on that.

Last year he re-read Greek Classics – Homer in Greek. He also had favourite corners, Bunyan, and small gems from medieval religious literature – but lately he was fascinated by the Czech novelist, Milan Kundera, and chuckled at Rushdie's comment on Kundera's *The Book of Laughter and Forgetting* – 'a masterpiece, full of angels, terror, ostriches and love.' He was aware of Kundera for years because of his association with the Czech New Wave films.

One of the books he read most recently was Kundera's *The Joke*, and on the second last page he underlined what follows: 'And what I said to myself was that although he would probably get over it, as the second fiddle had predicted, he would lead a very different life, a life under the watchful eye of death.' Such was Peter's life for the last few years. And on the last page, he underlined the very last line: 'Where a shiny ambulance with its headlights on stood waiting.'

That was the intellectual and the critic, but there was nothing 'shiny' about Peter Connolly, the country lad from Drumconrath in the County Meath, Maynooth priest, Oxford graduate, Professor of English Literature at Maynooth for thirty years.

For us of the more intimate historical Maynooth he is a diocesan priest less, and not to be replaced.

This lover of literature, remarkable film critic, and the author of more than one essay of critical and historical importance, was an astonishingly traditional priest: the Mass, the Sacraments, the Breviary, the Rosary. And since his retirement – the white lithe figure had to abandon the tennis courts earlier – he surprised us all by plunging into the pastoral life of Meath, his home diocese.

On this day when the bell tolls for Peter Connolly we remember that the poet he loved most was John Donne.

But today, somehow George Herbert speaks of Peter better:

> Heaven in ordinary, man well-drest
> The Milky Way, the bird of Paradise,
> Church bells beyond the stars heard, the soul's blood,
> The land of spices, something understood.

Requiescat in aeterna pace.

Judith, Patrick and Cliona Rossiter
**A brother and two sisters killed in a car crash in Wales
while on the way home to Dublin**
*Church of Our Lady of Perpetual Succour, Foxrock, Dublin
5 September 1987*

Parents can be asked to bear no greater loss than to see the children they bore, loved and cherished through so many years,pass before them out of this life.

I know that the great sympathy we all feel, the wish to be close, and to support you in this time of terrible grief over the loss of your three teenage children, my cousins, can do little to ease the pain of that wound in your hearts caused by the snatching away of those you love by death. Only time can ease the grief, a grief that we can only dimly share in.

An old saying had it that those whom the gods love die young. Is there some small ray of hope here that might open a crack of light to ease our grief? How often do we know people who have lived, tragically, long past their useful lives, and seen the sickness, infirmity of a pitiable kind, their disillusionment and helplessness? It is a state of affairs far removed from the active, productive and happy times they enjoyed in their prime, and it does help one to see the core of wisdom in that old saying.

To die young in the fullness of strength, beauty and vigour, with so many hopes, promises and aspirations unfulfiled, is always a tragedy of the worst kind – unless there be some serious thing in the future, known only to God, from which they were preserved. But on the other hand, in merely human terms there is really no suitable time to die. We depart from this life when we have experienced what it is we needed to learn, and I have often felt, on balance, that to be taken up to God at the time of your greatest happiness and promise is probably one of the greatest blessings that God could bestow.

This does not lessen our grief and loss, but I think it should give us some consolation and help to see things from a slightly different point of view, help to bear with the loneliness, the grief and the separation. Our Lord himself wept at the death of Lazarus his friend, even though he knew he was to set about raising him from the dead within a few moments. He also told us that between this world and the one where our destiny lies, there is a barrier which prevents communication. It is not, I am sure, that God has decided that there should be no contact between those worlds, but probably only because in this life we have not got the equipment in our poor meagre senses, to grasp the everyday realities of the world to come. It would be like trying to describe what a beautiful landscape is like to a person blind from birth, or trying to convey what a marvellous symphony sounds like to one who has never been able to hear.

There is a very old fable which puts that message well. It is about a group of little insects who lived in the mud on the bottom of a lake. Every so often one of them felt an urge to climb to the surface along one of the reeds growing in the water. None of them ever came back; the others wondered what had happened; they'd love to hear from them to know what things were like with them now. Eventually, they made an agreement among themselves, that the next one called to climb up the reeds to the world above would come back and tell the others about it. When it did happen to one of them he found was emerging from the dark and murky waters of the lake into a totally transformed world on the surface, bright with sunlight and vivid colours, more beautiful than they could ever have imagined below. It was a warm world filled with the most beautiful sounds of nature. He tried to go back down to tell his friends, but suddenly found he was being transformed from being a dowdy grub into a beautifully radiant butterfly, and was flying above the surface of the water. He tried to go back but could not, and in any case he wondered what use would it be? Who would believe that this now radiantly beautiful creature was the humble one they had known in the gloomy world below? This is an attempt to say what cannot be adequately said in human thought and language about our destiny, whose only gateway we know is unfortunately the grave. It was so even for Christ, just as the seed has always to die before the glory it contains can grow and be revealed.

Cardinal Tomás Ó Fiaich
Archbishop of Armagh and Primate of All-Ireland
Chairman of the College Trustees
Maynooth College Chapel, 11 May 1990

The readings we have just heard were those Tomás Ó Fiaich selected for the Mass of his consecration as Archbishop of Armagh twelve years ago.

How prophetic it has all been; the devotion to his little flock, so often scattered, in Ezechiel's words; the suffering that so often comes to those who speak out the truth of the Gospel, as described by Paul; the ministry which tried to unite all people in peace and justice, after the spirit of the Eucharistic discourse in the Gospel of John.

How integral a ministry when the words chosen at the start as a programme for action, can serve so beautifully for an epitaph at the end.

There is no need for me to rehearse his biography here. In the last few days the media have done it well for those of you who did not already know it personally.

He was a student of this College, a member of its Department of Modern History, Registrar, Vice-President and then President. He loved Maynooth in the truest sense of the word. It showed itself in the long hours of unremitting labour for its welfare, which so few know about, but without which very little of significance can occur. Only a few weeks ago when we last met here he was enormously enthused when I outlined to him the plans for the £11,000,000 expansion of facilities on both north and south campuses of the College. He was warm-hearted, anxious to be fair, deeply conscious of the culture and history that made a unity of the Catholic people of Ireland. He was a scholar, but also a bard and a scribe; the author of several of the best known hymns in Irish today.

He became Archbishop of Armagh at a very turbulent time for both State and Church, and it was tragic that his greatest gifts, love of people and place, and dedication to Irish culture and the Irish language, were often used quite unfairly to identify him as a person ambiguous in his attitude towards violence, and irretrievably antagonistic towards the Unionist tradition. Nothing could have been further from the truth. His speaking out honestly on so many complex and sensitive issues inevitably caused controversy, but it was not something he intended, and I never met anyone more anxious to be sensitive to the feelings of the Protestant traditions.

More deep even than his love of people was his love of place. He cherished the great Christian historic sites of Western Europe. He also loved this place. He took pride in the fact that he was the first person for eight hundred years from the area of County Armagh to have been appointed Archbishop of Armagh. The other was the great St Malachy, and it was on his feast day that Tomás Ó Fiaich was born. Above all he realised the irreplaceable jewel which the Irish language is, and how much it contributed to the Irish identity. With it and our history we can go into Europe and add to its cultural richness; without it we become just a distribution heading covering a small number of extra people on the far fringes of the Community.

If your mourning for the Cardinal is more deep than a passing emotion you must realise that the language has lost perhaps its most potent ally in him. Take up the torch that he has passed on to us, so that this irreplaceable and treasured element of European culture will not be lost.

One of the most precious things in the human heart must surely be attachment to one's own and to one's own native place.

In ancient Rome a distinguished administrator died, who had been instrumental in erecting some of the most magnificent buildings in the Forum. A few years later an important visitor to Rome was being shown through the Forum, and he asked to see the monument to that great man's memory. He was told there was none. But then one of the Senators said to him that it was unnecessary: '*Si monumentum quaesieris, circumspice*', 'If you are looking for a monument look around you' – all these are his monument!

We must take this further for there will be no monuments of even that kind at Maynooth to Tomás Ó Fiaich. It was not his style to try to erect great physical or institutional elements, which might accidentally serve later to map the passage of his career. He was a romantic, if by that we mean passion, imagination, love of origins, and the education of the senses in childhood landscapes. Memory men, remembrancers, are always loving men – memory after all gives its hundredfold only to those who feel greatly. Balzac said that O'Connell incarnated a people. Tomás Ó Fiaich incarnated a rich lode of our Christian and Gaelic past. History was no nightmare to him: it was his origins, anguish, beauty, neighbours, love unbroken. '*Si monumentum*' … thus it is that he will have a far more enduring monument in the minds and hearts of the people of Ireland, and particularly in the those of this College which was his Shambala for so long. They will keep his memory green long after those of us who were privileged to know him will have passed on after him into the fullness of hope.

The oldest piece of vernacular literature in Europe is a Gaelic manuscript in France, a country and language that he loved in themselves, and for the little Irelands on French soil. And it was the same with Austria, Belgium, Germany, Italy and Switzerland. For him the shortest road to Tara was via Clairvaux, Louvain, Bobbio or Würtzburg. He liked to quote De Gaulle's: 'All my life I have made for myself a certain idea of France.' And it was there he died, mirroring his only County Armagh predecessor in eight hundred years – the great St Malachy.

Tomás Ó Fiaich's last manu-script, taking the elements of the word consciously, was extraordinary. He literally died writing, filling out the details on a hospital entrance form, as a courtesy it would seem, to some clerk who could not manage the phonetics of 'Ó Fiaich.'

He wrote Ó Fiaich in Irish: then in English – or rather French – Thomas, which is probably the name as it was on his baptismal certificate. Next Ara Coeli, then Armagh. The last word he ever wrote was French. And how fitting that it was IRLANDE.

Lord, we give back to you the spirit of Tomás Ó Fiaich. We loved him greatly. We thank you for his presence in our lives, and the richness and treasured memories it left us.

Ar dheis Dé go raibh a anam dhil.

James O'Rawe
Student of Down and Connor Diocese
Maynooth College Chapel, 25 March 1991

The preacher must never speak for himself on an occasion like this, but for the sorrow and sympathy of the community. The Liturgy of the Church never countenances the mere memorial of an individual without also drawing a lesson from that life for our own.

There are many profitable lessons we could take from the life of James O'Rawe, and they hinge on generosity, and commitment. After a long and full life as a widely-respected doctor and family man in Belfast he set out to follow his dream of being a priest: a major decision at his age when the easy path of comfortable retirement lay before him. He was dedicated, quiet, kind and sincere, one in whom there was no guile.

In a place like this College we live in what is in many respects an unreal world in which, for the most part, the aged, infirm, the very young and the disabled find no place. It is over thirty years since a student died actually within the College; it brings us up short to find that death can be a part of life in Maynooth for a student.

It puts us thinking. We reckon it tragic that he died a week before receiving Diaconate, which was a part of his long dream of reaching the priesthood. In his case it was not even a matter of the labourer in the parable of the vineyard, at the eleventh hour receiving the same pay as the one who had worked from the beginning, for James had not even begun this particular work. To think like this is the reason why so frequently human calculation is annihilated by the divine.

Yesterday we celebrated Christ's triumphant entry into Jerusalem. It was the way things ought to have been; the way the Messiah ought to have been received, and the way it would have been were it not for the extent to which evil had possessed the hearts of men. Have you noticed how often in the life of Christ that human wisdom is outstripped by the divine? What prudent judge of human affairs would have counselled God to make his grand entry into the world in a stable? Or to leave it on the disgraced cross of a criminal? Yet out of the chaos of this disaster as viewed through human eyes emerged a higher order, the glory of the resurrection and the triumph of Christianity.

Who would have thought yesterday as James occupied his place here in the Chapel for the Palm Sunday Liturgy, that today we would meet to celebrate his Requiem? Today is the traditional date of the feast of the incarnation, when God's almighty Word forsook his throne in the realms of everlasting day to become man in the womb of Mary. What a paradox; the incarnation sandwiched between the triumph of Palm Sunday, and the betrayal by Judas and crucifixion. In human terms it should never have been, it made no sense, it was a complete disaster; and this was exactly how his disciples saw it. But how often what seems to be a failure, inappropriate, or out of place in the judgment of men, turns out to be the very opposite in the providence of God.

Faced with these mysteries such as the one we face today we know we must see further than just the tragedy and the loss. St Paul, faced with the same issues concluded his meditation in these words:

> O the depth of the riches,
> And of the wisdom,

And of the knowledge of God.
How incomprehensible are his judgments,
How unsearchable his ways.
For who has known the mind of the Lord,
Or who has been his counsellor?
Or who has even given him anything that had to be repaid?

In that spirit we give back to the bosom of its Creator the spirit of James O'Rawe, and we pray that he will soon share, not now in the diaconate of service, but in the glory of the day of triumph of the Easter King.

Anniversary of Cardinal Tomás Ó Fiaich
Maynooth College Chapel, 8 May 1991

Public figures are often seriously misunderstood; there was probably no better example of that than the man whose anniversary we keep today. The late Cardinal was a very private, a very wounded man, who suffered greatly. He was a man of deep loyalties and attachments, expecially to this College and its students and staff.

He was a man who loved origins; above all the origins of the Celtic race in Ireland; for him it was an essential component of *dúchas*. He was a prince of the Church, very well known internationally, but the title and description that appealed to him most was the *Coarba Phádraig*; Padraig's Coarb at Armagh.

We are here this morning to keep one of the most ancient customs of the faith; prayer for the dead at their anniversary. It is something that is at the heart of the Catholic faith; it is also something that is at the heart of our own sense as a people. The Irish race is a mixture of many strains; but the Celtic left its stamp on all who came before and after it in this land. The Celts saw God suffused in nature, close, near, relevant, interested in our lot, mirrored in the passage of the cycles of the seasons. They were fascinated by transitions, by in-between states; the move from darkness to light, from dusk to night, from one day to another at midnight; from one year to the next at Samhain. That was the deep mind of Tomás Ó Fiaich.

For the Celts the anniversary of death was a time when the departed came close once again to those left behind. If this be so I am sure Tomás Ó Fiaich is with us here this morning , for keeping his memory must surely also bring him close to us. He was the successor of Patrick, whom this College took as its Patron, and surely Maynooth is at the very heart of carrying on the apostle's work in Ireland. Almost all of his adult life the Cardinal was intimately linked to this College and few realise the labours he undertook for it, even up to the last. We are all in his debt, indeed in debt to the extent that only the things of the spirit can repay; and repaying is what our prayers for him are about this morning. And we pray that as his destiny was so closely linked with Maynooth in the past, we may also share with him his destiny in glory.

> From boyhood to Man; and from Age to Death
> In Christ's strong arms may we be embraced.
> From Death to Light, and to the Light of Lights
> May we be in step with Christ in Paradise.
>
> *O fhás go haois, is ó aois go bás*
> *do dhá láimh a Chríost anall tharainn,*
> *O bás go críoch, ní críoch ach ath-fhás,*
> *I bParrthas na ngrást go rabhaimíd.*

Kevin Bannon
First Divinity Student, Kilmore Diocese
Died at Washington, D.C., 12 September 1992
Maynooth College Chapel, 17 October 1992

'O Death, where is your victory; O Grave, where is your sting? Death is swallowed up in victory' (1 Cor 15). So said St Paul, the writer in the New Testament who reflected most on the mystery of death, and who linked its meaning always to the death, resurrection and ascension of Christ our Lord.

We are told the loss of a loved one in death only really strikes home after a while, and at specific intervals; principally about a week after the death, and again about a month later. For that reason, the Church in her wisdom, has the immemorial custom of the Month's Mind Mass, and we are privileged to have Kevin's family and close friends here with us today in this Chapel. This Chapel meant a great deal to him, and in it he so often offered up his youthful and generous aspirations to God, to whom he had made the supreme gift, the total dedication of his life.

In what I used to find the most puzzling and most profound statement of St Paul about our state in this world, we read in the Epistle to the Romans: 'It was through one man that sin came into the world, and through sin, death.' So it seems that if there had not been sin, there would have been no death; and further, even more strikingly, it seems that death was not intended by God to be part of our lot; that it is an unnatural thing. And when we look at the heart-break and loss that it brings, especially in the death of a person so full of the life and vigour of youth, we know in our heart of hearts that this could not have been the way things were meant to be. But as things stand now the heavy burden of grief and loss cannot be avoided, and we look for ways, through our prayers and comfort, by which we can support each other.

Above all today we want to help the one who has left us by our prayers; he has the immense advantage that his life basically had already been dedicated here at Maynooth to ideals that have their real basis and roots in what is the real world, the one beyond the material. So we pray with Christ in the Mass to help him to continue onwards in his journey towards God. Too much grief and mourning for him can hold that journey back.

There is no easy way to cope with the grief and loss brought by the death of one we love, but there are a few things that we can keep in mind that will help us start to bind up broken hearts.

Firstly, there is an aim and a purpose in all things that occur. Every person, every event in our lives, is there because we ourselves have drawn it there. Things do not happen in an aimless and senseless way. Must we not then dare to hope that our God takes us from this world when we are at the pinnacle of what we came into this life to achieve?

Secondly, as the most basic gift God gave us on this earth was our freedom, must we not also dare to hope that no matter how cruel and senseless the circumstances may seem to be, that there is, buried however deep down within us, a desire and a longing for the precise circumstances and time of our passing from this world into a different plane of existence?

Thirdly, because our vision is so limited, and our capabilities so weak, we cannot help but feel loneliness and inexpressible loss. But we know nevertheless that there is a different standpoint. We know that what we are all heading for is a transition and a transmutation into a higher realm, whether achieved in this life or later, as St Paul reminded us in the words I quoted at the start, when he linked us with the destiny of Christ the Lord of Glory.

Kevin has only gone on before us into the fullness of hope. It takes a really heroic effort not to be overly saddened by such painful goodbyes, for we very rightly wish they never were.

Crushed though they make us, farewells are sadly always necessary before we can know that unique joy which only meeting again can give. And meeting again, whether it be after moments, or years, or even whole lifetimes, is an absolute certainty for those who have been closely bound together in the bonds of love.

In the depths of this sorrow from which we cannot ever fully escape, it is the attitude, the vantage point, that counts. I suppose the real mark of our ignorance about the ways of God is the depth of our belief in injustice and tragedy. 'What the caterpillar or slug calls the end of the world, the spiritual master calls a butterfly.'

Sister Clare Gilligan
Daughter of Charity
Maynooth College Chapel, 13 November 1993

Sister Clare came to Maynooth only in the later years of her life. Though she lived very quietly in the Infirmary she loved the life of the College here, and particularly loved this Chapel. Even though few of us knew her we were all deeply touched by the suddenness of her passing from this world last week.

There is a purpose in all things, however absurd or meaningless they may seem. Death is but a new beginning, and if those who are left can go beyond the sense of personal loss and grief, then they too can share something of this new beginning.

Life continues. Eventually we will meet our loved ones again, and the relationship will be strengthened in spite of, or in one way because of, the separation and the lessons which have been learned from it.

Death is a subject that used to be very much taboo, but in recent years all over the Western world an enormous interest has begun to develop in what happens to us after death and during death itself. I suppose we could say our attitude to death is a fairly harsh barometer of the state of our faith in general; the more empty our faith is of any transcendence, the less we are able about talk about death, the next world, or offer any real consolation to the bereaved.

When the physical body dies, through accident, illness, or old age, the spirit enters into a new phase of consciousness, according to our Christian belief. The spirit becomes aware of a new plane of experience. Life in a physical body, in the world of matter, is life on one plane, in one world, but it is not the only world. We believe that the departed are still joined to us, on a different stage of that journey towards God which we call the Communion of Saints.

The liturgy forbids us quite rightly to eulogise the departed at a funeral mass; we comment on their lives only for the benefit and help it may give us ourselves.

Sister Clare was quiet, unassuming, gentle, kind and humorous. She was deeply interested in the happiness and welfare of others. I suppose when we have said that we have said it all and everything else is merely ornamentation.

Her patron saint was born eight centuries ago this year.

Having refused to marry at the age of 15 she was moved by the dynamic preaching of Francis of Assisi, and he became her lifelong friend and spiritual guide. At 18 years she escaped from her father's home by night and in the poor little chapel of Portiuncula received a rough woollen habit and exchanged her jewelled belt for a common rope with knots in it. Others joined her. They lived a life simple in the extreme, excluded from the world. The nuns went barefoot, slept on the ground, ate no meat, and observed almost complete silence. She was a woman to be reckoned with: no plaster cast saint. When even the Pope requested her to moderate her penances she said to him, 'I need you to absolve me from my sins. But I do not wish to be absolved from the obligation of following Christ Jesus.'

She served the sick, waited on tables, washed the feet of the begging nuns. She used to come from prayer with a face so shining it dazzled those about her. She was seriously ill for the last 27 years of her life. Popes, cardinals, bishops, often came to consult her. She never left the walls of the monastery of San Damiano in Assisi.

This was the life that inspired our Sister Clare. She too chose anonymity, not to flee the world, but to serve better its disadvantaged and deprived, following the teachings of Sts Vincent de Paul and Louise de Marillac, who so strongly emphasised the presence of God in us and in our neighbour.

Nearly ninety years ago Monsignor Daniel Mannix, President of this College, travelled to Paris to the Motherhouse of the Daughters of Charity, to ask for some sisters to be sent here to Maynooth to take care of the seminarians. This church was new when they first came here. They have continued to come to this day. I know it is difficult for the Sisters themselves, who have always prized being unobtrusive and private, to fully understand the place that the Daughters of Charity have achieved in the prayers and affection of the vast majority of the priests of Ireland who have passed through this College. Sister Clare has joined that long line of the Daughters of Charity who have died in the service of Maynooth, and as such has an everlasting claim to be remembered in our prayers here.

St Clare of Assisi was 41 years in the religious life. She had a passion for the simple literal gospel life that Francis had taught her; a life of courageous resistance to the ever-present pressure to dilute the ideal; a passion for humility, and ardent life of personal prayer, and a generous concern for her sisters.

On her deathbed she was heard to say: 'Go forth in peace, for you have followed the good road. Go forth without fear, for he who created you has made you holy, has always protected you, and loves you as a mother. Blessed be you, my God, for having created me.'

We know those were the ideals also of our own Sister Clare, and it is in that spirit we join our prayers for her with the sacrifice of Christ in this Mass, knowing she has gone on before us into the fullness of hope. May her great and generous soul reap the benefits of the dedicated life she led, and be an inspiration to those of us who were privileged to know her.

Ciarán Woods
Deacon of Clogher Diocese
Maynooth College Chapel, 7 April 1993

Who would have thought last Sunday, as Ciarán was Deacon here in the Chapel for the Palm Sunday Liturgy, that today we would meet to celebrate his requiem? I mentioned to him after Mass in the Sacristy, the death of James O'Rawe after our Palm Sunday liturgy two years ago. Little did we know how tragically soon the event was to be repeated.

The contrast between the two liturgies in which Ciarán was so centrally involved, last Sunday and today, have a message for those with the eyes to see it. Palm Sunday was a day of brightness, joy and triumph for Christ; a few days later the same friends of his mourned his tragic and horrible death. A few days later still, the friends and disciples were rejoicing in that newest of things in human history; a thing that changed the meaning of all death for ever more, the Resurrection, in which Christ the Lord of Glory returned from whence he came, and earned the right of all of us to share in it.

Four hundred years ago a great poet wrote:

All the world's a stage
And all the men and women merely players:
They have their exits and their entrances,
And one man in his time plays many parts.

These lines are as true today as when first written. Our eternal spirits incarnate on this earth to play parts, empowering roles, in the great drama of life. The spirit, the actor, plays many parts. The role dies with the play; the actor goes on to play many more roles.

For those of us who have been privileged to share in a birth or death, we will be aware of the separate presence of the soul at such times, and of how purposeless the physical body is without the energy of the spirit to empower it. That is why it is almost impossible to look at a baby and not to feel love for that little being; not because it is so weak and helpless, but because as you look into its eyes you see there the pure reflection of its spirit, as yet unsullied by the personality.

In the same way whatever pain or suffering a dying person experiences, as you look into their eyes you are aware of the presence of a very different being, a being of spiritual consciousness, that exists in a state of bliss. It is at times like that that you can differentiate very clearly between the actor and the role that has been played, between the body and the spirit.

If the awareness of the soul is so strongly there at birth and at death, why is it not always so obvious during the remainder of life? Why is it that so many people accept and cause so much pain and suffering? Why is there so much intolerance between the world's races and religions? Why are our spirits so incapable of manifesting their divine note? The answer is simple; it is because we have become so immersed in the physical body that we, in practice, almost believe it is the only reality. We have become almost convinced that we are the personality; that we are the role we are playing. We are all doing this to a greater or lesser degree. We are identifying with our roles in the physical drama, with our physical bodies on earth, rather than with what is eternal in us. This is why so many fear death; for what is death but the ending of the illusion, and a return to the reality, which so many of us deny for so much of our lives. This is why we apply that horrible phrase 'the dead' to those who have gone before us, as if they were in a lesser condition. For the dead are not 'dead' in that sense; if anything they are more alive than we, for they exist now on a higher plane of existence than the material.

Every single aspect of the physical is both mortal and fallible.

Everything comes from the dust and returns to it. Only one thing endures, only one thing is constant, that is our consciousness, or the force of the spirit in motion. It is consciousness that determines the note of our physical being. It is consciousness that is with us at birth, is with us throughout our lives, and is with us after death. Only the body knows death, not the consciousness. It is only the body that is limited by the physical restrictions of the plane of this earth, not the consciousness. The drama of life is played out on a very small stage, defined by our sensory organs. We are only in a school of learning here, it is not our true home. If what we are at heart is our consciousness, then we can never die; it is only that our realm of experience has changed.

It is difficult to accept the need for someone to die, especially when they are young in physical years and full of promise. It seems so senseless when there is so much potential unfilled, so many skills and talents to give to the world that sorely needs this assistance right now, so much joy to give back to families, relatives and friends. The death of a young person is almost always regarded as a tragedy.

In this Holy Week, let's spare a moment to reflect on the life and death of Jesus, where surely the apparent tragedies of immense promise and a life cut short in full bloom were never more highly accentuated.

Here was a person, who if he had but lived for, say, another forty years, would truly have transformed society in that time, for in terms of human estimation his work was just beginning. Yet he was condemned to death by the political and religious leaders of his time. Was this a tragedy? All of those on his side who saw it unfolding at that time undoubtedly though it so. Do we think his death was an act of blind fate, a very unfortunate occurrence? Was it not rather an event that was foreseen and agreed to, agreed to in the first place by himself, even though with tremendous fear and apprehension. It was an act of conscious sacrifice to demonstrate and bring about something of cosmic significance.

Jesus could have avoided his crucifixion at any time. He could have transported himself away from it at any time, as he did release himself miraculously from moments of great danger on a few occasions that we know of in the Gospels.

With the benefit of the passing years we can now see, as he saw in advance, what came of that sacrifice; for his death was the start of a great birth, the Christian religion, which has touched the hearts of countless millions of souls and opened for them an enlightenment

of which they could never otherwise have dreamed. It was necessary to release the old to initiate the new. Death is not only a great
transmutor, it is a great initiator. Death is not an ending, it is a
beginning.

But the more we have become attached to the physical, then the
more we will dread and fear and mourn in the presence of death.

There is no easy way to cope with the grief and loss brought by
the death of one we love: it is so easy to be trite and unfeeling; but
there are a few things that we can keep in mind that will help us
start to bind up broken hearts.

In the case of Christ's death we have the advantage of the bodily
Resurrection and Ascension, and the interpretation of countless
generations, to help see it in a very different light from the unmiti-
gated disaster it seemed to be when it was happening. Ciarán's
death we cannot, as yet, see in a larger scene. But there is an aim and
a purpose in all things that occur. Christ told us that not a sparrow
falls without God's knowing; that every hair on our head is numbered. Every person, every event in our lives, is there because we
ourselves have drawn it there, and nothing happens in an aimless
and senseless way. Must we not then dare to hope that our God
takes us from this world when we are at the pinnacle of what we
came into this life to achieve?

Of one thing we can be certain, that there is no way the significance of any life in God's eyes can be guaged in length of days; nor
can it be measured by how well it fits in with human plans and calculation.

We trust in Christ, above all in his very own painful example of
this Holy Week, and in St Paul's words pray:

> O the depths of the riches,
> And of the wisdom,
> And of the knowledge of God.
> How incomprehensible are his judgments,
> How unsearchable his ways.
> For who has known the mind of the Lord,
> Or who has been his counsellor?
> Or who has given him anything that had to be repaid?

CHAPTER 12

Epilogue

Conference of the Heads of the Irish Universities
**Function in honour of Msgr Míceál Ledwith
to mark his retirement as
President of St Patrick's College, Maynooth**
Dublin City University, 30 January 1995

Dear Friends, former Colleagues,

We all belong to a profession where one of the great hazards of life is long speeches that have few slack moments when no axes are being ground! I hope this delightful occasion is such a slack moment, and I want to register my appreciation to you for having this occasion for me to mark my retirement after a decade at the helm in Maynooth.

It was decade of enormous change on the Irish University scene as we all scrambled to keep pace with the extraordinary demands of a country whose resources were as scarce as its young people were plentiful. It's at times of great pressure such as this that the Universities can lose sight of the reason why they are there at all in the first place, and thus do themselves more damage than their worst enemies ever could. It can so easily happen if our concern is too exclusively for relevance, for the provision of marketable skills for our young people, and for respect for market forces. All these concerns are vitally necessary but to justify their existence the Universities have to provide as well, lasting values, which they themselves are best placed of all to provide. As President Mary Robinson put it so well last year, that means trying 'to uphold, and promote the free interplay of argument and discussion; a critical approach to the orthodoxy of the times; a passion for truth and freedom to express the ideas which emerge from the restless questioning surge of the human intellect' (At Adam Mickiewicz University, Poznan, 24 June 1994). Maurice Blondel put it more sardonically:

'He who marries the spirit of the age is soon a widower.'

I heard a fable a while ago in the US[1] and I thought it has a moral for us all.

Once upon a time the animals decided they must do something heroic to met the problems of the 'new world.' So they organised a school.

They adopted a curriculum consisting of running, climbing, swimming and flying. To make it easier to administer the curriculum it was decided that all animals should take all subjects.

The duck was of course excellent in swimming, in fact better than his instructor, but he made only a pass in flying and was quite poor in running. Since he was a slow runner he had to stay in after school, to practise running. This was kept up until his webbed feet were badly worn and consequently he became only average in swimming. But average was acceptable in the school, so nobody worried about that – except the duck.

The rabbit started at the top of the class in running, but had a nervous breakdown because he had so much make-up work in swimming.

The squirrel was excellent in climbing, until he developed frustration in the flying class where his instructor made him start from the ground up, instead of from the tree top down. He also developed problems from over-exertion, and eventually ended up getting only a pass in climbing, and a fail in running.

The eagle was a problem student, and had to be disciplined severely. In the climbing class he beat all the others to the top of tree, but he insisted on using his own way to get there.

At the end of the year, an abnormal eel that could swim exceedingly well, and also run, climb and fly a little, had the highest average and so graduated at the top of the school.

The prairie dogs stayed out of the school and fought the tax levy because the administration would not add digging and burrowing to the curriculum. They apprenticed their children to a badger and later joined the groundhogs and gophers to start a successful private institution.

I'm sure there's a moral for us all there as we struggle and stagger from one crisis to the next in Ireland today!

We are a small country and the seven universities in the Republic have a total population that is quite small by wider stan-

---

1 Canfield, Jack and Hansen, Mark V, *Chicken Soup for the Soul*, Florida, 1993.

dards. There are forces that greatly outnumber the universities' role in inculcating lasting values. In such a climate there really is no room for an unwise competition among us in which we allow the playing off of one against the other to the detriment of all eventually.

The seven universities in the Republic, despite significant differences in history, size and orientation, have done a marvellous job in pulling together towards a common goal, and the credit for that must mainly go to the organisation of CHIU. I'm sure that the greater need and importance of this Conference lies in the critical years ahead. It was a great privilege for me to be part of all of that with you in these past ten years.

The end of my own time as President ushered in dramatic new changes in Maynooth itself – the introduction for the first time of a new Head for the National University part of the College. It was a change that had of course been on the drawing board for several years, but nevertheless it was a major change for an old institution, and could have been quite a disruptive and unsettling process. It was a change that would not have been helped by a long transition period, which is why we felt it best to have a three months transition, which would take place during the Summer vacation rather than in the middle of an academic year. I am delighted to say the transition has worked well – a very satisfactory situation as Maynooth moves towards its Bicentenary this year – in June or in September 1995 – depending on whether law or geography has pre-eminence in your mind!

I greatly valued the help and assistance which so many of you gave me through this organisation during my time in office, and which we saw particularly at the time of the CRE Conference eighteen months ago in Maynooth. My one great regret at the end of my time was that new university legislation had not yet appeared, despite so many false dawns. I am confident that in this birthday year of three of our institutions here it will now be possible to bring in this long awaited boost to status and morale. I was extremely fortunate to have in the administration with me a small group of totally dedicated, hardworking, inspired and always loyal people, most of whom are here in this room today as members of this Conference: Seamus Smyth, Pat Dalton and Peter Carr. By and large in Maynooth we are fortunate in having a very positive and committed staff – I suppose the greatest treasure any institution could hope to have. I am delighted that Seamus has inherited that situation which he himself was so instrumental in building up.

My warmest thanks to you all – especially to the Chairman of

CHIU, Dr Art Cosgrove, President of UCD, for the kind and generous words in my regard which he has just now spoken, and to Dr
Danny O'Hare, President of this University, whose guests we are
today. A particularly warm word of thanks to Dr John Nolan,
Registrar of the National University of Ireland and Executive
Officer of CHIU, for so many things over the decade on which he
brought his perennial courtesy and efficiency to bear.

As Franklin D. Roosevelt once said in a cable to Winston
Churchill: 'It was fun being in the same decade with you!'

National University of Ireland
Function to mark the retirement of
Msgr Míceál Ledwith
as President of St Patrick's College, Maynooth
Dublin, 25 May 1995

Chancellor, Vice-Chancellor, Presidents and Registrars:

May I say how very honoured I am that you have invited me
here this evening for this function to mark my retirement, and especially that you have taken the time from debate on so many pressing
matters these days to do so? During my time as President I always
looked forward greatly to the meetings the administrations of the
National University Colleges had together – such as at Senate or
Standing Committee. Many of the problems that we were labouring
under at home were put into a better and more manageable perspective when you realised that nearly everybody else was grappling with the same issues or maybe worse, and a general encouragement was given to all.

But tonight it's all gain for me as I didn't have to go through the
long day of meetings the rest of you did, before coming to enjoy this
function.

I am very grateful for the very generous comments the
Chancellor has spoken in my regard just now. Charles William
Elliott retired in 1909 after a long session as President of Harvard
and at his retirement dinner the Chancellor congratulated him on
having achieved miracles in the University during his term: 'Since
you became President,' he said, 'Harvard has become a storehouse
of knowledge.' 'That's true,' said Elliott, 'but I can claim very little
credit for it. It is simply that the freshmen bring so much and the
graduates take so little away!'

It's true a very great deal has been achieved at Maynooth over the past decade. The threefold increase in student numbers, the doubling of staff and the new buildings on the north campus, are I suppose the more tangible and visible evidences of that, but I think the most significant development, which was facilitated by the ending of my own term as President, was the appointment of a separate head for the NUI part of Maynooth, and all that that implied. It might have seemed to be a relatively simple thing, but the implications were enormous, and it crowned the many positive developments in that area over the last decade or more. I am probably best placed to know the enormous role in all of that development that Seamus Smyth played and I know that no better person exists to guide the destinies of the College into its third century than he. He was to me a valued friend, trusted advisor and an inspiration in many more ways than I can count. It is not always the case that a person who has played such a significnat role in the development of an institution gets the opportunity to build on that with his own term of office as the Head, but I am delighted that it so turned out with Seamus Smith, and those here who have not yet had to chance to get to know him as well as I do will see how true my words are. I want to thank tonight also the Registrar during all of my time as President, Dr Peter Carr. Peter was also a true and loyal friend and supporter during all those ten years and I owe him a great debt.

All of us in Maynooth felt that the best way forward was the harmonious progression of all the three parts of Maynooth in a mutually enriching relationship. I have never tired of pointing out over the years that the Arts and Science courses at Maynooth didn't begin with the opening up of the College nearly thirty years ago, nor indeed with the beginning of Maynooth's association with NUI in 1910. They go back to the very beginnings of the College with very creditable courses indeed in the main range of the humanities then current in third level institutions, as well as in Mathematics and Physics. So Arts and Science at Maynooth are also celebrating their Bicentenary this year.

Ten years ago, Chancellor, when the President of UCD was retiring, I held a function for him in Maynooth, and I remarked then that you were the first Chancellor of NUI not to have been a member of the Maynooth staff!

I am very happy to say that that state of affairs still exists. May I say how greatly I admired the way in which you conducted the affairs of NUI during these past twenty years. Everybody knows that the affairs of any great body seldom run entirely smoothly, but

I always admired how you steered the meetings of the Senate and Standing and Finance Committees through many a stormy and treacherous passage, always unfailingly courteous and urbane. I never saw you become impatient or ruffled, despite the intense provocation you often received from us, and I know the National University of Ireland has been fortunate indeed to have had you at the helm in these very difficult years.

While there have been enormous changes in third level education in Ireland in recent years, I suppose at heart great issues seldom change radically. The great headline in ancient times at which all education aimed was that of Hippocrates, 'ars longa, vita brevis.' 'life is short, art is long.' How do you best understand 'art' in that sentence? I suppose it was meant to indicate skills, information, wisdom, knowledge, everything that went to define a civilised human being. When all the scramble for relevance to our times through which we must go has been finished, ultimately the test of any university must be how successfully it has crammed as much as possible of the *ars longa*, into the *vita brevis* – in our case normally a space of only four or five years. But they are very critical years for each individual and the policies of education impinge only very slowly on the public life of a country, so it is not easy to see we are making mistakes, nor to be quickly encouraged by the obvious value our policies are yielding.

In this regard I have so say how encouraged I was to see appear recently, the White Paper on education: 'Charting Our Education Future.' There is a strong commitment to 'amend', fortunately, rather than 'replace,' the National University legislation, on the basis of proposals submitted by the Senate. I am sure this will be to the advantage of all of us, especially in the commitment in the longer term legislation to preserve the diversity of the ethos and traditions of the Colleges, the commitment to research in all colleges, even if there is a strong emphasis on the two-tiered approach, the broadening of representation on the governing bodies, the question of quality assurance; are all issues that will engage a lot of attention during the immediate future. Maynooth I suppose has a lot to gain from this move, proportionately, I suppose more than any other College. The medieval theological postulate of Limbo has long drifted out of favour with theologians, and I hope the Limbo situation of NUI at Maynooth will soon follow suit.

I was always a little concerned at the implications that the interests of the state and the interests of the universities in relation to education, might not always coincide, but might in practice seriously diverge. In the White Paper there is a very strong insistence that while the traditional aims of higher education must be safeguarded, the universiites must also respond to the changing needs of society and the interests of the State. I feel that the interests of the State and of the Universities in relation to education should always be maintained in reasonable harmony, if not coincide. Earlier I said the impact of educational policies are slow to make a visible difference in society, and when they do it is often too late to avoid the negative consequences of them. But I think it well serves the best interests of the state to have as much as possible of the *ars longa* cast into the *vita brevis*, and short term policies can wreak a lot of destruction. None of us, having survived a single day in our offices, could ever dream that we were living in ivory towers, insulated from the real demands of the present day, and none of us would want that even if it were possible. I think the legitimate interests of the state and of the universities coincide a lot more than we have given them credit for, and if a university is really doing the task of truly educating, I think the state will be extremely pleased at the results.

I particularly appreciated President Michael Mortell's invitation to be with him for the Honorary Conferrings in Cork a few weeks ago. My warmest thanks to the Registrar Dr John Nolan, who organised tonight's proceedings. It was always a great pleasure to work with him, and to avail of the never-failing courtesy and politeness in which his efficiency was always so beautifully wrapped.

To all of you I owe a great deal, to some of you an extraordinary amount, and I thank you for it: the list would be far too long to mention in detail here.

It has been delightful to be back with you for a short while once again, and while I am realistic enough to know you have been over-generous in your praise, I am vain enough to be thankful for it, nevertheless.

May I wish all of you every success in the years ahead. They will be momentous years for NUI. I hope that this great institution which has done so much to preserve and forward the ethos and culture of this land will have an enhanced role in the new forms and structures that emerge from the present debate.